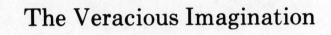

# The Veracious Imagination

# THE VERACIOUS IMAGINATION

## Essays on American History, Literature, and Biography

## Cushing Strout

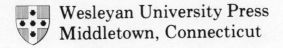

Wesleyan University Press
Middletown, Connecticut

Some of these essays first appeared in journals, and the author
is grateful for permission to reprint them to *History and Theory*
for chapters 2 and 12, *American Quarterly* for chapter 3, *Yale
Review* for chapter 4, *Clio* for chapter 5, *Prospects* for parts of
chapter 6 and chapter 10, *Daedalus* for chapter 11, and
*New Literary History* for chapter 13. Chapter 14 was originally
delivered in a much more informal and shorter form as a lecture
at a symposium in honor of Erik H. Erikson at Adelphi
University in 1977. All the published essays have been revised
to take account of repetitions or dated topical references.

The publisher gratefully acknowledges the support of the Hull
Memorial Publication Fund of Cornell University toward the
publication of this book.

Library of Congress Cataloging in Publication Data

Strout, Cushing.
    The veracious imagination, essays on American
history, literature, and biography.

    Includes bibliographical references and index.
    1. American literature—History and criticism—
Addresses, essays, lectures.   2. Literature and
history—Addresses, essays, lectures.   3. Historiography—Addresses, essays, lectures.   4. Psychohistory—Addresses, essays, lectures.   I. Title.
PS169.H5S85      813'.009'358      80-17436
ISBN O-8195-5048-5

Distributed by Columbia University Press
136 South Broadway, Irvington, NY 10533

Manufactured in the United States of America
First edition

To the memory of my father
Sewall C. Strout, 1894–1980

# Contents

# Preface

"Yes, it needs doing. Only it's getting too big."
"Don't worry about that, mun. Say your say."
Raymond Williams, *Border Country*

All of the essays in this book might be called border-country
pieces. They are preoccupied with the territory marked out by
the overlapping concerns of fiction, history, and biography.
Inevitably, looking at this territory requires shifts in perspective
derived from moving back and forth among different disciplines. Fitzgerald's narrator in *The Great Gatsby* concludes
that "life is much more successfully looked at from a single
window, after all," rather than from the outlook of "that most
limited of all specialists, 'the well-rounded man.'" But literature and history, which reflect on experience rather than merely
reflect it, need more than a single window to do justice to their
complexities. In this case my emphasis on "binocularity"
reflects my own experience as a teacher of both history and
English. It puts me on guard against the tendency to isolate one
from the other, as academic departmentalization tends to do.
But in this respect following E. M. Forster's famous advice—"only connect"—is also going against the grain of two
tendencies in our current climate: the historical suspicion of

literary evidence because it does not lend itself to the quantification of historical analysis and the aesthetic suspicion of history derived from the structuralist elevation of "synchronic" over "diachronic" perspectives. At the same time the development of analytical social history and the subversions of narrative in modern and "postmodern" novels have combined to put story telling, a common feature of histories and novels, into a dubious light. Yet, especially among Anglo-American philosophers since Collingwood, a valuable line of thought has rediscovered the truth-telling function of narrative in opposition to the long-standing positivistic assumption that only scientific laws provide genuine explanations. The first essay, "The Fortunes of Telling," written for this volume, explores the peculiarities of this intellectual situation and establishes the historical and literary themes of this collection. My own perspective is sympathetically (but critically) affiliated to the post-Collingwood tradition, as my early essays on historical causality and on William James's "unfinished arch" of "tychism" make clear.

In part 2 my essays on influential American political novels link history and fiction to counter the dominant critical tradition of overemphasizing the fabulistic, mythological, and metaphysical character of our classic writers, a habit whose ancestry I trace to Tocqueville's speculations on democratic literature. This interest in the symbolic, however, has led to the discovery of typology, and it has the merit of closing the gap between myths and symbols, on the one hand, and historical and social ideas, on the other. Typology connects symbolic forms with an idea of history and therefore with an orientation in time. My essays on millennial themes in the political novel reflect the stimulus of Erich Auerbach's *Mimesis*, which found a connection between biblical figuralism and modern literary realism in the idea of historical consciousness.

The essays in part 3 (not previously published, except for some of the material on Doctorow) focus on the recent revival of historical consciousness in the documentary drama, the memoir, and the historical novel, forms which have attracted among others such considerable talents as Arthur Miller, Norman Mailer, John Updike, William Styron, Gore Vidal, and E. L.

Doctorow. My polarizing of the "veracious" and the "voracious" imagination (an adaptation of George Eliot's phrase) points to the hazards involved in exploring the border country where fiction and history merge. The historicizing of fiction and the fictionalizing of history are very different things, but in an atmosphere where the "realistic" novel has lost prestige and everything is seen "structurally" in terms of rhetoric, the imagination can become imperialistic, as it does in *Ragtime*. My references to Aristotle, Virginia Woolf, and George Eliot show that the problem of the relation between the imaginary and the actual is an old one; but it is still something of an unknown territory in current criticism, which wobbles between too easy a triumph of imagination over everything, a surrender of imagination to fact, or a confusion of realms in such categories as "the nonfiction novel" and "the fictual." In exploring Mailer's memoir; Kipphardt's play on Oppenheimer, Gibson's on the Adamses, Miller's on Salem Witchcraft, Updike's on Buchanan; or Styron's novel on Nat Turner, Vidal's on Burr, and Doctorow's on the Rosenbergs, I have tried to explore at the same time the general issue of the role of the actual in the fictional without resolving one into the other.

Part 4 deals with the equally controversial area of "psycho-history." Working on American images of Europe[1] had alerted me to ambivalence as a concept, and later collaboration with Dr. Howard Feinstein, a psychiatrist, taught me much about psychoanalysis. Unfortunately propagandists have touted it as the key to open all historical locks, while skeptics have repudiated it with equal facility because one cannot literally put a dead person on the psychoanalyst's couch.[2] My position, responsive to Erikson's ego psychology, neither embraces nor spurns psychological analysis but seeks rather to integrate it within biographical (individual or collective) studies as a way of keeping both historical and literary discussion in touch with paradoxical conflicts that often mark the creative life of thinkers, doers, and artists alike and help to illuminate their thought and action. It is fitting that for both the uses and abuses of psychoanalytic insight my major examples involve both William and Henry James as subjects, for both of them touch on many of my own themes. The older brother was interested in evangelical religion and Freud because both tapped "the subliminal self," while the younger was not only fascinated as a novelist with the sense of the past, but also thought of the novel as a kind of psychological history.

As a theorist of history, Collingwood himself rejected both biography and psychoanalytic thinking; but in these respects I think he was false to his own best insights, and the affinity that clinicians like Erik Erikson and Roy Schafer have felt for Collingwood's stress on the "inner side" of history ought to correct his own prejudices. The case histories of Freud, as he confessed, read like short stories, though in a nonlinear, spiral form, because psychoanalytic therapy is a way of providing what neurotics can not give: "an ordered history of their life in so far as it coincides with the history of their illness." There is, of course, another side to Freud, the positivist who thinks of "sexual substances" as "chronic poisons" which may one day be understood as "chemical changes." But for the humanist historian, biographer, and critic what is most useful in him is his insistence that we must pay as much attention to "the purely human and social circumstances of our patients as to the somatic data and the symptoms of the disorder."[3] In this light the themes of this collection of essays form a circle by finding a family resemblance in biography, history, fiction, and psychoanalysis as modes of truth telling by complex narrative order.

No preface can prevent misreadings, but I particularly want to guard against one. In a recent sympathetic and valuable account of structuralist theory a colleague observes: "Notions of truth and reality are based on a longing for an unfallen world in which there would be no need for the mediating systems of language and perception but everything would be itself, with no gap between form and meaning." This critical description of the idea of literature as a form of intentional communication is part of the structuralist project "to divert attention from the author as source and the work as object" to focus instead on "writing as an institution and reading as an activity."[4] But an interest in truth and reality can be thus reduced to a naive realism only on the untenable assumption of an irrevocable gap between a pure subjectivity and a pure objectivity. To divorce interpretation from truth and reality merely takes for granted the ideal of the naive realist, even while denying the possibility of realizing it. But thought's acts—symbols—are not inferior substitutes for an original reality; they connect subject and object. "The symbol intervenes between subject and object," as a philosopher has put it, "and is directed towards both."[5] Unfortunately today, in some fashionable quarters, literary sophistication has come to mean "the disappearance" of "the thinking subject," the denigration of "representational justification" or description of the world, the inflation of textual meaning to a range of "infinite possibilities" and the narcisistic reduction of any text to "an exploration of writing," the goal of criticism being to show the reader, "by the acrobatics in which it involves him, about the problems of his condition as *homo significans*, maker and reader of signs."[6] These essays, on the contrary, seek to put in the foreground the person and his historical world, while legitimating some interpretations rather than others.[7] In my view this strategy is basic for humanistic study in history and literature, even though I am well aware that my discussion of texts, restricted by the purposes of my argument, cannot do justice in this context to the nonmimetic aspects of fiction, which are always part of one's experience of it, especially in stories that are not pertinent to the issues I explore.

Some of these essays were written in June 1978, at the Villa Serbelloni, Bellagio, Italy, home of the Rockefeller Study and Conference Center. It is a place where every prospect pleases and not even man is vile. I am grateful to the Rockefeller Foundation for the happy privilege of the experience, darkened only by the shadow of one's flickering awareness of the difference between that magical setting and the current historical torment of Italy.

I am in debt to several colleagues: to Dr. Howard Feinstein for close collaboration in research for chapter 11, to Meyer Abrams for a reference to Dr. Johnson, to Sander Gilman for a clinical clue to James's crisis, and to the section on the History of Psychiatry at Cornell Medical College for hospitality and stimulus to my ideas on psychological interpretation. Justin Kaplan has graciously permitted me to quote a letter of his to Albert Stone.

## Notes

1. Cushing Strout, *The American Image of the Old World* (New York, 1963).

2. For an assessment of psychoanalytic work in social science, literature, and history in American studies see the Bibliography issue of *American Quarterly* 28, no. 3 (1976), which includes my essay, "The Uses and Abuses of Psychology in American History," pp. 324–42.

3. Sigmund Freud, *Dora—An Analysis of a Case of Hysteria*, introduction by Philip Rieff (New York, 1963), pp. 31, 135, 32.

4. Jonathan Culler, *Structuralist Poetics: Structuralism, Linguistics, and the Study of Literature* (Ithaca, N.Y., 1975), pp. 131–32.

5. John William Miller, "On the Problem of Knowledge," in *The Paradox of Cause and Other Essays* (New York, 1978), p. 61.

6. Culler, *Structuralist Poetics*, pp. 29, 201, 246, 260, 130.

7. "Post-structuralism," the latest critical fashion from France, has arisen in the wake of structuralism, and its characteristic voices continue to speak (with cultish opacity of style) about the irrelevance of the author, the radical indeterminacy of texts, and the identification of history with fabulation. But in a recent collection of such voices Edward W. Said strikes a valuable dissenting note by arguing that texts place themselves in the world and so "impose constraints and limits upon their interpretation." See Said, "The Text, the World, the Critic," in *Textual Strategies: Perspectives in Post-Structuralist Criticism*, ed. Josué V. Harari (Ithaca, N.Y., 1979), p. 171. In a wide-ranging polemic against these "postmodern" tendencies Gerald Graff parallels my argument in calling for a historically oriented teaching of literature and for a recognition, in opposition to the radical skepticism favored by current literary theory, that it makes sense "to appeal to the facts when we assess the merits of conflicting interpretations, even though it is true enough that what the facts are is something that can be determined only by an act of interpretation." See Graff, *Literature against Itself: Literary Ideas in Modern Society* (Chicago, 1979), p. 202.

# PART 1
# Narrative Explanation

To know a story when we see one, to know
it *for* a story, to know that it is not reality
itself but that it has clear and effective
relations with reality—this is one of the
great disciplines of the mind.
—Lionel Trilling, *The Liberal Imagination*

# 1/The Fortunes of Telling

A decade ago Lionel Trilling remarked that the contemporary novel is unhappy with the narrative mode, "which once made its vital principle, and its practitioners seek by one device or another to evade or obscure or palliate the act of *telling*." He thought narrating was in difficulties because it took for granted the authority of the teller over his characters and his confidence in presuming to give counsel to the reader. "It is the nature of narration to explain," he observed, "it cannot help telling how things are and even why they are that way."[1] In his view the modern uneasiness over narration reflected a decline in the sense of history as providing either the sanction of a past or the assurance of a future. For him, story telling, historical consciousness, and explaining were all connected.

The fortunes of telling are much in dispute and have their own story. What Trilling joined together much of our current intellectual culture has rent asunder. Philosophers under the dominance of scientific models of explanation have tended to see stories as dependent upon nonnarrative causal regularities, rather than having any explanatory functions of their own. Many fashionable literary critics have been bent on subordinating the idea of temporal development to an ahistoric "structural" analysis. While some novelists have been deeply attracted to taking history seriously, others have been drawn to "deconstructing" it through parody. For many historians the traditional role of story telling has been downgraded in favor of sociological analysis, while a movement in Anglo-American analytic philosophy has sought to find in historical story telling valid forms of explanation that do not turn on scientific regularities.

Aristotle began the critical tradition that a story of an action must have a beginning, middle, and end, as a living organism does. A recent critic marks our distance from this classical standard by celebrating the category of the "post-war American non-fiction novel," which is said to see the world as a process "free from the meaning of a beginning or the significance of an end." [2] Another critic has seen the nineteenth-century novel's "imaginative involvement with history" as a departure from the outlook of earlier and later "self-conscious novelists," who emphasize the fictionality of their work, a tradition begun by Cervantes, Fielding, Sterne, and Diderot and continued by Joyce, Nabokov, and Borges. [3] Much modern writing subverts linear continuity. A recent historian of film finds a parallel between "the disruptive intentions of modern writers and artists" and "the increasing misgivings of historians and thinkers about the synthesizing narrative." Jacob Burckhardt in his history of the Renaissance, Siegfried Kracauer has remarked, was not much concerned with "the influences connecting the 'before' with the 'after'" and his account "time and time again escapes from the tyranny of the chronological order of things into more timeless regions where he is free to indulge in phenomenological descriptions, communicate his experiences, and give vent to his insights into the nature of man." [4] The most influential modern form of historiography has been the French *Annales* school, recently celebrated by an American social historian for signifying the replacement of narrative history by problem-solving, interdisciplinary study of slowly changing patterns in the lives of ordinary people. Fernand Braudel, the genius of the *Annales* movement, called himself a "structuralist" and emphasized "submerged history," changes of *longue duré* over vast sweeps of time, in contrast to the "conspicuous history" of political events. [5]

In current literary criticism the interest in narrative theory has coincided with a "structuralist" denigration of temporal process. Structuralism's founding father, the linguist Ferdinand de Saussure, as Jonathan Culler has pointed out, believed that explanation consists of relating an action "to the underlying system of norms which makes it possible." The special significance of this strategy lies in its move away from historical explanation:

> To explain social phenomena is not to discover temporal antecedents and to link them in a causal chain, but to specify the place and function of phenomena in a system. There is a move from the diachronic to the synchronic perspective, which one might speak of as an internalizing of causation: instead of conceiving of causation on a historical model, where temporal development makes something what it is, the historical results are detemporalized and treated simply as a state, a condition.[6]

For structuralists history is not man's essence; it does not hold his essential meaning; and it is not "a privileged means of access to the understanding of man."[7] It is just a chronological way of "encoding" the order of events, one possibility among many.

Trilling could have found evidence for his point in a contemporary American critic who has written extensively on both contemporary narrative theory and the structuralist movement. Linking the rise of the novel to the rise of historical consciousness, oriented toward actual events, he nevertheless betrays his structuralist interest in denigrating the diachronic when he speculates that the roots of our feeling for narrative structure are to be found not in the consciousness of historical sequences, but rather in the "rhythms of sexuality, the various periodicities of sperm production, menstruation, courtship, and coitus."[8] Pornography's absorption in sexual rhythms, displacing the traditional novel's focus on the particularities of person, place, and time, would seem to illustrate this speculation better than the love stories of the nineteenth century with their backgrounds of historical change.

In one quarter, however, the prestige of narrative has grown rather than diminished. Many postwar Anglo-American philosophers (R. G. Collingwood, William Dray, Alan Donagan,

Michael Scriven, W. B. Gallie, Arthur C. Danto, Louis O. Mink) have taken narrative seriously as the hallmark of historical understanding and explanation, distinguishing history from the abstract, deductive, and experimental style of natural science, which has dominated so much of modern Western philosophy. These thinkers do not see stories as "imperfect substitutes for more sophisticated forms of explanation and understanding," but rather as "primary and irreducible" ones. "It is from history and fiction," as Louis O. Mink has put it, "that we learn how to tell and to understand *complex* stories, and how it is that stories answer questions."[9] These philosophers, facing the prejudices of a positivist tradition of explanation, had to establish what Trilling took for granted—that narrative, history, and explanation are bound up together.

What stood in the way of this perception was the Humean philosophical tradition of identifying causality with correlations between similar types of events, a notion of causal connection difficult to find in the actual writings of historians whose generalizations usually have a different character. The philosophical narrativists challenged the positivistic demand that all valid explanation must have the character of summing up the necessary and sufficient conditions for an event through precise generalizations about the regular correlations between like events. They argued that historians do not characteristically establish laws or ordinarily appeal to them overtly because their generalizations are often merely truistic. They pointed out also that historical explaining is much broader than causal ordering and has many contexts, depending upon the presumed interests and ignorance of the reader.[10] Explanation by laws or by narratives serve different purposes. Narrativists do not rule out "causes," but they see them as specific judgments defining particularized, lawlike (but not lawful) attributes of "a response proceeding from the knowledge and character of the agents concerned."[11] Universal generalizations about human beings might guide the direction of research by pointing to possible connections, but historians do not use such lawful generalizations in explaining historical actions. They refer instead to the specific beliefs, purposes, and characters of particular agents, seen as elements of a story.

In the narrativist argument against causal explaining by lawful generalizations there was always the danger that this logical issue, more interesting to philosophers than to historians, would obscure the larger point that causal ascription is only one of the things narratives do. Even then, historians often use what one philosopher, Georg Henrik von Wright, has called "quasi-causal" explanations, which do not depend for their validity upon the truth of covering laws: "The events to which a causal role is attributed [like the assassination at Sarajèvo in relation to World War I] create a new situation and thereby provide a factual basis for practical inferences which could not have been made before." Actors assess the new situation in view of their existing intentions or reshape them because it has provided new opportunities. Some "quasi-causal" explanations, which are prominent in history, also have the explicative function, as von Wright has further pointed out, of helping us to understand "what something *is*" or "for which reason it happens" ["there was an uprising among the people because the government was corrupt and oppressive"], and their truth does not depend upon the validity of generalized connections between events [oppressive governments do not necessarily produce uprisings].[12] It is these "quasi-causal" (but valid) modes of explaining that histories include and develop. Von Wright briefly hints at the role of narration by noting that one could say that the intentionality of behavior is "its *place* in a story about the agent," because agents or their observers make behavior intentional by setting it in a context of aims and cognitions.[13] "Only in retrospective stories," Louis O. Mink has said, "are hopes unfulfilled, plans miscarried, battles decisive, and ideas seminal."[14] The historian J. H. Hexter has particularly enriched the controversy over historical explanation by pointing out that the most important part of the historian's work may not be the "processive" account of a sequence of events but rather the effort to show what it was like to be a person or a certain kind of individual or group in a particular place and time, a task demanding literary powers of evocation.[15]

Another danger in the narrativist strategy is that it might suggest too simple a view of both explanation and narrating. Hexter, for example, while repudiating the "fascinating errors" of Carl Becker's skeptical historical relativism, affirmed his "easy truths" about Mr. Everyman being "a specialist in history, because he has to be," doing research in his accounts in order to pay his coal bills. Even "a stupid six-year-old," Hexter maintained, could give an account of why he got his pants muddy and was late for dinner, so providing "the appropriate, adequate and complete explanation." [16] No covering laws need be invoked, only a simple story. Apart from the hidden role of custom in making these accounts intelligible to those who hear them, thus covertly presupposing some tacit generalizations, however familiar, in their narration, the trouble with these examples is that they do not resemble the problems historians worry their heads about. Sometimes telling part of a historical story might involve "easy truths" as simple as these, but the charm and challenge in studying history is more like the sophisticated traveler's effort to translate the speech and customs of a strange society, where the risk is not in making an error in computation, but in suffering culture shock. The stories of historians therefore are often made up with the help of ideas derived from economics, sociology, psychology, or anthropology, as well as those that come from practical experience and the familiar "logic" of a common situation.

The best narrativist arguments have recognized that analysis is part of making a narrative, not a substitute for it. Gallie's paradigm for understanding the historian's history is following a story full of surprises, accidents, and the unforeseeable, but oriented by previous necessary conditions and a vaguely promised culmination. But his comparison might fit too easily the tale of Jack and Jill. In revising his position Gallie concedes that history is "always much more than story" and includes impersonal trends as well as individuals, and must also contain—as aids to following the story—"interpretation, generalization, reflective discussion, and explanation." [17] Danto argues that narrative causality must depend on social generalizations about the constant conjunction of like events, which put events in a class, but he concedes that only knowing the agents' specific intentions can tell us in an overdetermined world *which* class is appropriate for a correct general description of the event to be explained. He also insists that any genuine narrative both "describes and explains at once."[18] Mink agrees that narratives answer "how" and "why" questions, as well as "who, what, and when" questions; and he emphasizes the point that understanding them is fundamentally a matter of seeing an event "as a response and therefore *as* an element in a story."[19] A narrative comprehends a moving pattern of reciprocal responses, as in a battle, with a beginning, middle, and end. It is not merely "one damn thing after another" in a bare chronicle of temporal succession, which disparagers of the diachronic perspective sometimes make it appear to be. Surely all these philosophers would agree that "Jack and Jill" falls short of being a history (even if their tumble actually happened) because we neither know why they wanted the water, how they fell, or what point there was in using vinegar and brown paper as a remedy for a broken crown.

At the other end of the spectrum even an enthusiastic spokesman for the replacement of narrative history by sociological, problem-solving analysis acknowledges the need to combine an emphasis on stable structures with "movement" and "trend" in a kind of "braiding" process, which must entail some element of narration.[20] Historians, as the English historian G. R. Elton has justly pointed out, may choose to focus analytically on dissecting a topic or on telling a story, and they may even do both within the same book. But no matter what form historical discussion takes, the questions "how" and "why"—not merely "what, where, when, and who," must underlie it, because historical truth is the product of a double process of "understanding what the evidence really says, and understanding how it fits together." This binocular perspective requires the historian to read "not only with the analytical eye of the investigator but also with the comprehensive eye of the story teller."[21] People talk of "straightforward history," Elton has remarked, "but what can be straightforward about a narrative which has to hold an infinity of threads in a single skein? What can be simple about a process which demands constant selection and rejection," trying to make prose represent history's complexity?[22]

It is ironic that Hexter should seek to root the validity of historical writing in the making of such simple narratives as the "stupid six-year-old's" account of why he got home late with muddy pants. Robbe-Grillet, pioneer of the bewildering *Nouveau Roman*, has also turned to young schoolchildren for his example because, before they are "conditioned by the narrative ideology of the society in which they live," their first attempts to "'relate the nicest day of your vacation'" produce stories that "are surely a lot closer to the style of the *Nouveau Roman* than to traditional novels, and the teacher immediately protests."[23] Only the teacher's instruction can bring "causality and chronology" into the child's mind as a form of "Balzacian order." The French writer romantically protests this development because for him "order itself is what is not endurable," and his own disjunctive "stories" are meant to subvert established order by calling attention through their own artificiality to the arbitrariness of all order. For him "the concept of truth in fact disappears" with respect to stories because he takes it for granted that "narrative has nothing to do with the referential."[24] But indirectly his example shows that doing historical narration is a relatively sophisticated skill, even in the "realistic" chronological and causal framework that he despises. Like a novel, narrative history tells a story that aims at "plausibility in depth"; like analytical history, "a novel may be much more than a narrative and much other," as a literary historian has observed, "and even when it is one, it may be expository."[25] Both forms describe, evoke, explicate, and explain.

Developments in the novel's form and in literary criticism have now complicated or threatened the narrativists' emphasis on story telling. Countering the contemporary fascination with social science, the historian C. Vann Woodward told historians "our kinship is actually much closer to novelists" than to social scientists.[26] But Hayden White, a historian responding to European literary theorists, derided the alliance for being based on an archaic tacit devotion to the linear time of a nineteenth-century novel,[27] displaced by the modern novel's increasingly complicated use of flashbacks, stream-of-consciousness techniques, and duplicitous narrators. Novels not only have become "increasingly saturated with history," as Woodward observed, they have also, as Joyce, Proust, and Woolf prove, increasingly come to "decompose" continuity over time. These new techniques need not contradict the historical consciousness modern novelists can still exhibit in their work, but White did not explain how historians could absorb such modern narrative sophistications. Historians might learn much, for example, from Freud's clinical method of retelling his story at different levels, as he unravels Dora's problems; but they can hardly do the same from the example of Nabokov's *Pale Fire*, which, according to one critic, is at least four novels and possibly an infinite regress of novels, "all different but all couched, oddly, in the same words." [28] Like novels, historical documents often have unreliable narrators, but written histories do not, unless the historian fails.

Structuralist French criticism has subverted the narrativist philosophers by assimilating historical discourse to its program for devaluing historical causality and the historical content of literature. Michael Lane, in an introduction to structuralism, has argued that structuralists explain changes in cultural configurations by "law-like regularities," rather than by historical processes of "cause and effect," while they demand that the present be fully known before any account be given of its development. [29] Lane also separates literature's "system of signs" from any content or "message." But historical discourse necessarily remains referential, and so for Roland Barthes, in French structuralist style, it is treated dubiously as "the only kind which aims at a referent 'outside' itself that can in fact never be reached." The modern "attenuation of narrative" thus represents in Barthes's view "a fundamental ideological transformation: historical narrative is dying; from now on the touchstone of history is not so much reality as intelligibility." [30]

Ironically, while the narrativist philosophers and their allies among the historians were becoming increasingly impressed by analogies between historical explanations and novels, structuralists undermined the point of this comparison by dehistoricizing literature and fictionalizing history. This dispute about narrative suggests the comedy about Mr. Box and Mr. Cox, who do not realize that they are inhabiting the same room because one of them rents it by day and the other by night, with the French critics and the Anglo-American philosophers being the boarders who pass each other on the stairs without speaking. Today, a military metaphor would be more appropriate, suggesting a French invasion of American shores. "There is no history, only fictions of varying degrees of plausibility," says the narrator of Gore Vidal's historical novel *1876*. A recent American study of narrative typically sees in the convergence of history, biography, and autobiography with the novel an expression of "a modern skepticism of knowing anything about human affairs in an entirely objective non-fictional way" because "all knowing and all telling are subject to the conventions of art." [31] In this light all narrative, whether in the novel or historiography, is "an unstable compound" of the fictional and empirical pressures which continually beset it.

Northrop Frye may seem to be a notable exception to this trend because he continues to believe that the distinction between fact and fiction is essential to sanity and even to newspapers, if not to literature, which by-passes the issue of credibility altogether; but his view of ordinary history relegates and degrades it to "a series of repetitions within a framework of compulsion and fatality" in which we know only by "seeing once again what we already know." Only the mythical imagination rises above this dreary round, and he separates the Bible from its historical matrix by declaring that if the biblical vision of life is "spiritually present in every event" as its "genuine form," it moves from the imaginative to the existential in "the opposite direction from the historical" by referring only to our own lives. Frye insists that it is "only the language of imagination that can take us beyond imagination." [32] But wherever it may take us, it is not located in history.

An American historian, Hayden White, has melded the Canadian Frye with the French structuralists and the German Karl Mannheim to create a theory of history that emphasizes its literary roots in the figures of classical rhetoric. White has applied Frye's literary categories—comedy, tragedy, romance, and irony—to the organization of all histories, while at the same time claiming that "different theories of the nature of society, politics, and history" are only appearances, veiling the ultimate reality of "figurative characterizations." [33] Seen in this garb as a muse of myths and tropes, Clio is transformed from Frye's greasy Joan, keeling the pot as a drab housemaid of compulsive repetitions, to a dark lady who speaks with a charming if somewhat artificial French accent. In his *Metahistory* White accuses the French of being "captives of tropological strategies of interpretation,"[34] but his own borrowing of four literary categories from Frye and four political categories from Mannheim to add to the four classical tropes of rhetoric will hardly strike historians as a blow for liberty, especially when it turns out that his categories are supposed to have predictable elective affinities for each other. White himself believes that "any linguistic protocol will obscure as much as it reveals about the reality it seeks to capture in an order of words."[35] It is rather like setting up Clio for a dazzling promenade with a figurative wardrobe of four garments in four shapes and four colors, none of which really seems to fit the restless lady. White's argument in the end asserts a self-styled linguistic "terminological determinism" of tropes, but he does not show concretely that the rhetorical design of the works of the "metahistorians" he examines are more fundamental and explanatory than their theories of society, politics, and history.[36] (Appropriately, it was French thinkers who originally made everything a matter of language, according to the principle of *Pygmalion's* Professor Higgins that "the French don't care what you do actually, so long as you pronounce it properly.")

White's strategy of finding fictive structures in historical writing is paralleled in literary criticism by a recent effort to redefine some American reportage of the 1960s as "the nonfiction novel." In this theory the category of "the fictual" is invented as a way of talking about contemporary American experience of reality as having "a disorienting fictiveness inherent in the facts," which are stranger than fiction.[37] This taxonomy is supposed to affiliate the nonfiction of Truman Capote's *In Cold Blood*, for example, with the flat characters, contrived plots, and antilinear stories of Thomas Pynchon's "transfiction" because both of them "accept the bizzare fictive nature of reality."[38] This category-mongering postulate of a "bi-referential" mode of writing, a tertium quid that can be called neither fact nor fiction, speciously presents itself not as a new interpretation, but only as an "inevitable" response to contemporary actuality. Actually, however, it reflects an influential political interpretation of America in the late 1960s as a country which, "having failed to cope with emerging urban reality," supposedly fell into "a total communal fear, estrangement, and paranoia." [39] Beyond these critical blurrings of the traditional Aristotelian distinction between history and poetry, between what happened and what might have happened, we enter the thicket where we are surrounded by fashionable hybrids of historical fact and literary fiction in such works as E. L. Doctorow's *Ragtime*, Alex Haley's *Roots*, and sundry TV "docudramas." These amalgams, which are somehow both more and less than historical novels, make us acutely uneasy about what standards would be appropriate for judging them. The two bestsellers are open to serious charges of historical distortion and also of copying fictional plots. [40]

What is lost in this fictionalizing mode is the sense of the "reciprocal pressure from reality upon consciousness, understanding, and a preordered mind set." [41] Structuralist "semiologists" assume that "no one can ever grasp exactly what another person might have had in mind," and it becomes unclear how we can make any discoveries about the world. [42] Both the theory of metahistory and the theory of the nonfiction novel give substance to the complaint that the temper of much vanguard discussion is the insistence on (in the words of Jeffrey Sammons) "the fictionalization of everything, the transformation of all reality into a literary text," in a climate of opinion where "language is regarded as controlling of the apprehension of the world rather than being ever and in any sense instrumental or referential." Where there is no tension between imagination and reality because everything is literature, as Sammons has further pointed out, "there is no category of the imagination." [43] Instead everything is swallowed up in that night in which all cats are not gray, but rather are as brightly painted as Henri Rousseau's animals.

For all their interest in stories the narrativist philosophers did not intend to make historical understanding fictional; on the contrary, they felt that so long as historians were justified only by their ability to make scientifically determined causal explanations, they would inevitably fail to meet such standards, thus leaving their field open to the condemnation of being impressionistic and arbitrary. Their interest was in finding valid forms of nonscientific explanation, rather than in imposing the paradigm of the laws of physics on historians. Indeed, influential relativists among historians, like Carl Becker and Charles Beard, were skeptics precisely because "they were still haunted by the abstract ideal of true explanation as the total reproduction of the past or the fixing of historical events according to laws." [44] They knew that historians could never realize this nineteenth-century ideal of knowledge, but they did not see that to let it stand as an unrealizable ideal was to make skepticism inevitable. They rightly insisted that it was a fallacy to think of the historian's mind as a mere mirror, reflecting the "cold hard facts" of the past; but they did not see that they were still trapped by the mirror metaphor in making the historian a relativist who could only project on the past his own time, writing history to make a usable past for the sake of political reform.

O History, as Carl Becker remarked, how many truths are committed in thy name! But there is no cynicism in this observation as long as it means that the course of events, like a moving train, provides new positions from which to survey the track left behind. Later events must inevitably refocus our attention on earlier ones. Similarly, all inquiry is guided by developing concepts that have their own history. But if the social pressures of the present stimulate historians to pose new questions about the past, those pressures cannot logically justify the answers that historians find, nor free them from the responsibility of distinguishing historically between their social hopes or fears and what the evidence obliges them to believe.

Some literary theorists have attempted to find in R. G. Collingwood's *Idea of History* a philosophical basis for the contemporary fictionalizing of history. Mark Weinstein, for example, finds in Collingwood's emphasis on the role of imagination in history conclusive evidence for the convergence of his philosophy with novels like Faulkner's *Absalom, Absalom!* and Thomas Pynchon's *V.* Weinstein sees these novels as a modern vision of history because they are ultimately ambiguous and agnostic about the truth of the questions their stories generate. In this reading of Collingwood the distinction between fiction and history disappears because both are seen as products of "the creative imagination," which is itself turned into a contemporary agnostic one. "The narrator of the novel," writes Weinstein about *Absalom, Absalom!*, "cannot give the true history because he does not know it." [45] Faulkner supposedly thus dramatized Collingwood's philosophy of history.

But the philosopher specifically insists upon the difference between novels and histories, for all their similarities in employing narration, description, presentation of motives, and analysis of characters. Both historian and novelist make the relation between a character and his situation so intelligible that "we cannot imagine him as acting otherwise," but the historian's picture of the past, Collingwood argues, is "meant to be true," a picture of things "as they really were and of events as they really happened." [46] For this reason histories, unlike novels, must be consistent with each other and rest on an "appeal to the evidence." Collingwood speaks of sources being "tainted," writers "prejudiced," and translations "misreadings," all needing to be "corrected" by the critical historian. He is not at all interested in making a case for what he called "historical skepticism." [47] He aims instead at destroying the fallacy that the historian passively reflects, as in a mirror, the facts given in documents, when in reality the historian has to use his critical thinking to infer from documents what the facts must have been if the evidence is to be understood in a "coherent and continuous picture, one which makes sense." [48] While Collingwood does not explain what coherent continuous sense means in history, it is at least clear that he in no way intends to suggest that historical thinking is "creative" in terms of invention. He himself was not only a philosopher but an archaeological historian of Roman Britain, working with traditional evidence.

Insofar as historical positivism treated events as mere happenings, detached from the mental outlook of participants, or ignored the existence of a history of history arising from the historian's being "a part of the process he is studying," Collingwood rejected it. But unlike the current fictionalizers of history he defined the study of history as "a science of a special

kind," and for him the historian's "business is not to invent anything, it is to discover something."[49] Moreover, far from licensing ambiguity as the characteristic result of historical interpretation, Collingwood thought it "wholly untrue" that historical argument is at best only permissive, never leading to certainty, only to probability. On the contrary, he believed one could make a historical argument which "left nothing to caprice and admitted of no alternative conclusion, but proved its point as conclusively as a demonstration in mathematics."[50] Nothing can be further from the spirit of the current fictionalizers of history.

Indeed, in some respects Collingwood is vulnerable to the charge of exaggerating the differences between fiction and history. He distinguishes art from history on the ground that the artist cannot formulate his problem until he has worked it out, while scientists, philosophers, or historians, like practical men, can be historically understood because they "proceed in their activities according to plans, thinking on purpose, and thus arriving at results that can be judged according to criteria derived from the plans themselves."[51] For this reason he concludes that there can be a history of artistic achievements, but no history of artistic problems. His concept of "re-enactment" as the historian's function highlights rethinking the reasons for an agent's choosing one alternative rather than another in an envisaged situation. To see his situation as one's own is not to perform an act of intuition or sympathy but to reconstruct a policy.[52] Yet Collingwood tends to contradict this view that only reflective actions, done on purpose, can be the subject matter of history when he also argues (as his critics have done) that "the extent to which people act with a clear idea of their ends, knowing what effects they are aiming at, is easily exaggerated. Most human action is tentative, experimental, directed not by a knowledge of what it will lead to but rather by a desire to know what will come of it." From this point of view artists are no longer in the special category Collingwood made for them and are more like most people in history, "embarking on a course of action without foreseeing its end and being led to that end only through the necessary development of that course itself."[5] Collingwood fails to resolve this tension in his position, but i

his antirationalist strain subverts an exaggerated emphasis on deliberate intentionality as the subject of history and undermines as well his view of the artist as a conspicuous exception to the rule, this conflict does not touch his refusal to merge history and fiction. Indeed, by praising Thomas Hardy for changing place-names in his novels, thus "recoiling against the discord of topographical fact in what should be a purely imaginary world," [54] Collingwood exaggerated the unhistorical nature of fiction and did not even consider what historical novels would do to his argument.

It can be argued, however, that narrativists have implicitly raised the issue of relativism by focusing on stories because, as one of them puts it, differences in literary form are "untranslatable into a common form to discover whether they are compatible or contradictory," since, their differences being not about theories or facts, but about imaginative structures, "one can prefer one to another only on aesthetic or political grounds." [54] Histories may be like stories, but stories notoriously do not agree with each other. Even within the world of a single novel, for example, there may be inconsistency, as in John Fowles's redoing of the nineteenth-century English novel in *The French Lieutenant's Woman*, where he introduces himself into the story as author and writes two different endings. Yet, even so, his novel reflects a deeply historical understanding of Victorian culture and exemplifies the modern writer's need to accommodate his historical consciousness and his aesthetic imagination without ignoring or compromising either one. Despite the trickiness of much contemporary narration and its absorption with subjectivity, alienation, absurdity, and linguistic self-consciousness, most serious novels still speak, however indirectly, to an actual historical situation, and sometimes they directly attempt to do the work of historians themselves, in part, by telling us how it was. Recognizing the historicity of fiction is, paradoxically, one way to forestall the vanguard tendency to reduce history to rhetoric, but without following quantitative historians in discounting narrative. The point is to appreciate the border country between history and

fiction without letting either one imperialistically absorb the other.

The overlapping territory between history and fiction is partly obscured by a venerable tradition tending to exaggerate their differences in favor of elevating the prestige of art over history. Ever since Aristotle, tradition has identified the historical with "what happened" and the fictional with "what could happen," and the distinction has usually followed Aristotle in finding poetry to be more serious than history because it gives "general truths" of probability or necessity. This invidious tendency to make one genre "descriptive" and the other "inventive" exacts the price of minimizing both the interpretive, explanatory function of historical story telling and the role of historical actuality in novels. One way of revising this traditional distinction is to defend the novel of manners on the ground that some "realistic" stories "can be read nearly as literally as history (much more literally than a great many history books)," [56] presumably inferior ones. Aristotle himself admits that the tragic dramatist may represent what has actually happened. Even so, "he is none the less a poet," he insists, "for there is nothing to prevent some actual occurrences being the sort of thing that would probably or inevitably happen, and it is in virtue of *that* that he is their 'maker.'" For him the realms of the probable and the necessary cover "the sort of thing that a certain type of man will do or say" and this typicality he contrasts with "particular fact," or "what Alcibiades did or what was done to him." [57] But surely one could point to poetry as the place where the particularity of experience is often most eloquently evoked; and Aristotle's concession itself acknowledges that in principle history can, after all, involve typicality. The soldier's historical experience of war, as Peter Munz has noted, includes not only the particulars of his time and place, but also the "universal drama of fear and triumph and of courage and cunning and anxiety pitted against evil obstacles," the same adventure that structures many novels. [58]

The most forthright way to revise Aristotle's distinction is to emphasize the point that the novel is "directly concerned with the nature of our situation in history, and with the direction in which that situation is about to move. . . . Implicit in the text of the novel are the propositions that man never lives by himself, and, above all, that he has a past, a present and a future. . . . The novel is the first art to represent man explicitly as defined historically and socially." [59] Surely the nineteenth-century novel is rich in evidence for this view, but what of those twentieth-century works in which authors deny "that structure, or 'history,' or the mechanisms of society can provide man with referents which enable him to know himself and the world"? [60] One strategy for dealing with them is to see them as also historical in representing a modern sociological reality of "dehumanization," even though the novel obsessed with dehumanized privatization may not see its material in a historical perspective.

If Aristotle's distinction survives in an invidious sense it is because of the formalist's claim that "the more closely great literature is examined, the remoter its connections turn out to be with any sort of history"; the "sweet birds" of art " inhabit no identifiable ruins; their songs refuse to acknowledge this or that ancestral origin." [61] All sweet birds sing in some choir, ruined or not, however, and their songs presuppose a tradition of singing which they continue or revise. Moreover, as well as participating in some literary tradition, novelists often engage in their own interpretation of their historical moment as an essential point of their art. The narrativist philosophers highlighted the explanatory function of stories withoug paying much attention to the historicity of fiction or the presence of artistic problems in the construction of histories. It has been historians, rather than philosophers or literary critics, who have responded to these issues.

C. Vann Woodward, for example, has emphasized the historical value of Southern novels, which have a consciousness of the past in the present without being conventional historical romances. "The historian is fortunate, I think," he remarks, "in sharing a period with literary men of great talent who share so many of his own values, so much of his own outlook and point of view, and so much of his own subject matter." [62] In this light the gap between fiction and history narrows, despite the point that histories, in principle, must be consistent with one another, while the worlds of novelists need not be. Among historians J. H. Hexter has written most persuasively on the importance of rhetorical skill in historical story telling not as decoration, but as a means of providing us with a way of recognizing "whether there was a historical story to tell, where the story should start, and roughly what the relative dimensions of its parts should be." [63] Decisions of this sort are precisely the ones that novelists have to make about their own stories, and they share as well the need for an ability to encourage "vicarious participation" in the lives of others, which can be an "indispensable part" of our understanding of the past as it actually was. [64] Furthermore, when Hexter gives historians the function of expanding consciousness not only to "a receptivity to a whole range of new experiences" but perhaps to "a permanent alertness" to "experiences even beyond that range," he speaks as a novelist often does about the aims of art. [65]

Yet Hexter also distinguishes Joseph Conrad's historically minded *Nostromo* from Oscar Handlin's novelistic *The Uprooted* on the ground that the worth of *Nostromo* would not diminish if the patterns of life Conrad ascribes to his imaginary Latin American republic were "quite remote from extrinsic actuality," whereas Handlin's presentation of immigrant experience, to be valuable, would have to be "something like" the immigrants' emotional response to their move to America." [66] Conceding that no historian has done any better than Conrad in showing effectively what a shaky Latin American republic (which he had never seen) was like, Hexter still thought it would be absurd to compare him as a historian with other historians because they have played different games with different rules. Only in a footnote does he acknowledge that a judgment about Conrad's success in portraying what such a republic was like might, after all, be an element in one's ultimate estimate of him as a fictive artist. [67]

As the historian John Lukacs has noticed, a *fact* originally meant something done, an action; and a *fiction* meant an act of fashioning or imitating. [68] The distinction therefore does not coincide exactly with the difference between something that happened and something that did not happen, because both words are rooted in the idea of an action. If taken literally, the traditional distinction between the actual and the possible as the dividing line between a history and a novel ignores the role of possibility in historical analysis and the role of actuality in the writing of novels. The proper response to the fictionalizing of everything is not to restore the distinction between poetry and history merely by negatively defining fiction as "what did not actually happen" and positively defining "fact" as "what really happened." This binary system leaves out the way in which a more complex series includes also "what might (could) have happened; what really happens; what might happen; what essentially (typically) happened/happens," and this series enters into the major forms of epic, romance, drama, and narra- tive.[69] By enlarging the spectrum Raymond Williams thus draws our attention to the "substantial overlap" of these cate- gories in histories, memoirs, biographies, dramas, epics, ro- mances, and novels. This recognition prepares us for a more imaginative response to historical writing and a more historical response to literature. There is an important sense, as Robert Weimann has said, in which "literature *is* history and history is an element of literary structure and aesthetic experience."[70] Marxists have made both of these observations, and the best Marxist theory can be an antidote to the recent intellectual tendency to aestheticize history and dehistoricize literature.

The point of this backward look at the recent status of story telling, however, is not to reassert a specific theory of history, particularly one which has the disadvantage of blurring the dif- ference between philosophy of history as reflection on how his- torical knowledge is possible and theory of history as a metaphysical view of how events come about not only in general but in particular. Such theory presupposes a grand design, a "superhistory," lurking behind the concrete story told by any actual historian, one which only the philosopher can explain. But this confusion of roles created hybrids, too empirical for the philosopher, too abstract for the historian, those centaurs of thought we find roaming the nineteenth century. The point rather is to see that the philosophers of history since R. G. Collingwood who have challenged the Humean mode of causal explaining, in order to see history as an affair of mind and will,

have been drawn inevitably toward looking at novels as including the sort of explaining, analogically, that histories also
provide. This analogy has now been subverted by the recoil in
art and criticism against the "realistic" novel of the nineteenth
century, by the analytical social history of the *Annales* school,
and by the structuralist devaluation of temporal process.
Resolving historical and literary discourse into rhetoric, as
structuralists have done, severs both from the historical
referents they share. The post-Collingwood tradition highlighted the territory where historical and literary perspectives
overlap but without engaging in much specific analysis of it;
the region is now something of a terra incognita among
philosophers, critics, and historians, though today journals like
*History and Theory* and *Clio* exist to fill some of "the
interstices between the intersections" created by the passion for
specialization that has isolated philosophy, history, and literature.

To consider the fortunes of telling at this moment is to appreciate the strangeness of our situation in which a French
literary analyst of "narratology" can conclude: "Today it is a
fact that it is no longer literature which provides the narratives which every society seems to need in order to live, but
film-makers tell us stories whereas writers deal with the play of
words." Another French critic has celebrated American "postmodern metafiction," with its "schizoid structures" and
"hallucinated subjectivity" as being essentially about "the subversion and the destruction of the narrative form itself." [71] Yet
in the 1960s, among writers themselves, there was a surge
of interest in the documentary drama, historical novel, and
imaginative journalism, a convergence emphasizing the overlapping of historical and fictional territories in contrast to the
Aristotelian tradition of separating them. These welcome
tendencies too often sponsor a theory, however, in which either
fact or fiction as a category is enlarged to engulf the other with
nothing left over, whether the gobbling be endorsed by novelists
or journalists. In this contemporary context post-Collingwood
philosophers should welcome an ally in what Collingwood did
not live to see, an Eriksonian "psycho-history" with a valuable
emphasis on the hyphen and the quotation marks as signs of

its ancillary and provisional role, a warning against reductionist engulfments. Ego psychology, in giving a more historical turn to Freudian psychology, has recently moved in a Collingwoodian direction, tending to see "causes" not as forces, but as redescriptions of an act in terms of an agent's reasons in order to make it more comprehensible. As the study of "both the person's reasons and the person's problems with reasons," current psychoanalysis is becoming congenially humanistic.[72] Like histories or novels, it also finds in story telling a form of discovering and stating human truths.

The territory of this overlapping of the realms of history, biography, and art now needs explorers who are, however, on guard against total mergers. Lives and texts, unconscious feelings and articulated goals, history and fiction, not only overlap; they illuminate each other because a vital tension keeps them to some degree independent as well as connected. To make a better balance current theory needs to historicize literature, rather than to fictionalize history by identifying it with mere particulars and encourage critics to grant art a freedom that severs it from history. But the scrupulous artistic imagination cannot transcend the historical imagination without ardently struggling to reconcile both of them. In the light of this encounter, where there are no easy victories for either one, we may learn better to mark out the boundaries of the border country between history and fiction.

Aristotle's separation will not remain as sharp a line as the one his quoters claim to find in his *Poetics*, but his idea of a distinction, suitably redrawn, can be valuable in opposing the fictionalizing of history and the "deconstruction" of literature's engagement with history. Even when both art and history, as they often do, focus on a historical situation, the historian's truth is bound to be more literal than the artist's, just as the artist's is bound to more figurative than the historian's. The one is constrained by public evidence while the other, even in a historical novel, has some vital freedom to invent and to draw on personal experience. Only specific analysis of concrete texts can illuminate the rationale of these differences when the artist and historian share a historical subject, but Aristotle was descriptively right to suggest a general difference as a matter of tendency. But he made the distinction invidious by granting a higher truth to art. In contrast, the historian John Lukacs counters that "it is more difficult to write a great history than a great novel," because documentary restrictions make the historian's artistic task even greater.[73] Rather than sponsor a contest between poetry and history for status, we should recognize instead the need for revising our critical and historical theories so as to take full measure of the border country that history and fiction share from their different perspectives. In that revision narrating can regain its power, being no longer separated from analysis and explanation. As the link between history, biography, and novel, narrating may then regain its status as a road to truth, which includes artistic evocation not as a byway, but as an essential part of the journey. Then what George Eliot once called for and celebrated as "the veracious imagination" may come into its own to counter the voracious imagination that today severs literature from history and resolves history into rhetoric.

## Notes

1. Lionel Trilling, *Sincerity and Authenticity* (Cambridge, Mass., 1973), pp. 134–35.

2. Mas'ud Zavarzadeh, *The Mythopoeic Reality: The Postwar American Nonfiction Novel* (Urbana, Ill., 1976), p. 87.

3. Robert Alter, *Partial Magic: The Novel as a Self-conscious Genre* (Berkeley, Calif., 1975), p. 89.

4. Siegfried Kracauer, *History: The Last Things before the Last* (New York, 1969), pp. 183, 186.

5. See J. H. Hexter, "Fernand Braudel and the *Monde Braudellien*...," *Journal of Modern History* 44, no. 4 (December 1972):480–539; David Hackett Fischer, "The Braided Narrative: Substance and Form in Social History," in *The Literature of Fact: Selected Papers from the English Institute*, ed. Angus Fletcher (New York, 1976), pp. 112–13.

6. Jonathan Culler, *Ferdinand de Saussure* (New York, 1977), pp. 76–77.

7. David Paul Funt, "The Structuralist Debate," *Hudson Review* 22, no. 4 (Winter 1969–70):639.

8. Robert Scholes, *Structuralism in Literature: An Introduction* (New Haven, Conn., 1974), p. 197.

9. Louis O. Mink, "History and Fiction as Modes of Comprehension," *New Literary History* 1, no. 3 (Spring 1970):557–58.

10. For a good summary of the argument see Rudolph H. Weingartner, "The Quarrel about Historical Explanation," reprinted in *Ideas of History*, ed. Ronald H. Nash (New York, 1969), 2:140–58.

11. Alan Donagan, "Explanation in History," in *Theories of History*, ed. Patrick Gardiner (Glencoe, Ill., 1959), p. 441.

12. Georg Henrik von Wright, *Explanation and Understanding* (London, 1971), pp. 155, 85.

13. Ibid., p. 115.

14. Mink, "History and Fiction as Modes of Comprehension," p. 557.

15. J. H. Hexter, *The History Primer* (New York, 1971), pp. 207–8.

16. Ibid., pp. 53, n.5; 50.

17. W. B. Gallie, *Philosophy and the Historical Understanding*, 2nd ed. (London, 1964), p. 3.

18. Arthur C. Danto, *Analytic Philosophy of History* (Cambridge, 1968), pp. 141, 232.

19. Mink, "History and Fiction as Modes of Comprehension," p. 555.

20. Fischer, "Braided Narrative," p. 121.

21. G. R. Elton, *The Practice of History* (Glasgow, 1969), pp. 109, 160.

22. Ibid., p. 115.

23. Alain Robbe-Grillet, "Order and Disorder in Film and Fiction," *Critical Inquiry* 4, no. 1 (Autumn 1977):4–5.

24. Ibid., pp. 6, 18.

25. George Watson, *The Study of Literature: A New Rationale of Literary History* (New York, 1969), p. 189. On the similarity between dramatic plotting and historical explaining see Michael Scriven, "Truisms as the Ground for Historical Explanations," in Gardiner, *Theories of History*, pp. 470–71; see also chapter 20.

26. C. Vann Woodward, "The Uses of History in Fiction," *Southern Literary Journal* 1, no. 2 (Spring 1969):58.

27. Hayden White, "The Burden of History," *History and Theory* 5, no. 2 (1966):126.

28. Peter J. Rabinowitz, "Truths in Fiction: A Re-examination of Audiences," *Critical Inquiry* 4, no. 1 (Autumn 1977):140.

29. Michael Lane, ed., *Introduction to Structuralism* (New York, 1970), pp. 17, 37.

30. Roland Barthes, "Historical Discourse," in Lane, *Introduction to Structuralism*, pp. 153–55.

31. Robert Scholes and Robert Kellog, *The Nature of Narrative* (New York, 1971), p. 151.

32. Northrop Frye, "History and Myth in the Bible," in Fletcher, *Literature of Fact*, pp. 16–19.

33. Hayden White, "The Historical Text as Literary Artifact," *Clio* 3, no. 3 (1974):299.

34. Hayden White, *Metahistory* (Baltimore, 1973), p. 3, no. 4.

35. Hayden White, "The Fictions of Factual Representation," in Fletcher, *Literature of Fact*, p. 36.

36. Ibid., p. 44. For White, great historians mediate between alternative tropological strategies, rather than using merely one, thus loosening up his system a bit, but he still dogmatically insists that what Tocqueville, for example, "means" by his terms "democracy" and "aristocracy" is *metonymy* and *synecdoche*. Ibid., p. 36. If tropes are ultimate, why should historians have to mediate between them? If his four patterns are intrinsically affiliated, why in practice are they so often mismatched?

37. Zavarzadeh, *Mythopoeic Reality*, p. 66.

38. Ibid., p. 45.

39. Ibid., pp. 42, 117.

40. For *Ragtime* see chapter 10. For *Roots* see Oscar Handlin, *Truth in History* (Cambridge, Mass., 1979), pp. 380–82.

41. Jeffrey L. Sammons, *Sociology and Practical Criticism: An Inquiry* (Bloomington, Ind., 1977), p. 155, n.

42. Culler, *Ferdinand de Saussure*, p. 125.

43. Sammons, *Sociology and Practical Criticism*, pp. xi–xii.

44. Cushing Strout, *The Pragmatic Revolt in American History: Carl Becker and Charles Beard*, 2nd ed. (Ithaca, N.Y., 1966), p. 159.

45. Mark A. Weinstein, "The Creative Imagination in Fiction and History," *Genre* 9, no. 3 (Fall 1976):272.

46. R. G. Collingwood, *The Idea of History* (Oxford, 1946), pp. 245–46.

47. Ibid., pp. 245–48.

48. Ibid., p. 245. Louis Mink asserts that Collingwood cares about how facts are *organized* into evidence rather than about how they are *established*; hence the "coherent picture" criterion deals with making evidence *intelligible*, rather than with *authenticating* it. Mink, *Mind, History, and Dialectic: The Philosophy of R. G. Collingwood* (Bloomington, Ind. 1969), p. 266, n. 10. But Collingwood does not make this distinction; he specifically argues that the historian's imagination is a "touchstone by which we decide whether alleged facts are genuine." Hence Collingwood rejects Suetonius's statement that Nero intended to evacuate Britain by saying: "my reconstruction of Nero's policy based on Tacitus will not allow me to think that Suetonius is right." Collingwood, *Idea of History*, p. 245.

49. Collingwood, *Idea of History*, p. 251.

50. Ibid., p. 262.

51. Ibid., pp. 312, 314.

52. Ibid., p. 283.

53. Ibid., p. 42.

54. Ibid, p. 246.

55. Louis O. Mink, review of Maurice Mandelbaum, *The Anatomy of Historical Knowledge*, in *History and Theory* 17, no. 2 (1978):222

56. Arthur Mizener, *The Sense of Life in the Modern Novel* (Boston, 1964), p. 268.

57. Aristotle, The Poetics, trans. W. Hamilton Fyfe (London, 1965), p. 37.

58. Peter Munz, *The Shapes of Time: A New Look at the Philosophy of History* (Middletown, Conn., 1977), p. 147.

59. Michel Seraffa, *Fictions: The Novel and Social Reality*, trans. Catherine and Tom Burns (Harmondsworth, England, 1976), pp. 10–11.

60. Ibid., p. 20.

61. F. W. Bateson, "Literary History: Non-subject Par Excellence," *New Literary History* 2, no. 1 (Autumn 1970):122.

62. C. Vann Woodward, *The Burden of Southern History* New York, Vintage Books, ed., 1961), p. 38.

63. "The Rhetoric of History," in J. H. Hexter, *Doing History* (Bloomington, Ind., 1971), p. 37.

64. Ibid., p. 43.

65. Hexter, *History Primer*, p. 108.

66. *Doing History*, p. 47.

67. Hexter, *History Primer*, p. 227.

68. John Lukacs, *Historical Consciousness or the Remembered Past* (New York, 1968), p. 105.

69. Raymond Williams, *Marxism and Literature* (Oxford, 1977), p. 148.

70. Robert Weimann, *Structure and Society in Literary History: Studies in the History and Theory of Historical Criticism* (Charlottesville, Va., 1976), p. 46.

71. Tzvetan Todorov, "The Principles of Narrative," *Diacritics* 1, no. 1 (Fall 1971):44; André Le Vot, "New Modes of Story-telling: Dismantling Contemporary Fiction," in *Les Américanistes: New French Criticism on Modern American Fiction*, ed. Ira D. Johnson and Christiane Johnson (Port Washington, N.Y., 1978), p. 117.

72. Roy Schafer, *A New Language for Psychoanalysis* (New Haven, Conn., 1976), pp. 210, 230.

73. Lukacs, *Historical Consciousness*, p. 127.

# 2 / Causation and the American Civil War

A specter haunts American historians—the concept of causality. After nearly a hundred years of passionate and dispassionate inquiry into "the causes of the Civil War" the debate is still inconclusive. Even more discouraging, according to the editor of a recent anthology of historical writings on the problem, "twentieth-century historians often merely go back to interpretations advanced by partisans while the war was still in progress."[1] Despite the impasse, historians are not often discouraged. Some take refuge in professional patience or the firm confidence that their opponents have simply hardened their hearts to truth. Others are reconciled to skepticism by the historical relativism, defended by Carl Becker and Charles Beard, which characterizes all historical interpretations as determined products of a temporary, dominant "climate of opinion." A few, like Beard himself, have drastically tried to cut the knot by surgical removal of the causal category itself from history, though his own practice of economic determinism flatly contradicted this Draconian proposal. When the investigation of the answer to a question has led to such frustrating difficulties, it is necessary to reexamine the question, even if it leads the historian into philosophical territory where he naturally fears to tread.

Historians are often vulnerable to Henry Adams's charge that their causal assumptions, "hidden in the depths of dusty libraries, have been astounding, but commonly unconscious and childlike,"[2] yet they can find no real help from the eccentric results of his own search for a historical physics which would unify the course of events under one abstract formula, "a spool upon which to wind the thread of the past without breaking it."[3] For all his brilliance his speculative theory has quite rightly struck most historians as an exotic hybrid of history and science, spoiling the integrity of each. The "scientific school of history" ended either in fanciful speculation about historical laws or a naive cult of fact-finding as the essence of scientific method. If even the scientist, at the level of subatomic particles, must substitute statistical probability for causal universals, the historian has always been embarrassed by the effort to discover conditions which invariably produce certain results not otherwise accounted for. He cannot discriminate with exactness constants and variables by experimentation on a past forever gone, nor can he always confidently turn to social scientists for causal rules when their findings, even when valid and relevant, are limited historically to particular times and places. Grateful as the historian may be for generalizations about, say, the voting behavior of Americans, he is ruefully aware that recurring evidence for the behavior of Americans in civil wars is fortunately not available.

The historian conventionally speaks of "multiple causes" because he knows he has no monistic formula to explain the course of history and no single generalization to cover all the necessary and sufficient conditions for a civil war. This fashion of speech is, however, misleading because he cannot escape his difficulties by multiplying them. If he does not believe that each of the many "causes" could have produced the Civil War by itself, then he must assume that the whole collection of them acted together as one in bringing about that effect. He is then left with the familiar problem of accounting for this causal relationship by reference to confirmed generalizations. What he

cannot do for one "cause," he cannot do for a set of them acting
as one.

Historians sometimes seek to avoid the problem of
generalized causal rules by talking of a necessary chain of
events.[4] Yet the events which are put into the so-called chains
clearly have more determinants than are recognized by so plac-
ing them, and the same event can be put into a number of
possible chains. The election of Lincoln, produced by a large
number of small events, might well appear in two alleged
chains of events which suggest quite different interpretations of
the coming of the war. The chains are not, furthermore, really
"necessary" unless their linkage is explained by theories or
generalizations which the makers of chains seldom make clear,
even to themselves.[5]

A deeper difficulty of the causal query is that it may be defined so as to conflict with the historical attitude itself. If the
historian were to deduce consequences from antecedents, there
would be nothing in the former not found in the latter. How
then could he speak of anything new happening at all? The special sensitivity of the historian is to the novel elements, the discontinuities, emerging in a situation. He discovers the relevant
antecedents retrospectively with the help of the illumination of
the consequences, which call out for a past. Looking backwards,
he discerns a process that does not logically or inevitably follow
from certain antecedents, but takes its life and form only from
its development. There is no point at which the historian can
declare that the Civil War became inevitable, even though he
might find it increasingly probable. Those who have said it was
inevitable have either deduced it from a dogmatic general
proposition about the "necessary" conflict of classes in society,
according to the determinism of historical materialism, or they
have pointed instead to the stubbornness of the slavery problem
and the moral and ideological imperatives which made certain
policies humanly "necessary" (granted their premises), rather
than historically inevitable in terms of an impersonal process.[6]
In studying the Civil War the historian must know about such
antecedents as the origins and expansion of slavery, for
example, but he cannot deduce the war from the existence of

that institution. "American historians have been too clever by half," Carl Becker once said, "in finding other causes of the Civil War,"[7] but the cleverness has been stimulated by knowledge of the fact that slavery existed and was eliminated elsewhere without civil war.

The serious difficulties of exact causal determination have led some thinkers to suggest that the historian make reasonable estimates of causes, based upon his judgment of what *would* have taken place in the absence of a particular factor being tested for causal relevance.[8] If the course of events would have been much the same, the factor is assumed to have had no causal significance. Some critics have replied that history is, as Beard maintained, "a seamless web"; but surely it is not so seamless that historians must follow Beard in believing that there is no more reason to explain American intervention in the First World War by reference to the German policy of un-limited submarine warfare than by reference to the Kaiser's moustaches.[9] This extreme position denies to the historian that realistic sense of relevance which the study of history and direct experience of human affairs have traditionally provided. Many explanations in history certainly do reflect and depend upon this trained sense of relevance.[10] Modern historians have stressed slavery rather than states rights in explaining the crisis of 1860 because they know that the legal position of states rights has often sheltered Northerners and Southerners alike, depending on the more substantial interests it has been designed to protect. Beard himself rejected Turner's stress on the importance of free land to American development on the ground that though slavery, capitalism, and free land were "woven in one national mesh," yet "slavery would have been slavery and capitalism capitalism in essence even had there been no free land with its accompaniment".[11] He could only ar-rive at this conclusion by imaginatively breaking the web he considered "seamless." (Even so, this procedure does not con-vincingly support Beard's thesis of the Civil War as a necessary conflict between capitalism and agrarianism, not only because the economic issue of the tariff had been gradually composed since 1832, but because it was during the competition for and debate over the western territories that relations between the sections became embittered to a state of crisis out of which the war came.)

Sidney Hook has persuasively argued for the importance of hypotheticals contrary to fact in establishing the interrelation of events. Yet he admits that though we have the right to make such predictions when they rest upon valid generalizations about individual and social behavior, still "we have no logical guarantee that they will continue to hold or that something new and completely unforeseen will not crop up." [12] The difficulty is that in dealing from a hypothetical point of view with a particular series of events we are assuming that it will not be intersected by other seemingly unrelated series of events. For this reason our calculations, even at their best, may be "well grounded and reliable but not certain." Is the process sound enough to justify our saying that slavery was the cause of the Civil War if by assuming its absence we could reasonably demonstrate that there would have been no armed conflict? We would then have to show that none of the other issues between the sections was intractable or explosive enough to generate war. The problem is that slavery was so entangled with the other grievances of a political, economic, and social character that it is artificial to separate it out, nor do we have at hand a confirmed set of generalizations about the causes of war to apply. Whatever our calculations might be, we could not satisfy the unknowns in the formula "if *a* and *only a*, then *b* and *only b*." We might well grant that though the North fought for the Union, and the South for the right of secession, still it was slavery which menaced the Union and needed Southern independence to protect its growth; even so, we could only conclude that the war was essentially fought *about* slavery, not that it was *produced* by it.

The hypothetical method of discovering causal relevance has awkward difficulties whenever the issues become complex. The historian is trained to think with respect to documentary evidence, which exists only for what did happen, not for what would have happened. He can reflect upon what might have happened in order better to evaluate what actually did happen, but to speculate on what would have happened often puts him in the position of building his hypothesis on a nest of bottomless boxes of untestable hypotheses. It is clear that the historian may sensibly ask if slavery might have expanded into the newly acquired territories in the 1850s and after. Whether or not Americans were quarrelling about "an imaginary Negro in an impossible place" has turned on a discussion of the relevance of a staple-crop system inappropriate to the arid lands of the West, the potential use of slavery in mining, the expansionist ambitions of Southerners, or the fears of some future technological invention as potent as the cotton gin in bolstering slavery.[13] The question serves to highlight the possibilities contained within the situation of crisis, and it has a bearing on the historian's appreciation of the Republicans' position of containment of slavery.

Doubt over the significance of an event tends to generate the conditional query as a way of resolving it. If the historian wonders why the South seceded after Lincoln's election, he might ask himself what would have happened if Senator Douglas had been elected. Since Southern Democrats had already rejected Douglas at the Charleston convention, they *might* have found him intolerable as president. The historian cannot be sure, but the question points up the South's demands and highlights the importance to Southern eyes of Lincoln being the leader of a sectional party committed to containment of slavery. Since men who act in history must calculate the possible consequences of various alternatives, the historian in trying to understand them is led to do the same. Questions of what would have happened can be answered, of course, only by judgments of probability based on knowledge of the actual situation. They emphasize the significance of certain happenings without pretending to an impossible certainty, specificity, or scope.

A merely utopian conditional question allows equally plausible but contradictory answers. It has, for example, been argued that if the North had let the South secede in peace, the two nations would have enjoyed future friendly relations, thus saving the terrible costs of war.[14] It is not surprising that a Southerner might find this assumption convincing, but it clearly includes too many imponderables to justify any firm judgment. To raise questions that cannot be reasonably answered is an exercise in futility unless they are treated only as the indirect means of drawing attention to elements of an actual situation. Asking what would have happened if the North had "let the erring sister go" only serves to force a weighing of Lincoln's policy reasons for holding a symbol of federal authority in the South, as well as of the nationalistic sentiments of the Northerners who supported him. Provided the historian maintains his primary interest in what actually did happen, he may with propriety, under certain conditions, ask what might have happened or what would have happened. Such questions are especially useful for evaluating policy.

The most frequent type of historical explanation usually appears in causal disguise, which helps account for the historian's reluctance to banish the idea of cause. *Cause* often functions as *reason* or *purpose*. Explanation in terms of purpose is the natural way participants in a situation account for what happens. Thus the interpretations of the Civil War that prevailed at the time were couched by the North in terms of the aims of a "conspiracy" of aggressive slaveholders and by the South in terms of the ambitions of a radical group of abolitionist "Black Republicans." These simple theses were too obviously partisan charges of blame to find acceptance by later historians, whose professional confidence is rightly based on the principle that those who come after an event can, with the help of emotional distance, awareness of consequences, and wider perspective, know more about it than any participant. But even later historians have extensively used the language of purpose. The "revisionist" thesis of a needless was produced by "blundering statesmanship" essentially interprets the war in that way, as the consequence of human judgments and passions, though it condemns them as "irrational."

The historian cannot dispense with "cause" in this sense because, as Becker put it, "men's actions have value and purpose; and if we write history in such a way as to give it meaning and significance we have to take account of these values and purposes, to explain *why* men behave as they do, what they aim to accomplish, and whether they succeed or not."[15] The critic might well say that a man's purpose may not be the cause of his action—yet apart from this "humanistic" concern history threatens to become a merely impersonal process which "might have occurred at any time and in any place, given a sufficient number of persons to operate the events."[16] It is this intense commitment to the purposive dimension of history which leads many historians to feel a strong sympathy with literature and a sullen suspicion of social science. The occasional philistinism and arrogance of some propagandists for the social sciences have made many historians understandably defensive.

Yet in cooler moments the humanistic historian must acknowledge that this purposive dimension does not exhaust history. Historians have also been keenly interested in the explanatory relevance to American history of such relatively impersonal factors as Tocqueville's "equality of condition," Turner's "frontier hypothesis," Beard's "capitalism and agrarianism," Potter's "abundance," and Hartz's "atomistic social freedom." These explanations need not be antagonistic when they are formulated without monistic claims. Turner, despite the dogmatism of his famous essay, was committed in principle to a "multiple hypothesis" approach; Beard was increasingly led to modify the monistic and deterministic implications of his economic interpretation; and both Potter and Hartz have explicitly repudiated the sufficiency of a single-determinant explanation.[17] The force of these various theories lies in their capacity to illuminate structure and continuity in American history, as demonstrated by specific historical illustrations, numerous enough to give significance to the generalizations. As such, they are not so much "causes" of specific events as they are ways of segregating out long-term conditions and tendencies of American culture and development. They give contour and meaning to the stream of events insofar as the historical evidence supports the generalizations.

The causal problem becomes acute when the historian faces the task of explaining a complex series of events which have the ideal unity of a single event, like the Civil War. The general causal question is then propounded: what was "the fundamental cause" of the event? The notorious disparity of opinion on the answer to this question should suggest that there is some fallacy in seeking to find a prime mover that can be abstracted from the process to account for it, like slavery, rival economic systems, or the "blundering statesmanship" of agitators and leaders. None of these alleged fundamental causes can be understood apart from their specific historical context, nor could any person be said to understand the Civil War who only knew that its fundamental cause was any or all of these things. Otherwise history would merely be a cookbook for those sworn to fasting. These judgments of fundamental causality are only retrospective assessments of a reconstructed story and never a substitute for it. Actually they should be taken only as clues to the story being told. The pragmatic meaning of the assertion that slavery was "the fundamental cause" is only that the institution was so deeply entangled in the issues that divided the sections that it provides a valuable focus for examining the skein of events which culminated in war.

The historian does his work in good conscience, despite the difficulties of causality, because so much of his labor does not depend upon causal judgment. Whatever some philosophers may say, he knows that explanation is broader than causal explication. He may tell his readers much about the issues between Lincoln and Douglas, the legal status of slavery, the structure of classes in society, the economic interests of the sections, the character of the abolitionist movement, the balance of power in the Senate, the social and ideological differences between North and South, and the chronology of events without venturing beyond descriptive analysis into causal judgment. Characteristically, the historian explains by showing how a certain process took shape, answering the "why" with more of the "what" and "how." "The careful, thorough and accurate answer to the question *How*," writes the English historian C. V. Wedgwood, "should take the historian a long way towards answering the question *Why*." [18] The historian is inescapably committed to narrative.

The relativists may quickly point out that the stories historians have told clearly reflect the "climate of opinion" in which they were constructed. Beard's economic interpretation grew out of a Progressive milieu in which the critics of industrial America had been drawn increasingly to economic analysis of contemporary problems; the "revisionism" of J. G. Randall betrayed some of the liberals' disillusionment with

World War I and the fear of involvement with World War II; Arthur M. Schlesinger, Jr.'s criticism of the "revisionist" thesis of "a needless war" openly compares the Nazi and Southern threats to an "open society" and reflects the postwar "hard" policy toward Soviet imperialism; and Avery Craven's latest analysis, a modified "revisionist" view, strikes a Cassandra pose by comparing the Civil War crisis to the frightening "cold war" situation of today, where huge power blocs compete for "satellites" and are deeply estranged from mutual understanding.[19] Inevitably, the historian's experience of present history will suggest questions and hypotheses, and in the attempt to relate his story to his public he will naturally try to find terms appropriate to his own age. Yet he must always be on guard against the insidious tendency of analogy to blur the important nuances of difference between a past age and his own. His fundamental premise as a historian must be that human experience significantly changes in its form and meaning, that his present is only a phase of a process which calls out for historical analysis precisely because it is not uniform and continuous. The historian may believe that while one generation passes away and another generation comes, the earth abides forever, but it is his special obligation to note that the sun also rises on a new day.

The relativism of Becker and Beard was a valuable attack on the pretensions of nineteenth-century historical positivism, but its force was blunted by remnants of the same determinism they challenged. Becker considered historical judgments transient and arbitrary because he saw the mind of the historian as a mere product of the social forces active in his setting, projecting onto the blank screen of the past his own image, shaped by the hopes and fears generated by his "climate of opinion." Beard was nostaligic for the dream of an omniscient grasp of the totality of all happenings. He knew the dream was utopian; therefore, he settled instead for an "act of faith" in historical progress toward a specific future as the basis for interpretation of the past, a prediction which future history would validate or refute. But one must reply: if involvement in present history gives the historian his need to know the past, it does not necessarily prevent him from having enough detachment to apply articulate and impersonal standards to the evidence he examines; if the historian cannot know everything, it does not follow that he cannot know anything of historical importance; if the future is opaque, the past cannot be illuminated from a source which, being still indeterminate, will not furnish any light; if the historian is truly honored, it is because of his power of hindsight, not his power of prophecy.

If historians seem to have rented out a large hotel of "rooms with a view" in order to tell their story of the Civil War, it should be remembered that the sign out front should often read, "philosophy, not history, spoken here." Much of the recent debate over the Civil War centers on philosophical issues about economic determinism or rationalist politics. The historical materialists reduce the political, ideological, and moral questions to the "inevitable" conflicts of classes in society; the "revisionists" assume that violence is abnormal and that an event as bloody and tragic as civil war must have been avoidable by "rational" men; their critics point to the intractability of moral issues and the normality of nonrational factors in history.[20] Historians cannot escape such philosophical questions, but they need not entail a skepticism about historical truth.

The philosophy of history in America, as Morton G. White has pointed out, has been a very poor relation indeed. (Not even the Pragmatists, who did much to stimulate interest in history, paid it the honor of systematic attention. It is therefore encouraging that White should seek to lead philosophers to consider the "special kind of discourse" which is narration.[21]) The causal problem would be greatly clarified if both historians and philosophers realized that in telling a story the historian is committed to the "logic" of drama. In explaining the Civil War he necessarily seeks to recreate the strife of opposing forces out of which the war came. The connective tissue of his account then has a dialectical form: a person or group takes a position and performs an action because of and in relation to the position or action of another person or group. The historian's story becomes a narrative of this reciprocal response. Thus, by a crude sketch, the explanation of the event would have this character: Lincoln saw in the South's proslavery position a threat to the democratic traditions of the American com-

munity; the South saw in his election the menace of future in-
terference with their "peculiar institution" and growing domination by an industrial North; Lincoln and the North saw in
Southern secession a challenge to federal authority and the
prestige of national union; the South saw in the provisioning of
Fort Sumter an intolerable danger to the independence of the
Confederacy. In such terms, but with much greater richness
and concreteness, the historian tries to reconstruct the dramatic
"logic" of a sequence of events which demands to be humanly
understood rather than scientifically explained.

This dialectical method does not entail any Hegelian
scheme or "bloodless dance of the categories"; on the contrary,
it keeps the historian in touch with the familiar existential
world of human action, too concrete and passionate for final
abstract accounting. Like the action of a novel or play, it can be
imaginatively experienced as a meaningful plot in which
character, events, and circumstances are woven together in a
process made intelligible in human terms of tradition, interest,
passion, purpose, and policy. This kind of historical action is
understood in the same way as a novel's plot is understood,
though the former must be faithful to given evidence and the
later to aesthetic standards. To ask the question "why?" is then
meaningful only as a demand for enlightenment on some
particular passage of the story which does not "make sense."
The general causal question remains at worst an irrelevant
basis for interminable disagreement, at best a generator of
hypotheses to stimulate research which may promote understanding by leading to a richer, more coherent story.

In reconstructing the dramatic "logic" of a situation which
eventuated in civil war, historians cannot expect to achieve a
flawless coherence in their stories. They have no warrant for
making history neat and tidy when experience itself has ambiguities. Often there is uncertainty about motives, even for the
actor himself, because the flaw lies not in the historian's impotence but in the documents or life itself. Even if historians
cannot agree, to cite a classic controversy created by conflicting
evidence, whether Lincoln sent a relief ship to Sumter in the
cunning expectation that the South would commit aggression

by firing on the fort, or, on the contrary, discovered by the attack how inaccurately he had measured the secessionist temper, nevertheless, they can still reach a common understanding of his policy reasons for risking war in the first place, whatever he expected or hoped would happen, after he had done what he felt had to be done. Historians will never escape the need for critical debate on their findings to help them move toward a consensus of understanding, but this fate is no ground for despair. It is rather the dogmatic insistence on scientific explanations, especially when they are beyond historical competence, that dooms historians to endless and fruitless contention.

White prophesies "a new era in the philosophy of history" when "the tools of linguistic philosophy" shall be brought to bear on "clarifying the logic of narration." [22] Sharp as these instruments are, however, they involve the risk that the operation may kill the patient. In explaining narration it may be forgotten that narration is a form of explanation, which aims not at logical rigor of implication but at dramatic comprehensibility, appropriate to the untidy, passionate, and value-charged activities of men. Historians may be said to be engaged in constantly teaching that lesson, yet, as much of the long inconclusive debate about "the causes of the Civil War" makes clear, without really knowing it. It is time they directly confronted the specter that haunts them.

(1960)

## Notes

1. Kenneth M. Stampp, *The Causes of the Civil War* (Englewood Cliffs, N.J., 1959), p. vi.

2. Henry Adams, *The Education of Henry Adams* (New York, 1931), p. 382.

3. Ibid., p. 472.

4. Adams described his own history of the United States as an effort to state "such facts as seemed sure, in such order as seemed rigorously con-

sequent," so as to "fix for a familiar moment a necessary sequence of human movement." Ibid., p. 382.

5. Mario Bunge, *Causality: The Place of the Causal Principle in Modern Science* (Cambridge, Mass., 1959), p. 126.

6. Arthur M. Schlesinger, Jr. sees the Civil War as a "log-jam" which had to be "burst by violence," a common feature of the "tragedy" of history; but surely only commitment to policy positions deemed necessary and worth the price of force explains the "log-jam" he describes. See Schlesinger's "The Causes of the Civil War: A Note on Historical Sentimentalism", *Partisan Review* 16 (1949):969–81. Pieter Geyl, who also attacks the "revisionist" thesis of a "needless war," carefully avoids making the claim that it was inevitable, leaving the issue moot. See Geyl's "The American Civil War and the Problem of Inevitability", *New England Quarterly* 24 (1951):147–68.

7. Becker to Louis Gottschalk, 3 September 1944, in Carl Becker, *Detachment and the Writing of History*, ed. Phil L. Snyder (Ithaca, N.Y., 1958), p. 88.

8. See Max Weber, "Critical Studies in the Logic of the Cultural Sciences", reprinted in English in *The Methodology of the Social Sciences*, ed. Edward A. Shils and Henry A. Finch (Glencoe, Ill., 1949), esp. pp. 164–88.

9. See Charles Beard's *The Discussion of Human Affairs* (New York, 1936), p. 79, where he characterizes causal judgments as subjective, arbitrary ruptures of the "seamless web" of history.

10. The relevance of training to the use of "guarded generalizations," neither purely analytic nor purely synthetic, is argued convincingly by Michael Scriven, "Truisms as the Ground for Historical Explanations," in *Theories of History*, ed. Patrick Gardiner (Glencoe, Ill., 1959), pp. 463–68.

11. Charles Beard to Frederick Jackson Turner, 14 May 1921, Box 31, Turner Papers, The Huntington Library, San Marino, Cal.

12. Sidney Hook, *The Hero in History: A Study in Limitation and Possibility* (New York, 1943), p. 132.

13. See Harry V. Jaffa, "Expediency and Morality in the Lincoln–Douglas Debates", *Anchor Review* 2 (1957):199–204.

14. Richard H. Shyrock, "The Nationalistic Tradition of the Civil War: A Southern Analysis," *South Atlantic Quarterly* 32 (1933):294–305. There is a useful extract in Stampp, *Causes of the Civil War*, pp. 45–49.

15. Becker to Gottschalk, 3 September 1944, in Becker, *Detachment and the Writing of History*, p. 87.

16. Carl Becker, "Harnessing History," *New Republic* 22 (1920):322.

17. For Turner and Beard see Strout, *The Pragmatic Revolt in American History: Carl Becker and Charles Beard* (New Haven, 1958), pp. 21–23, 105–6. For the others see David M. Potter, *People of Plenty: Economic Abundance and the American Character* (Chicago, 1954), p. 165; Louis Hartz, *The Liberal Tradition in America* (New York, 1955), pp. 20–23.

18. C. V. Wedgwood, *Truth and Opinion: Historical Essays* (London, 1960), p. 14.

19. Schlesinger specifically refers to the problem of dealing with a "closed society" in both periods. See Schlesinger, "The Causes of the Civil War." The

"cold war" analogy is extensively developed in Avery O. Craven, *Civil War in the Making, 1815-60* (Baton Rouge, La., 1959), esp. pp. xiii–xiv.

20. Illustrative examples of these three positions can be found in Stampp, *Causes of the Civil War*, pp. 56–65, 83–87, 113–22.

21. M. G. White, "A Plea for an Analytic Philosophy of History," in Morton G. White, *Religion, Politics, and the Higher Learning* (Cambridge, Mass., 1959), p. 74.

22. White, "Plea for an Analytic Philosophy of History," p. 74.

# 3 / The Unfinished Arch: William James and the Idea of History

There is a persistent piece of professorial folklore about William James. His contribution to philosophy, according to the myth, was Pragmatism, a typically American reduction of theory to practice, which merely provided James and the tightfisted folk of the New World with a philosophy for getting along without any philosophy. Others have ably defended James as an individual from the ridiculous charge of opportunism by pointing out that this perpetual champion of the underdog and hater of bigness was a passionate foe of the American worship of "the bitch goddess SUCCESS" with its "squalid cash interpretation" and "callousness to abstract justice."[1] What requires even more emphasis is that for all his conversational tone and impatience with academic technicality James profoundly needed philosophy. In the crisis of his depression of 1870, marked by an ebbing of the will to live, he was characteristically saved, through the French philosopher Charles Renouvier, by conversion to the philosophical doctrine of free will. After the formulation of his famous method of Pragmatism, he moved steadily toward the construction of a metaphysics. "I think the center of my whole *Anschauung*," he wrote in 1909, "since years ago I read Renouvier, has been the belief that something is doing in the universe, and that novelty is real."[2]

The pressing concern of his last years was to complete the architecture of his "tychism," for which he had laid the foundation in *Radical Empiricism* and *A Pluralistic Universe*. In the month before he died in 1910 he wrote in a memorandum directing the publication of *Some Problems in Philosophy*, published posthumously in its fragmentary and unrevised condition: "Say that I hoped by it to round out my system, which now is too much like an arch built only on one side."[3] If James hated "the abstract rigmarole in which our American philosophers obscure the truth," it was not because he had any animus against metaphysics or systematizing, but because he was too much the artist to tolerate "that kind of oozy writing."[4] (As Santayana remarked, James not only did not talk like a book, he did not even write like a book—except like one of his own.) While his death cut short the completion of the arch of his bridge, the structure still stands as a provocative monument to a dynamic view of reality. As it hangs there in the air with the pathos of the unfinished, it tempts the charmed spectator to speculate on how it might have fulfilled its intention.

James was confident that the Pragmatic movement marked a new turn in thought, "something quite like the protestant reformation," which was destined for "definitive triumph."[5] Recent scholarship has clearly demonstrated the broad American impact of what Morton G. White has called "the revolt against formalism" in philosophy, law, economics, and history, and H. Stuart Hughes has saluted James as "the revivifying force in European thought in the decade and a half preceding the outbreak of the First World War."[6] Yet fifty years after his death the philosophical scene seems to lack Jamesian landmarks. Logical positivism, symbolic logic, linguistic analysis, dialectical theology—none of these powerful currents of thought has a Jamesian source, direction, or character. He stubbornly opposed the limitation of meaningful discourse to scientific statements; he mistrusted logic, hated verbalism, scorned the intellectualistic ingenuities of dialectic, and condemned the omniscient and omnipotent God of theology as "a disease of the philosophy-shop." If the imagination can conjure up the picture of James at a contemporary convention of professional philosophers, it boggles at conceiving how he would be able to contain himself. This hostile confrontation of James with present philosophical tendencies is, nevertheless, a misleading half-truth. There is one very modern philosophical interest with which James would profoundly sympathize: philosophy of history. (In his ethics James seems, because of his emphasis on an ultimate challenge to "our total character and personal genius," very close to existentialism, but characteristically without its tragic despair.) It is not, I hope, farfetched to imagine that if he were to complete the arch he had so brilliantly begun he would have had to move toward a philosophy of history.

The phrase "philosophy of history" is unhappily ambiguous, and I hasten to say that he would not have found himself sympathetic with grandiose efforts to see in the course of events some vast design decipherable only to the prophet's eye of faith. He would have had as little respect for a spiritual historical determinism as he showed for the pseudoscientific effort of Herbert Spencer to discount the role of great men in history by a monistic appeal to "the aggregate of past conditions" or the pseudoscientific ambition of Henry Adams to justify his pessimism by the application of the second law of thermodynamics to human history.[7] What he would have sympathized with, I think, is a philosophy of history that makes time intrinsic to reality, sees in history the place where man makes himself in actions and institutions, and finds in it the morality of responsibility for commitments to finite enterprises. He would appreciate too the effort to provide explanations for past events without recourse to historical laws. From this point of view it is permissible to believe that James would have found nourishment in the writings of such varied modern historical thinkers as R. G. Collingwood, Ortega y Gasset, Raymond Aron, K. R. Popper and Isaiah Berlin. If James had been able to finish his arch, perhaps it would not be so difficult as it now is to find an American name in any list of significant philosophers of history.

These speculations of mine are based on a vivid and durable thread running through, to use one of his brother's phrases, "the figure in the carpet." This motif is always relevant to the idea of history, and it appears in his conception of psychology, truth, and metaphysics. To see its place in the design may help give us a better sense of what the unfinished arch needed for its completion.

The most celebrated and fruitful concept in *The Principles of Psychology* is James's idea of "the stream of consciousness." By it he exposed the poverty of the traditional view of consciousness as a blank stare without orienting interest, temporal horizons, or a penumbra of vagueness. This richer sense of the movement and complexity of awareness in the individual has had, of course, an extraordinary development in literature, of which Gertrude Stein, one of James's most devoted pupils, is the first and most bizarre example. But the conception also influenced the writing of history. James spoke of the "specious present" of the individual's stream of consciousness as "no knife-edge, but a saddle-back, with a certain breadth of its own on which we sit perched, and from which we look in two directions into time."[8] Carl Becker, in his classic study *The Heavenly City of the Eighteenth-Century Philosophers*, applied this concept of the specious present to the mind of an age, or its "climate of opinion." Thus he showed how historians like Gibbon and Voltaire created an image of the past which made the writing of history a weapon in the warfare against tyranny and superstition. This same concept of the specious present he also used to dramatize the making of an American revolutionary in that witty amalgam of history and fiction, "The Spirit of '76." This charming essay tells the story of Jeremiah Wynkoop's conversion to reluctant rebellion, and Becker unifies the tale by focusing on the hero's "little world of opinion and conduct, held together by recollection of the past and hope for the future."[9]

The ideas of William James profoundly influenced historical theory as well as practice. Becker's first statement, in 1910, of his revolt against "scientific" history challenged historians to accept for their own field the implications of Pragmatism. Certainly in *The Principles of Psychology* he could have found a basis for his own attack on the notion of "reason cut loose from will and emotion, from purpose and passion."[10] In his well-known presidential address to the American Historical Association, "Everyman His Own Historian," Becker elaborated his historical relativism through the concept of the specious present. The value of history, he argued, is its enlargement and enrichment of the "specious present" of Mr. Everyman. Becker gave the idea a characteristically skeptical turn: memory of the past and anticipation of the future go hand in hand in the construction of historical knowledge, as they do with Mr. Everyman himself, and in the end it is not the historian who imposes his story on Mr. Everyman; it is rather Mr. Everyman "who imposes his version on us, compelling us, in an age of political revolution, to see that history is past politics, in an age of social stress and conflict to search for the economic interpretation."[11] The bent of the historian's mind is, in short, determined by the dominant social forces of the day. Becker's private notes document his belief that James's picture of experience as a dynamic "going concern" (as portrayed in *A Pluralistic Universe*) had destroyed any final absolutes.[12]

Becker's relativism, which grew out of a revolt against "scientific" history with its cult of "cold, hard facts," "definitive" histories, "impersonal laws" and "objective detachment," closely parallels James's sustained polemic against the abstractions of old-fashioned empiricists, rationalists, and idealists with their passive, spectatorial view of consciousness, their static timeless Truth and their "block universe" of spiritual or mechanical determinism. Pragmatism was a recognition of the historical nature of the truth-making process, just as relativism was an acknowledgement of the history of history.

James's influence on American historical theory was, however, like Pragmatism itself, of ambiguous value. Clearly, all truth has a history, and the growth of man's techniques for finding it has no calculable limits. The writing of history has a special dimension of growth because the continuing process of historical change perpetually opens up to view new relationships between an unfolding past and a moving present which seeks to maintain its orientation by resurveying its altered perspectives. Yet just as Becker substituted for a sterile pseudoscientific conception of history a skeptical relativism which dangerously blurred the necessary distinction between history and propaganda, so also did James replace an artificial rationalism with a pragmatic theory that tended to obscure the responsibility of truth-finding procedures.

Becker transformed the history of history into a basis for skepticism by speaking of the past as "a kind of screen upon which we project our vision of the future; and it is indeed a moving picture, borrowing much of its form and color from fears and aspirations." [13] From this point of view written history becomes part of a struggle for survival, an instrument for moving practical programs into the future. The fact that practical historical problems stimulate the need to study the past is misread into a warrant for construing the past in terms of present hopes and fears.

In similar style James moved in his theory of truth from a plausible premise to a dubious conclusion. He insisted that truth happens to an idea, that a true idea performs a mediating function in relating old knowledge and new experience with "a minimum of jolt, a maximum of continuity." In finding truth men are obliged to take account of three aspects of reality: sensations, relations among particulars (both the external ones of date and place and the internal ones of mathematics and logic), and previous truths of experience. Yet the human mind is intrinsically selective, and so there is a human element in all truth, and man's truths, like his actions, make genuine additions to a reality which is still "in the making." [14] This position, as broadly stated, can be taken as an accurate picture of the actual development of knowledge, which presupposes active curiosity, working postulates, chosen hypotheses, and revisable conclusions. But James went on to stress that the mediating ideal's successful working is a matter for individual appreciation, and each person is also entitled to take as truths any ideas which are "helpful in life's practical struggles," if they do not clash with other beliefs having "vital benefits." In this way he opened the door to a personal relativism and the determination of truth, in at least one sense, by a belief's therapeutic value.

Both Becker and James were, of course, responsible intellectuals. Becker recognized, for example, that Algie M. Simons's history of the United States was really only socialist propaganda, written "without fear and without research," and it is likely that James, the friend of heresy, would have been depressed to see his concept of the "will to believe" transformed into the contemporary cult of "faith in faith," so prominent a part of current conformity. Yet neither man made it clear that a humanistic account of knowledge need not license an arbitrary subjectivity, subversive of the scruples of truth-seeking. In this respect Pragmatism was not humanistic enough. The demand which we impose on ourselves that our thought be responsible to what the evidence obliges us to believe is a precious human interest, and its assertion is what gives to thought its rigorous ardor. James was especially sensitive to the heroic element in life, but it was the price of his voluntarism that he could so eloquently praise "the stern and sacrificial mood" of character in action without responding equally well to the courageous integrity of the thinker's struggle to maintain his code of responsibility.

Thought and will need each other, but for both Becker and James they are not kept in the necessary tension. When they are merged, the pursuit of truth is subordinated to practical needs and action is deprived of the valuable guidance of knowledge. As a historian, Becker was understandably sensitive to the immersion of written histories in the historical milieu of a past period and its problems, and James, being a doctor and a psychologist, was naturally perceptive of the life-enhancing role of "over-beliefs" in the lives of troubled individuals. But the logic of truth-statements cannot be reduced to their practical function in a social or personal context without indulging in a form of the genetic fallacy. It is a familiar frustration in the life of thought that every valuable revolt against a dominant orthodoxy can only make its way by a powerful polemic that tends to overstate its case.

If James's Pragmatism can be seen as an effort to give a historical account of the process of knowing, his Pluralism was also deeply responsive to the centrality of history in human experience. "We humans," he affirmed, "are incurably rooted in the temporal point of view."[15] It was the nub of his objection to the Absolutes of Spinoza, Bradley, and Royce that they made no direct contact with individual sympathies, remaining abstractions forever foreign to human ways:

> As absolute, then, or *sub specie eternitatis*, or *quatenus infinitus est*, the world repels our sympathy because it has no history. *As such*, the absolute neither acts nor suffers, nor loves nor hates; it has no needs, desires or aspirations, no failures or successes, friends or enemies, victories or defeats. . . . I am finite once and for all, and all the categories of my sympathy are knit up with the finite world *as such*, and with things that have a history. . . . I have neither eyes nor ears nor heart nor mind for anything of an opposite description, and the stagnant felicity of the absolute's own perfection moves me as little as I move it.[16]

James came close to affirming the secularity of all experience. "All 'homes' are in finite experience," he wrote in *Pragmatism;* "finite experience as such is homeless. Nothing outside of the flux secures the issue of it. It can hope salvation only from its own intrinsic promises and potencies."[17] This is as bold an assertion of the absoluteness of human experience as one can find in modern literature. It is qualified only by James's charming but inconsistent conception of a finite God. (If God were not finite, he would have no history and so not need us.) If James was sympathetic to the religious effort to refer human life outside of itself for ultimate meaning, he characteristically built upon it only a kind of halfway house.

A consistent secularism would, I suggest, have been more compatible with James's affirmation of history. In a pregnant note to his famous essay "The Dilemma of Determinism" he wrote: "To say that time is an illusory appearance is only a roundabout manner of saying there is no real plurality, and that the frame of things is an absolute unit. Admit plurality, and time may be its form."[18] The idea of history as a plurality of histories with no extratemporal justification or interpretation would have been thoroughly in keeping with his attack on all monisms. History would then have many centers of meaning; men would have their "homes" in particular historical communities; History as a whole would be "homeless." James's Pluralism would then define the intellectual perspective of the modern historian.

The historian cannot help but feel a profound sympathy for James's Pluralism because by it he sought to make room for real possibilities, beginnings, endings, crises, evils, and novelties—in short, for the world of history. The monistic vision of a thoroughly rationalized or mechanically determined world, in which the meaning of the parts is given by a prior unity, is based on the illusion that the world can be viewed from the outside as a total fact, as if man were capable of an omniscient perspective. "Something is always mere fact and givenness," James maintained.[19] For him the ultimate import of the free will issue was whether or not novelty could "leak" into the universe by way of the actualization of real possibilities:

> Our sense of 'freedom' supposes that some things at least are decided here and now, that the passing moment may contain some novelty, be an original starting-point of events, and not merely transmit a push from elsewhere. We imagine that in some respects at least the future may not be co-implicated with the past, but may be really addable to it, and indeed addable in one shape or another, so that the next turn in events can at any given moment genuinely be ambiguous, i.e., possibly this, but also possibly that.[20]

What James defended is the world the historian presupposes in his work—a world of happenings and actions in which particular events and decisions make an actual difference to the situation and might have been some other way. On this premise, as Isaiah Berlin has brilliantly argued, all efforts at historical judgment depend, for the historical sense of evaluation is acquired by putting what did happen in the context of what could have happened.[21]

In his last years James worked to round out his metaphysics of "tychism"—a world whose order is really in the making, like that of the historian's. He felt, as the historian must, the defects of the traditional view of causality in which the effects are said to be somehow contained within the causes, so that nothing new ever happens. James believed that Hume's famous skepticism about causality, based on the fact that no separate percept of connection, power, or efficacy ever turns up in experience, was due to the perversion of his empiricism by intellectualistic prejudices which could not do justice to actual experience where both terms and their relations are found together in solution. Nor could he accept Kant's account of causation as the application of a categorical rule of uniformity because it still left the connection of events mysterious. The positivists were equally unsatisfactory because they stripped causality to the generalization of facts by laws.[22] James's solution, consistent with his radical empiricism, was to look for a perceptual experience of "the kind of thing we mean by causation," and he found it in the individual's personal "activity-situations" where he strives to sustain a purpose against obstacles. Wherever causal agency may be actually *located*, a problem James did not pretend to settle, its *characteristics* are clearly revealed, he argued, in these personal endeavors:

> The transitive causation in them does not, it is true, stick out as a separate piece of fact for conception to fix upon. Rather does a whole subsequent field grow continuously out of a whole antecedent field because it seems to yield new being of the nature called for, while the feeling of causality-at-work flavors the entire concrete sequence as salt flavors the water in which it is dissolved.[23]

James's discussion was tantalizingly incomplete. He hinted at the possibility of a pan-psychism in which we would have to ascribe even to physical causality "an inwardly experiential nature." Certainly such a bizarre conclusion would not have embarrassed him. He was a psychologist with a personal and scientific interest in sick souls, the mystical claims of unconventional religions, and the "spook-haunted" phenomena of physical research. But much as I admire his openness to persons and ideas beyond the pale of respectable society, I have no wish here to follow his speculation in this odd direction. I wish instead to emphasize what might have been a less dubious fulfillment of his metaphysical purpose. Ralph Barton Perry, his most knowledgeable and sympathetic interpreter, surmises that James might have later spelled out a rational account of the "leaking" of novelty into the universe in this way:

> Event *a* would look forward to, and in some measure anticipate, *b; b,* when it came, would in some measure fulfill this anticipation and look back upon *a.* The prospect of *a,* and the retrospect of *b,* would overlap; *a* would be qualified by *b*-about-to-come, and *b* by *a*-just-past. . . . Each event would come as an unfolding, as something 'called-for' or 'looked-for,' but would also have in it an element of surprise.[24]

This would have been the fulfillment of what James finally called, under the influence of Bergson, his *"synechism."*

James believed that to be faithful to the later movement of his thought he would reluctantly have to give up logic and accept Bergson's intuitionism. This desperate solution troubled him as it has troubled later philosophers, who were unfortunately thus given some cause to shake their heads sadly about James's impressionistic style of thought. I find it striking that no one seems to have noticed that the conception of causality for which James was groping has a firm basis in the actual procedure of the historian. In history significant events, like the American Revolution or the Civil War, are not deduced from antecedent circumstances, though these are always relevant to an understanding of such crises, nor does the historian's power to explain them depend upon his ability to have been able to have predicted them from a given set of past events. The historian's accounting is always hindsight, which requires the occurrence of the event. Looking backward with the benefit of the perspective provided by the event having happened, he tries to see the event as a complex fulfillment of active tendencies never quite working out according to plan. However helpful the social scientist's generalizations about regularities may be to the historian, he must fall back in the end upon this dynamic view of causality. Yet it is a conception that has still to make its impact upon contemporary discussion of the nature of historical explanation.

The historian can exploit this view of change only by the technique of narrative, which runs counter to the modern prejudice against story telling as an evasion of analysis. Those who have this bias are enthralled instead with psychological generalizations, *supra*historical myths, or sociological categories. From their point of view narrative is identified with the merely entertaining chronicle of fortuitous events, like the detective story. But the essential ingredient of plot, in literature or history, is the particular impact of the action upon particular agents. Narration for the historian is not a matter of telling "what happened next"; it is a way of defining and dramatizing the conflict of forces in their reciprocal response. To narrate this kind of happening is not to set the stage for a later explanation from outside the action; it is instead to make the action itself comprehensible through the drama of dialectical tension. To relate means to connect as well as to tell, and the historian's telling is a kind of connecting which finds in change the dynamics of development. This idea forms a link between James's "synechism" and the historian's work.

"I live in apprehension lest the Avenger should cut me off before I get my message out," James wrote his brother in 1906. "It is an aesthetic tragedy to have a bridge begun," he added, "and stopped in the middle of an arch." [25] More than that, it is a loss to the philosophy of history in America that James could not finish what was, so far as it had been built, a structure eloquent in the wit of unpretentious candor, the grace of a humanistic temper, and the high tension of an original mind.

(1961)

Notes

1. James to H. G. Wells 11 September 1906, in *Letters of William James*, ed. Henry James, 2d ed.; 2 vols (Boston, 1926), 2:260.

2. James to James Ward, 27 June 1909, in *The Thought and Character of William James*, ed. Ralph Barton Perry, (2 vols. (Boston, 1935), 2:656.

3. Quoted by Henry James Jr., prefatory note, *Some Problems in Philosophy: A Beginning of an Introduction to Philosophy*, ed., H. James Jr. (New York, 1911), p. viii.

4. James to Dickinson S. Miller, 6 December 1905, in *Letters of William James*, 2:237.

5. James to Henry James 4 May 1907, in *Letters of William James*, 2:279.

6. H. Stuart Hughes, *Consciousness and Society: The Reorientation of European Social Thought 1890–1930* (New York, 1958), p. 397. See Morton G. White, *Social Thought in America: The Revolt against Formalism* (New York, 1949) and Strout, *Pragmatic Revolt*, especially pp. 26–28.

7. See James, "Great Men and Their Environment," in William James, *The Will to Believe, and Other Essays in Popular Philosophy* (New York, 1897), pp. 216–54 and James to Henry Adams, 17 June 1910, in *Letters of William James*, 2:344–47.

8. William James, *The Principles of Psychology*, 2 vols. (London, 1891), 1:609.

9. See Strout, *Pragmatic Revolt*, pp. 68–85, for a discussion of this dimension of Becker's writing.

10. "Detachment and the Writing of History," *Atlantic* 106 (1910):527.

11. Becker, "Everyman His Own Historian," in Carl Becker, *Everyman His Own Historian: Essays on History and Politics* (New York, 1935), p. 253.

12. Miscellaneous Notes, drawer 15, Becker Papers, Cornell University.

13. Carl Becker, "What Are Historical Facts?" *Western Political Quarterly* 8 (1955):337.

14. William James, *Pragmatism: A New Name for Some Old Ways of Thinking* [1907] (New York, 1919), pp. 244–57.

15. William James, *A Pluralistic Universe*, ed. Ralph Barton Perry (New York, 1943), p. 40.

16. Ibid., p. 48.

17. James, *Pragmatism*, p. 260.

18. William James, *Essays on Faith and Morals*, eds. Ralph Barton Perry (New York, 1947), p. 181.

19. Preface to *The Will to Believe*, reprinted as an appendix to Perry, ed., *Essays on Faith and Morals*, p. 330.

20. James, *Some Problems in Philosophy*, pp. 139–40.

21. Isaiah Berlin, *Historical Inevitability* (London, 1954), p. 31.

22. See James, *Some Problems in Philosophy*, pp. 189–207.

23. Ibid., p. 218.

24. Perry, ed., *William James*, 2:666.

25. James to Henry James, 10 September 1906, in *Letters of William James*, 2:259.

# PART 2
# The Political Novel
# and the Idea of History

What we see here is a world which on the one hand is
entirely real, average, identifiable as to place, time,
and circumstances, but which on the other hand is shaken
in its very foundations, is transforming and renewing
itself before our eyes.

—Erich Auerbach, *Mimesis*

# 4 / *Uncle Tom's Cabin* and the Portent of Millennium

"Everybody's Protest Novel," James Baldwin called it in 1949, in order to condemn it and its descendants. Looking at it through the eyes of a modern Negro, he found it a hysterically moralistic melodrama of stereotypes with a cast of genteel mulattoes and quadroons whose lightness of color betrayed Harriet Beecher Stowe's revulsion against blackness. "Tom, therefore, her only black man," he asserts, "has been robbed of his humanity and divested of his sex. It is the price for that darkness with which he has been branded." Her fear of the dark, Baldwin charges, is "a theological terror, the terror of damnation; and the spirit that breathes in this book, hot, self-righteous, fearful, is not different from that spirit of medieval times which sought to exorcise evil by burning witches; and is not different from that terror which activates a lynch mob." The bill as drawn is as plausible as it is unhistorical, as provocative as it is astigmatic—half right for all the wrong reasons.

It is true that Stowe was hot about the crime of slavery and fearful of the doom of her country, as Baldwin is hot and fearful with equally good reason about the race problem today, but her novel deliberately aimed to undercut self-righteous moralizing. While she succumbed in part to the sentimental tradition of the paternalistic plantation with its childlike slaves and their indulgent owner, she did not blink the fact that the inept benevolence of her planter St. Clare could not prevent his wife from selling his slaves down the river. Baldwin takes Miss Ophelia from New England as the author's mouthpiece forgetting that Stowe has St. Clare accuse her of a Yankee prejudice against Negroes, "wanting them out of your sight and smell." The author's postscript lays the heaviest burden of guilt for slavery on the "people of the free states" who have "defended, encouraged, and participated, and are more guilty for it, before God, than the South, in that they have *not* the apology of education or custom." Her fabled villain, Simon Legree, is a Yankee. If she stacked the cards, she did not deal all the good ones to any section or group, particularly not to her own.

Reading Stowe out of her context, Baldwin misses the relevance of the relative whiteness of her blacks in the novel. Their color dramatizes Stowe's sense of the great horror of slavery—the breaking up of families for exploitative reasons. In a culture which idealized the home as much as hers did, the sexual crossing of the color line, promoted by the system of slavery, was a vivid symbol of evil because the white man who exploited a black woman violated the integrity of two families, his own and hers. It is the tragedy of Misse Cassy, Legree's mulatto mistress, that she has been sold by a white man whom she loved and by whom she bore two children. The planter St. Clare suffers from an unhappy marriage to a coldly respectable woman who breaks up the family life of his slaves, and that sugary confection, little Eva, prefers the Southern plantation to Vermont because "it makes so many more round you to love, you know." The mulatto George, Eliza's husband, begins to recover his faith in the justice of God only when he lives for a while in the Quaker home of Rachel Halliday, who had "so much motherliness and full-heartedness even in the way she passed a plate of cakes or poured a cup of coffee, that it seemed to put a spirit into the food and drink she offered." Stowe gives her the accolade: "This, indeed, was a home,—*home*, a word that George had never yet known a meaning for." Trust in

God's providence soon begins to "encircle his heart, as with a golden cloud of protection and confidence." St. Clare on his deathbed, envisioning "the gates of eternity," knows he has come "Home, at last," and his final word is "*Mother!*" This unpalatably Victorian cult of the family gags the contemporary reader, but its power to move her audience had much to do with the effectiveness of Stowe's indictment of slavery as an institution which deprived Negroes of their rights to recognized marriage and a stable family. The paleness of her Negro characters dramatically underlined this connection, a heritage from slavery which the controversial Moynihan Report (1965) to President Lyndon Johnson emphasized in the unsentimental sociological language of our own culture.

Baldwin is understandably appalled by Stowe's sentimentality, but he entirely loses sight of the sources of it. This "ostentatious parading of excessive and spurious emotion," he concludes, is "the mask of cruelty," a propensity proved by the fact that her sometimes terrifying story is a "catalog of violence." The linkage of sentimentality and cruelty is common in those journalistic exposés which contrive to titillate the feelings they editorially censor; but the violence in *Uncle Tom's Cabin* has an extremely realistic basis. Stowe not only relied on documentary accounts of the horrors of slavery, but she was familiar at first hand with the violence of her own period of history. Edmund Wilson points out that on the day her father and her husband were read out of the Presbyterian Church for heresy by the General Assembly in Philadelphia, one of the city's new buildings, dedicated to abolitionism, was burned down by a mob. In 1841 when Harriet began writing stories, a man hiding a runaway slave attacked the owner, a local farmer was murdered by Negro thieves, a white woman was raped, and race riots erupted for a week. When a cholera epidemic broke out in Cincinnati, Harriet lost her most recent baby. She later recalled that it was at his grave that she learned "what a poor slave a mother may feel when her child is torn from her." Much that is in *Uncle Tom's Cabin*, she felt, "had its root in the awful scenes and bitter sorrows of that summer." Violence was not something she vicariously experienced through her writing; it was part of her life which served her imagination as a writer. Wilson puts it with his usual felicity: "*Uncle Tom*, with its lowering threats and its harassing persecutions, its impotence of well-meaning people, its outbreaks of violence and its sudden bereavements, had been lived in the Beecher home, where the trials and tribulations, as they used to be called, of the small family world inside were involved with, were merged in, the travail of the nation to which it belonged."

These qualifications, however, do not strike at the heart of Baldwin's misreading of the story as social propaganda with its theological meaning reduced to a medieval terror of witches. Wilson comes much closer to the truth in *Patriotic Gore* when he points out that the tale "has registered the moment when the Civil War was looming as something already felt but not yet clearly foreseen: an ambiguous promise and menace, the fulfillment of some awful prophecy which had never quite been put into words." Wilson does not extend this crucial insight to the details of the story itself, but he puts the reader on the right track by observing that millennial expectations of a religious nature "blazed up against the twilight of the Calvinist faith, at the beginning of the Civil War." *Uncle Tom's Cabin* is a great document of the millennial temper of American Protestantism in the first half of the nineteenth century, a prime source for understanding its philosophy of history and revivalist theology.

Traditional Calvinism predicted great trials for the church before the millennium, which would be inaugurated by the Second Coming of Christ. Jonathan Edwards and his New England followers, Joseph Bellamy, Timonthy Dwight, and Samuel Hopkins, preached instead the more radical doctrine of a golden age on earth to be fulfilled before Christ came to earth in order to wind things up for the Last Judgment. This more optimisitc postmillennial view of the Second Coming was, as Stowe wrote in *Poganuc People*, "the star of hope in the eyes of the New England clergy; their faces were set eastward, towards the dawn of that day, and the cheerfulness of those anticipations illuminated the hard tenets of their theology with a rosy glow." This "little bit of a woman, about as thin and dry as a pinch of snuff," as she described herself, grew up in this New England world of modified Edwardsianism. Appropriately, her preface foresees "another and better day dawning," foreshadowed by the signs that "the hand of benevolence is everywhere stretched out." The contemporary movement for humanitarian reform which linked the ideals of piety and benevolence was augury of a coming millennium. The turbulent current of the Mississippi River in *Uncle Tom's Cabin* symbolized the "headlong tide of business" on which her countrymen were afloat, carrying with it "a more fearful freight, the tears of the oppressed, the sighs of the helpless, the bitter prayers of the poor, ignorant hearts to an unknown God—unknown, unseen and silent, but who will yet come out of his place to save all the poor of the earth!" Her passionate faith in the Second Coming wavered between the optimistic hopes of the postmillennialists and the apocalyptic fears of the premillennialists, but the eschatological expectation is always present as a reverberating note of the novel's major thematic chords.

In her pages Negro Christians live in hope, whites live in fear. St. Clare's mother told him of a millennium that was coming, "when Christ should reign, and all men should be free and happy." He concludes that "all this sighing and groaning, and stirring among the dry bones foretells what she used to tell me was coming." He reads the signs in "a mustering among the masses, the world over," a singular observation for a plantation master. St. Clare wonders: "But who may abide the day of His appearing?" His creator completes the portentous quotation in her postscript: "for that day shall burn as an oven: and he shall appear as swift witness against those that oppress the hireling in his wages, the widow and the fatherless, and that *turn aside the stranger in his right:* and he shall break in pieces the oppressor." Christians might pray for the coming Kingdom, but they should remember in fear and trembling that in this last convulsion "prophecy associates, in dread fellowship, the *day of vengeance* with the year of his redeemed." The rhetoric is, of course, like that of the storefront Negro churches in Baldwin's *Go Tell It on the Mountain,* and its judgment on inhumanity is kin to his own apocalyptic preaching in *The Fire Next Time.*

Stowe was no Calvinist, despite the fact that Calvin was the name of her husband, a professor of biblical literature at Lane Theological Seminary which her father had founded in Cincinnati. Her novel was in large part a protest against the

Calvinist doctrine of human inability to merit salvation. One of her brothers had been deeply disturbed by Jonathan Edwards's case against free will, and her sister Catherine had suffered badly from the doctrine of predestined election of the saints. Harriet herself agonized over the fate of the unregenerate soul of her drowned son. By the time the novel was written, the influential revivalist preacher, Charles G. Finney, had assimilated Calvinism to an optimistic Arminianism, emphasizing human ability to work out one's salvation, that would have seemed both heretical and sentimental to Jonathan Edwards. Finney thought men could become converted "in the space of a few minutes" if they only listened to the promptings of the heart instead of to the voice of theological reason. This voluntaristic emotional Protestantism saved Stowe and suffused her story.

The unlettered faith of Uncle Tom, who got religion at a camp-meeting revival, is the true hero of her book. "We does for the Lord when we does for his critturs," he says in the spirit of Finney himself. When Misse Cassy, imprisoned on Legree's brutal plantation, asks why the Lord should have put some people in a situation where "we can't help but sin," Tom replies, "I think we *can* help it." Even Legree was almost once persuaded by good angels: "his heart inly relented,—there was a conflict,—but sin got the victory, and he set all the force of his rough nature against the conviction of his conscience." Swift conversion, in Finney's fashion, is part of the sentimentality of the novel. Eliza's husband George finds, again in the Quaker house of Rachel Halliday, that there his "dark, misanthropic, pining atheistic doubts, and fierce despair, melted before the light of a living Gospel, breathed in living faces." Tom's faith not only converts St. Clare to a pledge of manumission, but four pages later, suffering from a knife wound inflicted during a tavern brawl, the former agnostic dies with a hymn on his lips and Tom's hand in his own. When Tom himself dies from his beatings, like "One whose suffering changed an instrument of torture, degradation and shame, into a symbol of glory, honor, and immortal life," his triumphant Christian victory over sin and death instantly converts two of the "imbruted blacks" on the plantation belonging to the atheist Simon Legree. The spiritual discipline of Calvinism had become too intellectually rigorous and morally severe for a sentimental people. Stowe's book exemplified the convergence of the popular cults of home, love, and instant salvation which transformed protestantism into a culture-religion.

Baldwin finds in her instead that same "medieval spirit" which burns witches and activates a lynch mob. Stowe's simplistic conception of villainy is exemplified in her picture of Legree as an atheistic, profit-minded, slaveholding alcoholic, a catalog of sins out of the Protestant tracts of her own day. But, though she believed the Bible provided the faithful with an absolute morality, she rose above the tractarian limits of her material in her portrait of the amiable skeptic St. Clare, who complains that "this whole business of human virtue is poor mean trash," because it is "a mere matter, for the most part, of latitude and longitude, and geographical position, acting with natural temperament." As for her superstition, it is Legree's literal fear of the dark which the author exploits as a means to engineer the escape of the slave girls from his plantation. Playing the part of ghosts, they terrify him into his fatal alcoholism, which seemed "to throw the lurid shadows of a coming retribution back into the present life." It is indeed that shadow, which menaces her readers as well for their complicity in the guilt of slavery, that saves her novel from being swamped in the milk of Finney's revivalistic benevolence. Her eschatology strikes the note of judgment which broods over the story, linking it to the Calvinism she hated.

Surprisingly, Baldwin misses his one chance to score directly on target with his charge of a "fear of the dark." He does not relate it to her concluding plea for colonization of the freed Negro in Africa. Stowe's abolitionism was far more conservative than that of her colleagues in the antislavery movement. The churches of the North, she urged, should defy the Fugitive Slave Law of 1850 by taking upon their shoulders the Christian duty of educating escaped slaves until they had sufficient "moral and intellectual maturity" to be assisted in their passage to Liberia, where they could "put in practice the lessons they have learned in America." This morally evasive solution conveniently suited a society in which racial prejudice against freed Negroes was strong everywhere in the Union. Stowe's rejection of "integration" was rationalized on the ground that while American Negroes as an injured group *ought* to have "*more* than the rights of common men," only a nation of blacks could have the power which effectively would "break their chains." This argument seemingly prefigures the Black Nationalism of Marcus Garvey in the 1920s and of the Black Muslims in the 1960s, but Stowe believed with Eliza's husband that "'a nation has a right to argue, remonstrate, implore, and present the cause of its race,—which an individual has not.'" Only black power could *justify* Negro protest.

Unlike her distant descendants' views, Stowe's Black Nationalism was linked to her identification of the Negroes with Christian virtues of suffering and tenderness. For this reason "the highest form of the peculiarly *Christian life*" would be exhibited in Africa when God had chosen it, "in the furnace of affliction, to make her the highest and noblest in that kingdom which he will set up, when every other kingdom has been tried and failed; for the first shall be last, and the last first." Liberia was to be the fulfillment of the expectations which little Eva and Uncle Tom dreamed of in their devoted reading of Revelation or of Tom's heavily marked passage from Matthew describing the Second Coming and the Last Judgment, which inspires his master to manumission and conversion. The dated, conservative policy of colonization was thus buttressed with the radical doctrine of the millennium and rationalized by an inverted racist division between "the hot and hasty Saxon," who would dominate America, and the "affectionate, magnanimous, and forgiving" Negro, who would build a Christian republic in Liberia. This mixture of sentimental piety, millennial hope, romantic racism, and political conservatism not only helps to explain the novel's enormous appeal, but marks its distance from the framework in which responsible thinking about the Negro's position in America must be done today. It is understandable why "Uncle Tom" has become the stereotype of the submissive Negro who plays the role acceptable to his oppressors, rather than the Christian hero who conquers sin and death by the power of his faith, just as it is understandable that the movement which is closest to her ethics of piety and benevolence, Martin Luther King's Christian nonviolent reformers, should heroically struggle for the integration of Negro Americans into their native society. It is in her policy of exporting free Negroes, which Lincoln also accepted, that she betrays a moral evasion of the deeper dilemmas inherent in the history of American race relations.

Protest novels, in Baldwin's phrase, "are a mirror of our confusion, dishonesty, panic, trapped and immobilized in the sunlit prison of the American dream." For the historian such confusion, however, can be of enormous documentary value. To misread *Uncle Tom's Cabin* is not to commit an aesthetic crime, but it is to suffer a major failure of historical comprehension. Baldwin warns us to remember, in defiance of the conventions of protest novels, that "the oppressed and the oppressor are bound together within the same society; they accept the same criteria, they share the same beliefs, they both alike depend upon the same reality." That awareness is precisely the strength of Stowe's novel and the source of its author's agony. Her story dramatizes the confused anxieties of her time with genuine power. She idealized a dream of domesticity which miscegenation and the slave trade ruthlessly violated. As a Christian she responded to the opposite ideal, however, of the hymn sung by slaves on Legree's plantation: "O there'll be mourning, mourning, mourning, at the judgment-seat of Christ! Parents and children there shall part! parents and children there shall part!" For true believers natural bonds, like racial differences, mean nothing. "In the gates of eternity," she believed, "the black hand and the white hold each other with an equal clasp"; yet in this world, she concluded, Negroes must find their home in a separate nation of believers. George, Eliza, and Cassy excite the reader's sympathy by their struggles to escape from slavery; yet Uncle Tom is honored above all for his stoically resigned acceptance of his sufferings. The vector of these contrary forces and feelings is Stowe's escapist dream of a Christian republic in Liberia which will make faith and freedom inseparably one. The postmillennialists were confident of a coming utopia. Stowe fervently hoped it would come, but she transferred it to Africa, fearing in her own country a vast convulsion as punishment for "unredressed injustice."

Stowe's millennialism would in a few years after the publication of her novel be set to martial music in "The Battle Hymn of the Republic" as Yankee soldiers sang of "the glory of the coming of the Lord" who had "trampled out the vineyards where the grapes of wrath are stored." That "fateful lightning of His terrible swift sword," which she had dreaded, was loosed at Fort Sumter. In the beginning it was more like the apocalyptic pessimism of traditional Protestantism than the post-millennial optimism of the religion of her day. Yet the end of the war did bring an end to slavery. The ambivalence in her sense of the future was justified. Now that our own present seems to hold the same ambivalent possibilities of fulfillment or destruction, reinforced by the nuclear dilemma, perhaps we can afford to read her with some sympathy for the poignant tension in which her novel holds conflicting anxieties in dramatic solution. To do so, however, we shall have to be as willing to reconstruct historically her religious tradition as she was anxious to bring it to bear upon the dilemma of slavery in a presumedly Christian and democratic society.

This much historical sympathy may have the paradoxical effect of freeing us from our own tendency, which Baldwin himself has succumbed to, of indulging in apocalyptic thinking. The substitution of abstractions for characters is not the result of what Baldwin calls her "fear of the dark"; it is implicit instead in the eschatological effort to transcend the concrete limitations and responsibilities of the specific demands of the historical hour. To read *Uncle Tom's Cabin* in this critical way is to see that its confused anxieties and emotional power, as well as its intellectual limitations, stem not from racial prejudice but from the ambivalent encounter of the American Protestant imagination with history. *Uncle Tom's Cabin* is not "Everybody's Protest Novel"; it is rather the expression of a specific religious imagination in its desperate attempt both to meet and to escape the dilemmas of American culture in the antebellum years. Baldwin connects it with *Little Women*, *Gentlemen's Agreement*, and *Native Son*. But Stowe's "intense theological preoccupations," as he quite correctly calls them, connect her novel much more relevantly to *The Pilgrim's Progress*. Read in this light, *Uncle Tom's Cabin* is not a fantasy, "connecting nowhere with reality," as Baldwin charges, for its images, rhetoric, and ideas are deeply connected with the ideological tensions of the most critical period of our history. The immense popularity of the novel is not only testimony to its power to make slavery a religious and moral issue in antebellum terms. It is proof as well of the pressure Americans felt—and still feel—to exaggerate their guilt, while minimizing their political responsibility, through a vision of history which wavers between a nightmare of doom and a dream of utopia. In this sense *Uncle Tom's Cabin* is surely one of the most American books in our literature and Baldwin is finally right—for the wrong reasons—in connecting it with our panic and confusion in "the sunlit prison of the American dream."

(1968)

# 5 / Radical Religion and the American Political Novel

Erich Auerbach, in his account of the representation of reality in Western literature, finds an anticipation of modern literary realism in the Bible stories. "When Stendhal and Balzac took random individuals from daily life in their dependence upon current historical circumstances and made them the subjects of serious, problematic, and even tragic representation," he argued, they were doing in a modern way what the biblical stories do: portraying ordinary people "caught in a universal movement of the depths which at first remains almost entirely below the surface and only very gradually . . . emerges into the foreground of history, but which even now, from the beginning, lays claim to being limitless and the direct concern of everybody." Biblical characters live in an identifiably localized world, shaken in its foundations and "transforming and renewing itself before our eyes." [1]

Auerbach's *Mimesis* scrupulously recognizes as well, however, that the Christian view of reality "differs completely from that of modern realism" insofar as it insists on a "figural" or "typical" way of connecting events, not causally but as signs that promise and fulfill each other. This mode can be es-

tablished "only if both occurrences are vertically linked to a
Divine Providence, which alone is able to devise such a plan of
history and supply the key to its understanding." The here and
now thus becomes "simultaneously something which has always
been, and which will be fulfilled in the future; and strictly, in
the eyes of God, it is something eternal, something omni-tem-
poral, something already consummated in the realm of fragmentary earthly event."[2] In this sense the medieval view is not
only anticlassical but also antimodern.

In Auerbach's judgment the French Revolution first fostered the modern consciousness of society being made and
unmade through convulsive processes of history. In the nineteenth century the emergence of socialism reinforced this
awareness and sponsored a secular theory of history as an evolv-
ing process of stages in development. Yet by the end of the
century social theorists in France's Third Republic had discovered structural similarities between Christianity and socialism, analogies which could be underlined from either a
conservative or a radical point of view. Whether because of the
erosion of Christian civilization, according to the disapproving
Gustave Le Bon, or because of having a common source in the
"peculiar dynamic character of western civilization, obsessed
by the desire for change and haunted by the notion of the
infinite," according to the approving Henri de Man, the
psychology of socialism was explained as an expression of an
essentially religious spirit.[3]

Modern scholars have tended to use the concept of displacement in accounting for secular religions. Freud used the
term to describe the unconscious transfer of an emotion to a
substitute object, masking the real locus of concern; it is one of
the devious ways in which the troubled ego seeks to relieve itself
of the burden of conflicting feelings. Useful as the concept is in
individual psychology, it does not provide a historical explanation for the social process that nurtures political religions. For
this reason the pursuit of analogies may not tell us very much
about how and why in a particular situation religious feelings
and attitudes have been carried over into nonreligious beliefs.
The danger in such efforts is to minimize the extent to which
new points of view establish real discontinuities with earlier

outlooks and have influential effects because of these differences. Even so, calling attention to similarities is a valuable
reminder of how influential biblical categories have been on the
imaginations of Western writers, Jewish and Christian. This
point is itself a historical one—and easily missed by readers no
longer familiar with the Bible. Finding anticipations, as Auerbach did, poses the same kinds of dangers as finding displace-
ments, but either strategy is illuminating so long as distinctions
are not forgotten.

The linkage between the biblical idea of a movement in
history and modern consciousness of social conflicts and change
is found best in novels that grasp the dynamism of millennial
and apocalyptic ideas. These categories may appear in stories
that lay claim to the label "realism" because they explore the
relations of individuals to the workings of a social system. A
prime candidate in nineteenth-century American literature is
*Uncle Tom's Cabin* with its ambiguous pairing of a hopeful
millennial vision of changed hearts ending slavery, on the one
hand, and an anxious fear, on the other, that a legalistic har-
dening of hearts may bring apocalyptic vengeance on a sinful
nation. Harriet Beecher Stowe's eschatological vision was split,
however, between the private, Christian, nonviolent resignation
of Uncle Tom and the political hopes of Eliza's husband for a
Christian republic in Liberia. Ultimately, for all its impressive
exploration of the system of slavery, the novel emotionally
comes out in favor of the sentimental hope of a loving, sacrificing family as the remedy for the race problem, and in this
respect it is more evangelically Victorian than biblical or
modern.[4] Stowe later organized a story around a militant slave
rebel, modeled on the same Nat Turner whom William Styron,
over a century later, made the messianic hero of doomed revolt,
although in *Dred* her Mosaic leader of the black Israelites is, as
a character, too much reduced to a bombastic symbol of vengeful "monomania" and none of her other characters has any real
relation to him.[5]

Auerbach was interested in the Bible stories for their elements of incipient literary realism. To reverse his strategy
would be to look for biblical elements of historical consciousness
in modern writers of realism. One might expect to find a

luminous example in the founding father of American realism William Dean Howells, because he was inspired by the Christian socialism of Edward Bellamy, Tolstoy, and William D. P. Bliss's Church of the Carpenter in Boston. Howells in *A Hazard of New Fortunes* (1890) did dramatize a violent strike in which his protagonist, a magazine editor, sees in the accidental death of a capitalist's son, a pacifistic settlement house worker, an emblem of the principle of Christlike suffering for the sins of others. Yet the editor rejects the strikers' actions and, in reflecting on the capitalist's grief, concludes that penitence is the way to keep evil at bay and to restore "the order of loving kindness, which our passion or our wilfulness has disturbed." This resigned acceptance of the workers' social defeat belies Howells's later prefatorial recollection of 1909 that when he wrote the novel "the solution of the riddle of the painful earth through the dreams of Henry George, through the dreams of Edward Bellamy, through the dreams of all the generous visionaries of the past, seemed not impossibly far off." [6] The novel entirely lacks the millennial passion of Bellamy's *Looking Backward* and reflects more accurately Howells's own stoical coming to terms with the private tragedy of his daughter's death during the composition of his story. Strong as it is in presenting a variety of socially located persons with differing ideologies and values, the novel is weakest in its sentimental and sketchy portrayal of the two social workers who have to do duty as futile, pale symbols of nonviolent Christian anarchism.

After the turn of the century political reform and literary realism flourished together. American writers were reporters before they were novelists. The investigative journalism of the muckrakers popularized stories about the real workings of social, economic, and political processes and morally evaluated them in terms of the shameful failure of moral and political ideals. The most influential and talented of these journalists, Lincoln Steffens, linked idealism and realism in his own flamboyant way, but the combination of them was characteristic of the muckrakers. Grandson of a Methodist preacher, Steffens wore a gold cross on his watchchain and dramatized his mediator's role in the McNamara bombing case of 1911 as the intervention of a true Christian who changed the issue from the guilt or innocence of the bombers to one of merciful accommodation in the interest of better labor–capital relations in the future. Persuading the employers to his view, but not the churches or the court, Steffens was confirmed in his belief that only a vision of the future could make men decent and that "sinners" rather than "the righteous" were the only ones capable of responding to its appeal with good will. When he enthusiastically hailed the Russian revolution in *The Nation* a year after Lenin came to power, the muckraker wrote under the pseudonym "Christian," John Bunyan's Pilgrim: "The revolution in Russia is to establish the Kingdom of Heaven here on earth, now; in order that Christ may come soon; and coming, reign forever."[7] His *Autobiography* (1931), however, is cleverly constructed so as also to illustrate and develop the theme that "a new culture, an economic, scientific, not a moral, culture," was fortunately emerging in the Soviet Union as the wave of the future. Steffens's Christian social gospel without God was matched by a pseudoscientific historicism that admired both Mussolini and Lenin as men of action who were supposedly empirically studying "the workings of elemental forces, and they hitch their wagons to these—not to stars, but to historically discovered and experimentally proved going concerns," which they "prophesy and steer by" instead of judging men and events. Steffens finally explained American corruption, which he had once called "the shame of the cities," in nonmoral terms as being merely "evidence of friction in the process of pouring new wine into the narrow necks of old bottles,"[8] making over an agrarian people into an industrial one. Steffens moved easily from a secularized Christian socialism to a "scientific" historicism because both positions enabled him to criticize either conservative or liberal American attitudes.

A mixture of "tender-minded" idealism and "tough-minded" realism in both politics and literature was characteristic of Ernest Poole, muckraker, settlement house worker, and member of the Socialist party. His political novel *The Harbor* (1915) converted syndicalist politics into an implicit, covert millennialism, couched in revivalist rhetoric, and presented overtly as the new realism in literature. Naive and didactic in style, *The Harbor* was a popular success and a monument to the radical populistic hopes of the Progressive era before they were shattered by World War I. For its hero Billy, the harbor he sees from Brooklyn Heights is not the quiet, safe haven idealized in a preacher's rhetoric. It is instead a harsh reality-principle, introducing him to all those aspects of life left out of his mother's genteel and pious world: prostitutes, immigrants, class conflict. It is also the world of his father's warehouse, the big companies of his girl friend's father, and the scene of the dockyard workers' strike. Each of these dimensions of the Brooklyn harbor is a stage in the growth of the narrator, defining also the movement of history from the mercantile dreams of his father to his father-in-law's vision of big business efficiency and planning, and culminating in the syndicalist politics of Billy's college friend, Joe Kramer, who was modeled on an I.W.W. organizer.

The novel blends this periodizing scheme with a psychological theme of the narrator's troubled efforts to reconcile the idealism of his mother and the tough-mindedness of his father. For the journalist hero the reality-principle is always intrusively harsh, seamy, and prosy, whether in his father's business, the syndicalist's activist contempt for creeds, the past, and art, or the grim conditions of the workers in the stoke-holes of ocean liners. The resolution of this conflict of legacies lies in Billy's growing identification with a vision of "a world for all the workers," a dream in which hope and realism are allegedly fused. This synthesis also defines his emergence from the gentility of his mother's culture into a career in muckraking journalism and the ambition of writing a realistic autobiographical novel, detailing the major changes in his ideals, the very story Poole's readers followed in *The Harbor*.

*The Harbor* is best understood as a conversion novel in which the narrator's story reflects a slowly achieved orientation toward the meaning of his own life and the history of which he is a part, an outlook formed through the failure of a series of false idols. In this light the syndicalist figure of Joe Kramer functions as a prophet, constantly intervening to tutor the narrator in the right perspective on reality and the meaning of the future. Billy struggles against Kramer's censure as he takes up each new idol, but the prophet always arouses Billy's guilt by accusing him of complacency or tender-mindedness. The religious paradigm becomes even more apparent in the climactic dock strike. At first the strike is not the "miracle" of organized mass action Billy hoped for but only "mobs of angry men." The harbor, he thinks, "held no miracles," yet soon he witnesses the birth of "the great spirit of the crowd." The ensuing description of the strikers' meeting turns it into a camp meeting when a stenographer vocally joins the cause, her life thereafter becoming "as utterly changed as though she had jumped into another world." [9]

Whenever he is emotionally identified with the crowd, Billy sees the world in millennial terms: "And again the vision came to me, the dream of a weary world set free, a world where poverty and pain and all the bitterness they bring might in the end be swept away by this awakening giant here—which day by day assumed for me a personality of its own." Striving to feel multitudes "fuse together into one great being," he encounters another god, who is great enough to swallow up in the conflicts of labor all the other wars. Jailed in the strike, Billy overcomes his doubts and feels himself belonging to "the crowd" with "a deep, warm certainty." [10] Billy confesses that he lacks the syndicalist's belief in the imminence of a general strike, and he has a wife and child to support by writing for conventional magazines. But his primary goal is to write a novel about how, through his struggle with the reality-principle of the harbor, he has gained a "deeper view of life," that is, of the possibilities of mass action.

Poole was forced by history to confront the actuality of the first World War and the cruel fact that the socialists in Europe "had been swept on with the rest." But his political religion was immune to countervailing evidence because of the nonrational power of his millennial faith. The new god was only sleeping to gain new strength, Billy concludes, and he sees again "in gleams and flashes" the world for all the workers as "the vision of the end." Though he accuses Kramer of being tied to a stiff syndicalist creed as much as the reporter-novelist is to a wife and home, the narrator still identifies with the mystical community of "the crowd"; he feels apocalyptically that "all the changes in the world seemed gathering in a cyclone now." He finally envisages Kramer sailing to Europe with his revolutionary gospel, and he hears the horn of the ship bellowing the end of "little creeds and gods." But in Poole's view of reality its message blends shock and "a dazzling passion of hope." The war was not enough to dissuade him from believing that it *might* be true that "the time was near when this last and mightiest of the gods would rise and take the world in his hands." [11] The political religion that dominates the construction and the language of the novel at its critical moments testifies to his secular version of a millennial faith.

The religious dimension of secular politics became most vividly evident in the 1930s. It found its roots in the despair over the worth of Western democracies, as they floundered into a world depression, and in the totalistic form of social hope promised by the Communist party. Communists seemed to present an image of courageous disciplined action justified by a rigorous philosophy of history. Whereas the rebels of Poole's generation treasured freedom of thought and speech, Communists guarded orthodoxy. "I belonged to a political party resembling a religious order," the German Communist Gustav Regler later observed, "in which acceptance and obedience, not speculation, were the first and last requirement. The intellectuals in particular were made to understand that only their talents were required of them, not their thoughts. We were all under the spell of the Russian code, which, discarding the substance of religion, the more rigorously applied its form." [12]

Even those immune to the lure of the Party could feel in the thirties that they were part of a dynamic historical movement that defined the emerging meaning of individual and collective life. The literary critic Alfred Kazin had defined this mood with retrospective eloquence:

> History was going our way, and in our need was the very lifeblood of history. Everything in the outside world seemed to be moving toward some final decision, for by now the Spanish Civil War had begun, and every day choked with struggle. It was if the planet had locked in combat. In the same way that unrest and unemployment, the political struggles inside the New Deal, suddenly be-

came part of the single pattern of struggle in Europe
against Franco and his allies Hitler and Mussolini, so I
sensed that I could become a writer without giving up my
people. The unmistakable and surging march of history
might yet pass through me. There seemed to be no division
between my effort at personal liberation and the apparent
effort of humanity to deliver itself. Reading Silone and
Malraux, discovering the Beethoven string quartets and
having love affairs were part of the great pattern in Spain,
in Nazi concentration camps, in Fontamara and in the
Valley of the Ebro, in the Salinas Valley of California that
Steinbeck was describing with love for the oppressed, in
the boilers of Chinese locomotives where Chiang Kai-shek
was burning the brave and sacrificial militants of the
Chinese Communists. Wherever I went now, I felt the
moral contagion of a single idea." [13]

The American novel of the 1930s that best captures that
decade's idea of political religion is John Steinbeck's *In
Dubious Battle*, published in 1936 when the Popular Front and
the Spanish Civil War began to enthrall the emotions of so
many intellectuals. Steinbeck was no Party member, and his
behavioristic intellectual perspective in the novel reflects much
more of his friendship with a marine biologist than it does the
dialectics of Marxism, despite the fact that the story is about a
Communist-led strike of migrant workers in California. The
Miltonic title from *Paradise Lost* points, nevertheless, to the religious dimension of the struggle which participants on both
sides see as God and the Devil, contending "on the plains of
Heaven." The distinction of Steinbeck's precisely worked out
story is that instead of making rhetorical or polemical appeals it
engages the reader in a troubling analysis of the difficulties
inherent in the Party leaders' strategy for organizing and leading the workers in a struggle for justice. The Modern Library
jacket cover, ignoring the title, piously refers to the "heroism"
of people engaged in "a common cause" as the essence of the
story, but it is rather the dubiety of the conflict that is most
heavily underlined by the actual course of emplotted events.
Steinbeck knew that both the Communists and their bourgeois
enemies would hate his book, because he presented neither the

"ideal communist" nor the "thoroughly damnable communist" but human Communists capable of both weakness and strength. He thought of his "brutal book" as being all the more so because "there is no author's moral point of view." [14] Certainly there is no moralizing authorial voice in it, nor does he resolve in any "solution" the ambiguities of the actions dramatized. But the novel is not merely a neutral report either. It clearly sympathizes with the migrants' efforts to resist their exploitation by the growers, while at the same time it develops an extended religious metaphor as a way of understanding the strengths and the weaknesses of the radical leaders.

The structure of the novel turns around a continuing dialogue between a new member of the Party, Jim Nolan, and an old hand, Mac, who tutors him in the Party way of looking at things. Mac's strategy depends upon a ruthless subordination of means to the end of winning converts, a result that may follow from actions which are immediately harmful to the workers. Thus Mac hopes for intervention by the National Guard: "The troops win, all right! But every time a guardsman jabs a fruit tramp with a bayonet a thousand men all over the country come on our side. Christ Almighty! If we can only get the troops called out." [15] The relationship between doctrinal pupil and teacher does not remain static, however, because the teacher is shown to be increasingly vulnerable to human doubts about his faith, while the pupil eventually emerges as a more certain believer than his tutor.

As the story proceeds, detailing the price of Mac's strategy in terms of human suffering, the leaders come under the skeptical questioning of Doc Burton, a sad-eyed sympathizer. Doc expresses a quasi-clinical curiosity, without "blinders of 'good' and 'bad,'" about the strike, which he compares to a wound, a fever, an infection that has gotten into "group-men," who merely use ideologies to rationalize their instinctive energies. Apart from this pseudoscientific skepticism, he is convinced that "the end is never very different in its nature from the means." Steinbeck uses overtly, even bluntly, the contrast between him and the Communists to point up the religious form of their atheism. Doc notes the religious gleam in Jim's eye and calls it "the vision of Heaven." When a girl invites Jim into her tent while her man is gone, the ascetic Jim passes her by, seeing her with his secular faith as reminiscent of the figure of Mary he had seen in his mother's church. In the climax Jim is shot dead "kneeling in the position of Moslem prayer." [16]

The other side of Doc's sad skepticism is his loneliness. He thinks of Jim's newfound political faith as supplying a coherent sense of meaning to life, one that, unlike Doc's biological speculations, provides emotional satisfaction in identifying with a cause, making "a group of men be God." Doc, having "nothing to hate," pathetically feels himself to be "working all alone, towards nothing." [17] As a character, he seems to reflect some of that self-defeating self-contempt that intellectuals in the thirties were prone to feel for not being sufficiently engaged in manning the barricades, but Doc's lament does not make him (as it did many others) vulnerable to the temptation to rationalize the brutalities of the Party. "We cast off our intellectual baggage like passengers on a ship seized by panic," Koestler later wrote of Party intellectuals, "until it became reduced to the strictly necessary minimum of stock-phrases, dialectical clichés and Marxist quotations. . . . To have shared the doubtful privilege of a bourgeois education, to be able to see several aspects of a problem and not only one, became a permanent cause of self-reproach. We craved to become single- and simple-minded." [18] Doc keeps his critical-mindedness, but pays the price of the reproach.

The power of the story is that it shows us what Jim's hate and faith concretely mean. His certainty of belief and identification with the cause become increasingly impersonal, even shocking, to Mac, who finds his pupil becoming "a proper son-of-a-bitch," a good Party man whom everybody would hate. [19] Jim accuses Mac of letting his personal hatreds and sympathies influence his conduct because he shares Sam's desire for revenge against the vigilantes who have burned a man's barn, just as he feels sorry for the victim, instead of subordinating everything to considerations of tactics and strategy. By the end of the strike Jim is eager to use his own wound to spill blood for the cause by stirring up the crowd to fight instead of voting to settle the strike. When he is used that way by Mac in the last scene, Jim is dead, a corpse with no face, his lack of indi-

viduality highlighted by Mac's praise: "He didn't want nothing for himself—" This last line of the book underlines the point that Jim has arrived at a pitch of fanaticism for which the anonymity of martyrdom is the only appropriate fulfillment. Even his death is swallowed up by the imperatives of Communist tactics.

In the debate between Doc's skepticism and the Communist's confident faith, Jim's martyrdom is problematic. He was shot because he and Mac went out looking for the missing and wounded doctor. This errand of mercy is never justified by any tactical considerations. In fact, Mac earlier had urged Jim to go back to town because it would be "bad economy" to waste his "genius for the work" in "a two-bit strike." The wounded Jim had angrily rejected Mac's suggestion, accusing Mac of protecting him not for the Party but for his own reasons. The reader becomes more sympathetic to Mac because his personal feelings are not always repressed, as Jim's increasingly are. As events unfold, the reader comes to see with increasing clarity that the Communist leaders are not able to plan and contr things with the far-sightedness they claim to have. When M learns that the crowd's sight of blood has enraged them to point of tearing down a barricade, at first he exults: "They n blood. That works." Then he reconsiders and begins to v Doc's skepticism about group-men's predictability. "It do want the same things men want—it's like Doc said—an don't know what it'll do. . . . Jim, it's swell when we can but we don't know enough. When it gets started it mig anything." [20] Doc's unbelief has gradually subverted belief, while Jim's belief grows more inflexible all the When in the very last scene Mac has propped up Jim's b corpse to dramatize a speech to the crowd, we no longer whether it is personal bitterness or Party tactics that expressing.

Following closely the turns of the plot, the attenti is inevitably plunged into a thicket of doubts. Does I when he is acting from personal as opposed t considerations? Does he have any consistent view of t stances under which it would be useful to let the blood? At one point Mac fears that the men will

who turn upon and rend a wounded member of the pack, if Jim rips off his bandage to excite the crowd. Is this fear only a rationalization of his personal feeling for Jim, or has Mac become persuaded by Doc? "It's kind of like Doc says to me one time," Mac cautions Jim, "Men hate something in themselves." Jim as a true believer will have none of it, scorning Doc's ideas for being as futile as he is. Does Mac's later turnabout in using Jim's corpse expose Mac's earlier tactic as a rationalization? Or, if Doc is right, doesn't it make Mac's melodramatic speech to the crowd a risky tactic whose unpredictability may defeat its purpose? The force of these accumulating events reinforces the dominating idea that the strikers are indeed opposed "in dubious battle on the plains of Heaven." The final effect is to subvert the premise that Marxism constitutes a science of history capable of planning its course with a confident faith. Nothing in the story refutes Doc's charge that Mac is a crazy mess of "cruelty and hausfrau sentimentality, of clear vision and rose-colored glasses." [21]

In historical retrospect, *In Dubious Battle* is a novelistic version of Reinhold Niebuhr's point, made a few years earlier in *Moral Man and Immoral Society* (1932) from a Protestant perspective, that Communism was "a secularized but still essentially religious version of the classical religious dream" of a new heaven and new earth "emerging from catastrophe." Like Steinbeck, Niebuhr warned that any absolutism would be "a dangerous guide in immediate and concrete situations," but "a splendid incentive to heroic action," for only the "ultrarational" hopes of true believers could provide the needed energy and courage to transform a desperately troubled society in a time of massive unemployment. [22] Neither the novelist nor the theologian reconciled these paradoxical assertions; they simply expressed them, tempted to believe that only uncritical fanatics could act.

By the end of the Spanish Civil War and the signing of the Nazi–Soviet pact of 1939 Western intellectuals were increasingly on guard against millennial expectations based on the Soviet Union's example. European writers on the civil war, such as André Malraux, Arthur Koestler, and Gustav Regler, severed their relationships with the Communists. Hemingway's *For*

*Whom the Bell Tolls* (1940) was begun as Madrid fell to the fascists, and it was already an elegy for a cause whose failure, derived from inner betrayals as well as from foreign interventions and noninterventions, meant that the bell also tolled for the Western democracies, now weakened by the lost cause as the fascists were strengthened by success for a second world war. Hemingway's liberal hero looks back nostalgically to his religious feeling of "consecration to a duty toward all of the oppressed of the world which would be as difficult and embarrassing to speak about as religious experience," a sense of taking "a part in something that you could believe in wholly and completely and in which you felt an absolute brotherhood with the others who were engaged in it," like the feeling "you expected to have and did not have when you made your first communion." [23] But the present time of the novel is a much more dubious and troubling moment, symbolized by his conversations with the cynical Russian journalist Karkov at Gaylord's hotel. Karkov's intimations about the political machinations of the Party against Trotskyites and anarchists, as well as the scathing dramatization of André Marty's political paranoia as bureaucratic chief of the International Brigades, display Hemingway's use of Gustav Regler's inside information about the Russian operation in Spain. Hemingway caustically portrayed, as Regler observed, "the spy-disease, that Russian syphilis, in all its shameful, murderously stupid workings, writing with hatred of the huntsman for the poacher." [24] Remembering his earlier religious feeling of political dedication, Jordan now speculates instead on his forebodings about whether the "dual controls" involving Russian military advisers in Spain would be gone after the war.

Jordan does not resolve his doubts. He accepts Soviet military discipline and organization on practical grounds without any ideological commitment to Marxism; and he concludes pragmatically from Karkov's tutoring that "the things he had come to know in this war were not so simple," and "if he were going to form judgments he would form them afterwards." Jordan can remind himself of his American belief in the Jeffersonian verities of "Life, Liberty and the Pursuit of Happiness," but concretely it is his love for Maria that impresses him as being "the most important thing that can happen to a human being." He characteristically imagines that sleeping with Maria has had the salutary effect of clearing his mind of political cant, stopping him from becoming "as bigoted and hidebound about his politics as a hard-shelled Baptist." The novel dramatizes the betrayal of the cause by Spanish failures of solidarity even with Jordan's partisan band, and the wounded hero's consciousness, as he waits alone to ambush a fascist officer, is much more engaged with his psychological struggle to avoid repeating his father's suicide than it is with any solacing sense of communion with his fellow partisans.[25] Political religion in Hemingway's novel is a nostalgic memory of lost innocence, a prelapsarian faith.

The revival of religion in the 1950s made something vital out of the political dimension of Christian traditions only in the millennial expectations of a promised land of full equality, as voiced by the Baptist preacher Martin Luther King, Jr., in leading the nonviolent civil rights movement. In the next decade, tragically scarred by the assassination of black and white leaders and the devious conduct of a hyperbolically violent and futile foreign policy in Southeast Asia, apocalyptic political attitudes became widespread. Thousands of protesters concluded that the ordinary functions of society lacked legitimacy and had become deeply corrupt. The New Left developed a wide spectrum that included Students for a Democratic Society, which was torn between "participatory democracy" and manipulative politicizing, Black Nationalists, Catholic pacifists, urban guerrillas, and parodic, publicity-seeking "action freaks," such as Jerry Rubin. The war, imperialism, and racism were the common targets, but there was no unifying ideology or program, and in practice the various factions came together only in a confrontation style of opposition to "the system," that is, officials in government or on the campus. One of the most influential of early spokesmen against the "establishment" on behalf of the young, Paul Goodman, was later impelled by the proliferation of opposition to characterize the scene in 1969 as being "like 1510, when Luther went to Rome, the eve of the Reformation." Adolescent conversions were "recurring as a mass phenomenon."[26]

Looking back at the decade from a near vantage point, the American novelist E. L. Doctorow explored the interconnections between an older political religion of the thirties and the New Left of the sixties in an imaginative and powerful novel, *The Book of Daniel* (1971). Doctorow found a focus for his historical meditations by novelistically reconstructing the impact of the Rosenberg espionage trial (1951) on the executed Communists' two children, who developed their own relationship to the New Left movements of the sixties.

The biblical Daniel wrote during the Maccabean Revolt as encouragement to Jews who had been robbed of their liberties and persecuted for their faith under Antiochus Epiphanes. The American Daniel grew up in the cold war climate of the fifties when his parents, alleged atomic spies, were put to death. Like the Old Testament tale, the novel is also partly epistolary and replete with historical theorizing. Its didactic sections are appropriate to the narrator as a child of a fervent, simpleminded Popular Front Marxist, who has taught his son to become "a psychic alien" by seeing the political point of everything, from comic strips to baseball. The novel is something of a detective story at the level of plot, and some of *Daniel*'s legends also have the flavor of ancient detective stories in which a sage upsets the judgments of less discerning folk, as in the story of Susanna, whom the biblical Daniel defended in court by extracting conflicting testimony from her accusers. Similarly, the protagonist of the novel, which involves a trial for conspiracy to commit espionage, based on dubious testimony more than on hard evidence, eventually develops his own theory of what really happened to his parents. Danny concludes that his father and his betrayer, idealistically conspired (to his mother's dismay) to cover for another couple, more highly placed in the Party, whom they believed were actually involved in espionage.

Doctorow has an acute sense of his story being about political religion. All of his characters, major and minor, are Jews; and his novel explores three generations of frustrated hopes. Danny's mother's Communism has something of his senile immigrant grandmother's ghetto faith.

It was something whose promise was so strong that you

> endured much for it. . . . The coming of socialism would
> sanctify those who had suffered. You went out and took
> your stand, and did what had to be done, not because you
> expected anything from it, but because someday there
> would be retribution and you wanted just a little of it to
> bear your name. If she had been religious like her Mama,
> she would have conceived this as a memorial plaque on the
> back of one of the pews in the Synagogue. [27]

Similarly, the lawyer for his parents "perceived in the law a
codification of the religious sense of life," finding irrationality a
sin and witch-hunting a form of paganism. A conservative
himself, he emotionally identified with Danny's parents during
the trial (as the Rosenbergs' lawyer did) because "Ascher
understood how someone could forswear his Jewish heritage and
take for his own the perfectionist dream of heaven and earth,
and in spite of that, or perhaps because of it, still consider
himself a Jew." [28] Danny's world, like the biblical Daniel's, is
desperate: his parents are executed when he is only a young
boy, damaging his own psychic stability; his sister, discovering that the name of her dead parents means nothing to
a new generation of anti-intellectual, media-conscious "action
freaks," determined to put down oppression with "put-ons,"
kills herself in despair; and Danny himself is finally ousted
from the library at Columbia University, where he is working on
his thesis, by the SDS takeover of the building. An account of
the making of a Jewish-American radical, who inherits his
father's Old Left rationalism, while uneasily joining the New
Left's antiwar march on the Pentagon, *The Book of Daniel*
wavers between a first and third person narrative mode, reflecting its protagonist's struggle to make sense out of the terrors of
his life. [29]

Doctorow names the third part of his novel "Starfish" after
an obsolete astrological sign implying the unity of belief with
intellect, language with truth, life with justice, a symbol for the
millennial fulfillment of the aspirations of political religion.
The starfish is also a creature capable of regenerating lost por-
tions of itself, even when cut in two. It points to the regenera-
tion of the Isaacson family, devastated by the death of the

grandmother, the eloctrocution of the parents, and the suicide of Danny's sister. Danny's honoring of his sister's unquestioning political faith by his own more devious emergence as a troubled radical illustrates the point of the symbol. The fictional family name suggests its biblical ancestor not only because of God's demand that Abraham be willing to sacrifice his son Isaac (as Paul Isaacson risked his family on his Popular Front faith), but also because Isaac's favorite, his firstborn son, Esau, is the one with the problem about preserving his inheritance, rather than selling it for a mess of pottage. Danny's sister charges him with selling out because he does not accept the family myth of their parents' total innocence. But in his own fashion he is faithful to his radical upbringing. Danny dresses like "a cafeteria commie" of the thirties in blue prison jacket and dungarees, and he interpolates in his narrative analyses from New Left "revisionist" histories of the cold war. His radical political understanding of the trial that convicted his parents brings him to accuse even the reformers and moralists who protested the execution of his parents of being complicit with "the system." From a *New York Times* reporter he first learns of the probability that, despite the biased trial, the Isaacsons were guilty of some kind of "third-rate operation" that made them "feel important." [30]

Danny's point of view transcends the Stalinism of the 1930s, the anticommunism of the 1950s, and the Yippies–anarchism of Arnie Sternlicht's movement to "overthrow the United States with images." Danny has his father's passion for political analysis and can think of only one event—a balloon flight to the North Pole in 1897—that might conceivably be "invulnerable to radical interpretation." Characteristically, he thinks his sister died "of a failure of analysis." Tracking down his parents' seeming betrayer to Disneyland, Danny spins out a witty political analysis of the amusement park's sinister implications, its substitutions of thrills for education and experience, its techniques for handling large crowds, its use of exhibits by major corporations. It is all spun off in the same spirit as his father's didactic penchant for political collage of the ads on cereal boxes, the history of dissent, the stereotypes of comic strips, and the public uses of baseball—"My father always gives you more of an answer than you bargained for." [31]

At the same time Danny tries not to be in thrall to his father's disappointed but persistent expectations for America, his anguish over his country's failures to preserve liberal and democratic ideals. Danny sees his mother as "the more committed radical" because she "wasn't to be surprised from the day they were indicted." Her politics were "like Grandma's religion—some purchase on the future against the terrible life of the present."[32] At the end of the novel Danny expresses a sense of his own link with Jewish history by hiring "little old Jewish men" who make their living in cemeteries to say the ancient prayers not only for his dead sister but for his parents, whose names he now puts in Hebraic form.

In keeping with this spirit he ends his own account of his shattering experience, sardonically entitled "A Life Submitted in Partial Fulfillment of the Requirements for the Doctoral Degree in . . . Arch Demonology, Eschatology, and Thermal Pollution," with direct quotation from the biblical *Daniel*. The radicals who have produced a mini-apocalypse at Columbia University claim to have "liberated" Danny, and he smiles as he closes his book to leave the library, for "it has not been unexpected." The campus revolution parodies and echoes the universal apocalypse prophesied in *Daniel* for the chosen people. The biblical apocalypse is "a time of trouble such as never was" when the people "shall be delivered, everyone that shall be found written in the book." Meanwhile, however: "Go thy way Daniel: for the words are closed up and sealed till the time of the end."[33] Before that moment there can only be false messiahs. For Danny neither Russia nor America can be the promised land.

Facing a world in which both Communist and democratic ideals have been betrayed, Danny lives out a biblical theme: "The drama of the Bible is always in the conflict of those who have learned with those who have not learned. Or in the testing of those who seem that they might be able to learn."[34] This is also the literary form of the story Doctorow's Daniel has told, and in this sense the biblical story of Daniel as a "Beacon of Faith in a Time of Persecution" is a true "type" of the growth of Danny's political perspective. Poole's hero learns to hope; Steinbeck's Mac struggles against his doubts; Doctorow's

Daniel has to transcend his family's radical pieties in his pursuit of the truth and his own political identity, as an heir of the Old Left and of a traditional Jewish search for social justice.

At the end of *Mimesis* Auerbach described a new form of "experimental" realism emerging between the two world wars. He hoped that by exploiting a multipersonal consciousness, multiple time strata, and random everyday occurrences, rather than great turning points, the techniques of vanguard novelists would eventually bring to light "the elementary things which our lives have in common." They would transcend "the controversial and unstable orders over which men fight and despair"—and about which older realists wrote novels—by lessening the differences between ways of life and forms of thought.[35] If so, the transformation of an older realism would have a happy issue. It was, as it has turned out, too much to expect from modern literature, nor did his hopeful prophecy count on the persistence of an older realism that would be attracted to the specific forms and differences of those unstable orders over which men fight. It forecast instead what is recognizable now as a widespread antihistorical strain in much modern writing. The idea of political religion as a structuring principle, however, was bound to bring into focus precisely those movements which, in emphasizing mass action and group differences, emphasized the common only in the context of conflict and disruption. At the same time, however, it has become clear that the techniques of the moderns, first made familiar by Woolf, Proust, and Joyce, can also be applied to historically oriented stories.

Doctorow's novel is "experimentally" modern in its open-ended conclusion of three possible scenes, its broken interior monologues, its frequent use of flashbacks, its form as the hero's own notebook. Because of its biblical allusiveness it also comes close to giving its horizontal view of reality a vertical dimension of figural or typological connections. Yet most fiction, by reason of symbolic devices and thematic concerns, suggests an overlay of more than causal connections between events without thereby taking a "typological" view of reality in the medieval sense. Doctorow's mind remains modern in this respect because the religious aspect of his novel derives from its grounding in a Jewish yearning for social justice, a form of political religion available to humanistic, not only to supernaturalistic, believers. Poole's lapsed Protestant hero, Billy, Steinbeck's lapsed Catholic, Jim, and Doctorow's lapsed Jew, Danny, are politically "religious" in a secular sense. Danny's account of his life resonates with the Bible's *Daniel* because the religion of his people is traditionally less involved with theological propositions than it is with radical hopes for fulfillment on this earth. Yet for all three protagonists, the religious backgrounds of their rejected pasts are alive, unrecognized and transformed, in their "unbelief" precisely because it has the shape of political religion. Animated by the passion for encompassing the process of history in an overarching scheme of moral meaning, these radicals draw on millennial and apocalyptic forms of thought within the framework of the realistic novel.

(1976)

## Notes

1. Erich Auerbach, *Mimesis: The Representation of Reality in Western Literature*, trans. Willard R. Trask (Princeton, N.J., 1974), pp. 43, 554.

2. Ibid., pp. 73–74.

3. Quoted in Donald N. Baker, "Seven Perspectives on the Socialist Movement of the Third Republic," *Historical Reflections* 1 (winter 1974):177.

4. I have discussed the novel at length in Cushing Strout, *The New Heavens and New Earth: Political Religion in America* (New York, 1974), pp. 177–84.

5. Alice Crozier, *The Novels of Harriet Beecher Stowe* (New York, 1969), p. 40.

6. Quoted in Strout, *The New Heavens and New Earth*, p. 233.

7. Quoted in Justin Kaplan, *Lincoln Steffens: A Biography* (New York, 1974), p. 219.

8. Lincoln Steffens, *The Autobiography of Lincoln Steffens* (New York, 1931), pp. 796, 817, 862.

9. Ernest Poole, *The Harbor* (New York, 1942), pp. 315, 320.

10. Ibid., pp. 321, 344.

11. Ibid., pp. 381–82, 386–87.

12. Gustav Regler, *The Owl of Minerva*, trans. Norman Denny (London, 1959), p. 168.

13. Alfred Kazin, *Starting Out in the Thirties* (London, 1966), p. 83.

14. Quoted in Peter Lisca, *The Wide World of John Steinbeck* (New Brunswick, N.J., 1958), p. 114.

15. John Steinbeck, *In Dubious Battle* (New York, 1936), p. 33.

16. Ibid., pp. 143, 253, 342.

17. Ibid., pp. 254–56.

18. Arthur Koestler, "The Initiates," in *The God That Failed*, ed. Richard Grossman (New York, 1951), p. 49.

19. Ibid., p. 266.

20. Ibid., pp. 337, 316–17.

21. Ibid., pp. 232, 206.

22. Reinhold Niebuhr, *Moral Man and Immoral Society* (New York, 1947), pp. 61, 199.

23. Ernest Hemingway, *For Whom the Bell Tolls* (New York, 1940), p. 235.

24. Regler, *The Owl of Minerva*, p. 293.

25. Hemingway, *For Whom the Bell Tolls*, pp. 248, 136, 305, 164.

26. Paul Goodman, *New Reformation: Notes of a Neolithic Conservative* (New York, 1970), pp. 60–61.

27. E. L. Doctorow, *The Book of Daniel* (New York, 1971), p. 42.

28. Ibid., p. 119.

29. For the politics of the Rosenberg children, see chapter 9.

30. Doctorow, *Book of Daniel*, p. 214.

31. Ibid., pp. 140, 301, 69.

32. Ibid., pp. 40, 42.

33. Ibid., pp. 302–3.

34. Ibid., p. 11.

35. Auerbach, *Mimesis*, p. 552.

# 6/Politics and the American Literary Imagination

Two of the most influential theorists of American literature, surprisingly, have been a French sociologist and a transplanted English poet: Alexis de Tocqueville and W. H. Auden. Stranger still, their influence is traceable in one case to a few remarks that are not about American writers as such and in the other to a footnote in a poem that is not about America. Tocqueville's *Democracy in America* contrasts aristocratic and democratic literatures by emphasizing the concern of the former with heroes, deeds, and legends, while the latter is said to be fascinated instead with "passions and ideas." In a commonplace egalitarian world democratic poets, he argues, will be forced to look "beyond external appearance and palpable fact to glimpse the soul itself" in "the hidden depths of man's spiritual nature"; therefore they will have a propensity to describe "man himself, not tied to time or place, but face to face with nature and with God." He gave as actual illustrations, however, not American, but French or English examples: the creators of Faust, Childe Harold, René, and Jocelyn—that is, Goethe, Byron, Chateaubriand, and Lamartine. Moreover, he warned that one should not always confuse American with democratic characteristics, and he predicted that American literature would be different from its present character. "No one," he said, "can guess that character beforehand."[1] Critics have found it irresistible, nevertheless, to look at American literature through the spectacles he put on for reading European democratic literature of the Romantic movement.

About a hundred years later, a provocative footnote in Auden's *New Year Letter* (1942) reinforced Tocqueville's point by generalizing about American literature in these terms: "The American literary tradition, Poe, Emerson, Hawthorne, Melville, Henry James, T. S. Eliot, is much nearer to Dostoievski than to Tolstoi. It is a literature of lonely people. Most American books might well start like *Moby Dick*, 'Call me Ishmael.'" Our books, he concluded, are "parables, their settings even when they pretend to be realistic, symbolic settings for a timeless and unlocated (because internal) psychomachia."[2] (In 1947, as an undergraduate at Williams College, I used this passage as a theme for my honors thesis, "A Literature of Lonely People," but I had no idea how much the zeitgeist would move in this direction.) Anyone familiar with American literary criticism since then will recognize in Auden's remarks the germ from which grew the more elaborate and influential theorizing of Lionel Trilling, Marius Bewley, Richard Chase, and, most recently, Quentin Anderson, all professors at Columbia University. The result has been to establish as orthodox a contrast between the English novel and the American romance, though the crucial examples keep changing their position in these categories.

In *The Liberal Imagination* (1949) Trilling made an influential distinction between Hawthorne's romances, lacking in "social texture," and James's novels, defined by "social observation." The novel in America, Trilling argues, had diverged from its classic intention by creating mythic characters representing abstract ideas. Ten years later Chase wrote a study of the American novel, elaborating Trilling's point and making a bow to Tocqueville on the abstractness and generality of the democratic imagination. Summing up his book in a later article, he declared: "The classic writers lack not only a sense of history but, as I have said, a sense of society and culture." In

1963 Marius Bewley followed Tocqueville, Auden, Trilling, and Chase in claiming that America supplied its artists "with abstractions and ideas rather than with manners," for the democrat is "the loneliest man in the Universe." By 1969 Joel Porte's *The Romance in America* could take it for granted that Chase had provided "a solid theoretical basis" for "the importance of romance as a nineteenth-century American genre" developed "sharply at variance with the broadly novelistic mainstream of English writing." In 1971 Quentin Anderson (in *The Imperial Self*) pointed out that there had been nothing mythically abstract about the vocabulary of our founding fathers, but he also aligned himself with his Columbia colleagues by quoting Tocqueville on abstractness as a property of our classic literature. Anderson located its roots, however, not in Hawthornian romance but in the Emersonian antinomian, individualistic stress on the "unconditioned abstractness of the self which creates its world instead of acting on it," leaching out "the compelling character of history, generational order, places and things."[3]

A comic element in this extended tribute to Tocqueville's literary observations is its use of Henry James. For Auden "the James drawing-room is not a real drawing-room, his Paris not a real Paris, his duchesses not real duchesses," any more than Moby Dick is a real whale. For Trilling the stories of James are, on the contrary, proof that the heights of the novel can only be scaled by social observation. For Chase the figure of James had become a link between the romance and the novel so that in his work "one catches hold of the romance only just as it is disappearing into the thicket of the novel." For Anderson everything has come full circle with a vengeance: *The Scarlet Letter* is "more closely akin to the novels of Jane Austen, George Eliot, or Trollope than it is to the late James." In Anderson's view James was "the bearer of an exemplary neurosis" who followed Emerson and Whitman in dramatizing "the dispensability of that world of the self and the other, or rather, the necessity of making it subordinate to the world of the undivided consciousness," to the autistic, sexless, artistic imagination.[4] The distinction between Hawthorne and James, so impressive to Trilling, had now been stood completely on its head. The belief that the

historical secret of a distinctively American literary tradition
can be found in a distinction between romance and novel
threatens to inspire a parlous game that any number can play
according to a constantly shifting set of rules.

In 1964 A. N. Kaul had revised Trilling by emphasizing the
role of perfectionist, communitarian idealism in our fiction, yet
Kaul still conceded that "personal and metaphysical relations"
dominated the American imagination. In the next decade
Nicholaus Mills challenged Trilling, Chase, and Kaul alike by
subverting the romance/novel distinction, but he also restated
it by reducing it to a matter of emphasis. Not only were questions of social considerations important to Hawthorne, Cooper,
and Melville, he pointed out, so also for George Eliot and
Dickens class and status were frequently of secondary rather
than primary interest. Similarly, myths and symbols were often
crucial to Scott and Hardy, as well as to our classic writers.
Despite his dissatisfaction with the romance/novel polarity,
Mills himself wound up by conceding that Cooper, Hawthorne,
Melville, and Twain gave "an ultimate importance (and textual
dominance) to certain ideational or visionary concerns that
finally makes these concerns superior to or situationally
transcendent of the social context in which they appear," while
Scott, Eliot, Hardy, and Dickens had just the reverse emphasis.[5] Thus more carefully and soberly stated, the original
contrast lives on in American literary criticism, like a deposed
monarch who has lost his crown without losing his prestige.

The time has come to emphasize the fact that loneliness
and symbolic settings, either before the Civil War or after it,
have not been in conflict with profound literary attention to historical realities and social issues. Our classic writers, in fact,
pioneered in exploring many of the same political questions
that would occupy our post–Civil War writers. James Fenimore
Cooper's obsessive concern with the plight of the gentleman in a
democratic republic reappears more democratically as the main
theme of John De Forest's *Miss Ravenel's Conversion from
Secession to Loyalty*, which is always cited as the beginning of
American "realism," and Henry James explores the plight of a
"poor gentleman" amid a group of feminists in *The Bostonians*.
Hawthorne in *The House of the Seven Gables* and "My

Kinsman, Major Molineux," for example, ruminates symbolically on the costs of inequities in property ownership and of violence in the Revolution, issues which James reexamines in an English context in *The Princess Casamassima*; while Melville in *Benito Cereno* deploys symbolism to brood upon the shadow of a slave mutiny darkening the republic's future and to furnish Ralph Ellison not only with an epigraph, but a precedent for the idea of the black man's invisibility to whites.

I have begun with this small skirmish against critics from whom I have learned much only to clear the way for talking about the political dimension of our literary tradition without having to apologize for it, as if the political novel were alien—something ordinarily found only on the continent of Europe along with feudalism, revolutions, and an intelligentsia, not to mention those outdoor cafés in which the last can argue about the first two. It survives even though our writers, as Irving Howe remarks, seldom see politics as "a distinctive mode of social existence, with values and manners of its own." How it exists is the burden of my remarks, for this tradition needs to be acknowledged as well as the Emersonian one in which, as Quentin Anderson says, the individual "walks about with a skylight in his head," and what this enables him to see "must in every case take priority over what he and his fellows did or said to each other."[6]

Trilling claimed that American contempt for society was not based on an ideal future but on "disgust with the very idea of society." He was talking about Theodore Dreiser, Sherwood Anderson, and Sinclair Lewis, in whose work he found no standard of what society might be and no sense of the "reciprocal actualities of society and personality."[7] Our political novelists vary widely in their ability to imagine such relations, but it is clear that their criticism of society arises not only from a sense of what society might be, as viewed in the light of the future, but even more often through an idealized memory of what it once was. This is true even with writers whose books seem to express a final revulsion against politics, such as *Democracy*, *The Gilded Age*, or *U.S.A.* The anguish in these works arises from a feeling of betrayal, a sardonic result of their encounter with the traditional political idea of American exceptionalism.

The new republic, it holds, would serve as an example to humanity because at its founding it had taken account of the measures necessary to prevent it from succumbing to the usual corruptions in the fall of states. This was the faith of the founding fathers.

Henry Adams's *Democracy* and Mark Twain's *The Gilded Age* are notable cases in point. The condemnation of political corruption in these books arises from disappointed political expectations. Adams and Twain both invoke an earlier political time, whether in George Washington's day or the Missouri towns-people's before the Civil War, respectively, when political virtue was supposedly a reality. Even though they propose no political remedies for the evils presented in their novels, a major point of their stories is that something historical has happened to disassociate Americans from these earlier modes of political life. Bernard DeVoto has hailed Twain as a writer who "fiercely championed the democratic axioms; they are the ether of his fiction and the fulcrum of his satire." Neither *The Gilded Age*, with its ferocious contempt for juries and public opinion, nor *A Connecticut Yankee in King Arthur's Court*, with its sardonic portrayal of the self-deceptions of a nineteenth-century republican technocrat, however, is democratic in outlook; they are even more suspicious of the ordinary man's capacity for judgment and good will than the most conservative of the founding fathers. DeVoto puts it better in saying that Twain's work registers the conflict between the assumptions and limitations of democracy, "between the ideal of freedom and the nature of man,"[8] an issue that was also basic for *The Federalist*.

Jefferson had suggested a national seal with the Israelites on one side, and Lincoln had spoken of an "almost chosen people." Comically invoking this tradition, Twain's Colonel Sellers is complacently sure that Congress's failure ever to convict any of its members of wrongdoing nevertheless has "a good moral effect" on foreign countries because the inquiry itself proves the purity of the model.[9] Adams has his heroine flee to Europe because she has become convinced that democracy is like every other form of government, while her own character has become tainted by a thirst for power in her fascination with the senator who confuses his own and his party's interest with the nation's. The Southerner who represents "George Washington at thirty" is dispatched to a minor diplomatic post, and the Bulgarian minister ridicules the exceptionalist's belief that the city of Washington is exempt from the "operation of general laws." In spite of these subversions of American exceptionalism, the novel treats Washington, the historical figure, as a charismatic hero, virtually outside history, who is admirable not for his policies but for his scrupulousness about money matters. Washington, Adams tells us in his autobiography, was "like the Pole Star" and "alone remained steady, in the mind of Henry Adams, to the end." [10]

Adams belonged to an ancient republican tradition, as old as Polybius, which stressed the importance of virtue to a republic. This "civic humanism," as J. G. A. Pocock has called it, holds to an ideal of mixed government in which change is always feared as a degeneration from a precariously balanced system with the consequent alienation of the individual from his moral concern for the general good. [11] While his heroine abandoned politics, Adams did not. An independent Republican, interested in civil service reform and scornful of regular party politics, he urged Carl Schurz to lead a free-trade movement. Adams later finished the last page of his nine-volume study of the administrations of Jefferson and Madison with the personal "gloom and depression" induced by the tragic suicide of his wife; but his history also reflected his philosophical confidence that although America was not exempt from "the common burdens of humanity," yet, "the experiment of embracing half a continent in one republican system" was the one great step America had taken "in advance of the Old World." [12]

John Dos Passos in *U.S.A.* might seem to be decisive proof of the American writer's obsession with a solitary survivor of a decaying society. Nowhere else in our modern social novel is the idea expressed with such relentless passion that people are doomed to be defeated (if they are decent) or corrupted (if they are not) by a potent but banal commercially organized society, which warps the life of the heroic and unheroic, the dissenters as well as the opportunists. Nowhere does *U.S.A.* assert, as

Trilling believed English stories do, that "initiation into society is possible, fascinating, and desirable"; instead, it says throughout "that virtue lies in alienation from society,"[13] whether in the sketch of Thorstein Veblen, who "couldn't get his mouth around the essential 'yes'" or in the fictional Ben Compton, the Communist organizer expelled from the party for the heresy of "exceptionalism." Characteristically, the trilogy ends with an isolated tramp hitting the road to nowhere in particular.

But Dos Passos had a lifelong encounter with the idea of American exceptionalism, both as angry young man who voted Communist in 1932 and as angry old man who voted for Goldwater and Nixon in the sixties. Even in 1932 Dos Passos thought Walt Whitman was "a hell of a lot more revolutionary than any Russian poet" he had ever heard of, and he protested against "imported systems" as a curse on the country. He warned fellow radicals that they could not "junk the American tradition" and would have to "Americanize Marx," which he did in his own mythological way by identifying Sacco and Vanzetti, the heroes of *The Big Money*, with the early Pilgrims, and, in the spirit of Whitman, calling for the need to "rebuild the ruined words worn slimy" in contemporary mouths and to remember the "old words the immigrants haters of oppression brought to Plymouth." When Dos Passos dreamed of the future, it was through his biographical sketch of Frank Lloyd Wright, who built for human "uses and needs" and "towards the American future instead of towards the painsmeared past of Europe and Asia."[14]

As Jean-Paul Sartre has pointed out, Dos Passos narrates in historical rather than fictional time: "Everything is told as if by someone who is remembering."[15] Dos Passos said that after Sacco and Vanzetti were executed he had "seceded" in his "private conscience like Thoreau in Concord jail." It would be more accurate to say that by the middle 1930s he had found some historical ground under his feet. At the end of 1934 he was telling Edmund Wilson that the Anglo-Saxon institutions of jury trial and common law would survive American capitalism as they had Tudor absolutism. "It would be funny," he remarked in an unconscious prophecy of his later conservatism, "if I ended up an Anglo Saxon chauvinist—Did you ever read my father's *Anglo Saxon Century?*" [16]

It is easy to miss the future-directed dimension of our political novels because it usually appears only paradoxically by reference to a modern version of an ancient historical idea, which makes the past existentially pertinent to present despairs and future hopes. Erich Auerbach has pointed out that the Bible shares with the realistic novels of Stendhal and Balzac the portrayal of ordinary people caught up in an emergent social movement, active in a localized world, which is shaken to its foundations, "transforming and renewing itself before our eyes." [17] The point can be reversed, as I have argued, to show how nineteenth- and twentieth-century writers, working in a realist tradition, have been able to use biblical ideas of apocalypse and millennium to interpret slave rebellions, labor strikes, and radical parties, as in Harriet Beecher Stowe's *Uncle Tom's Cabin*, William Styron's *The Confessions of Nat Turner*, Ernest Poole's *The Harbor*, John Steinbeck's *In Dubious Battle*, and especially E. L. Doctorow's *The Book of Daniel*, which mixes its narrative modes with Old Testament and modernist techniques. [18]

Norman Mailer began as a political novelist in *The Naked and the Dead* with a despairing projection of a coming fascism, although he could not find a credible social context for it in the civilian lives of his characters. Nor could he find a historical moment to fit his apocalyptic sensibility until the late sixties made one to order. *The Armies of the Night* calls to mind *The Education of Henry Adams*. Adams insisted on the need for "a new social mind," adequate to the world of modern science and politics, and, given the rapid acceleration of "the movement from unity into multiplicity, between 1200 and 1900," he warned, the human mind would "need to jump." [19] Mailer's novelistic account of his participation in the march on the Pentagon in 1967 is a true descendant of Adams's autobiography. Like his forerunner, whose sense of the "doubleness" of life led him to call himself half seriously "a conservative Christian anarchist," Mailer dreams of being both Hemingway and Trotsky, with a dash of Victor McLaglen and Harpo

Marx, and defines himself as a "Left Conservative," mingling radical politics with conservative cultural attitudes. Presenting himself as a profane clown or ludicrously inept idealist in his political role as public speaker, this comic, but "not unheroic," narrator is ambiguous enough in his own proportions, as he says, to deal with a political event as ambiguous in its tactics and point as a symbolic demonstration against the Vietnam War. Only an egotist obsessed with his public image and being televised for the BBC throughout his adventure could be "at home in a house of mirrors" in the "crazy house History" of 1967. Like Adams's rather fanciful byplay with the "Virgin" and the "Dynamo" as historical terms, Mailer is also seduced by polar thinking and defines the division in America as a "schizoid" conflict between "neo-fascists" and "villainous hippies," working-class soldiers and middle-class dropouts, small-town "cold warriors" and urban "peaceniks," techno-logical totalitarians and political nihilists—at last, between the abstractions of "Christianity" and the "corporation." [20]

Mailer's "growing sense of apocalypse in American life" is linked to a tradition of personifying America, which is as old as Cotton Mather's biography of John Winthrop. [21] *The Armies of the Night* as a modern jeremiad incorporates a biblical sense of history with its profound sense of the present moment as being one of supreme crisis and decadence, its prophetic confidence in a cataclysmic coming renovation, accompanied by an elect who will be the agency of redemption. So this "history-as-novel" ends with admiration for the Quaker "saints" who redeem America's sins by refusing all compromise with the government and dehydrating themselves on the floors of their prison, while its rhetoric thrills with the extravagant hope that there is some "hint of a glorious future" in the "spoiled children of a dead de-animalized middle class," the young protesters who climbed "the moral ladder" much higher than Mailer himself by staying on at the Pentagon steps to be beaten up by the federal marshals. Spurred by walking in Washington arm in arm with Robert Lowell to recall "ghosts of Union dead" and to feel the stab of his own patriotism, Mailer envisions his country as a land where "a new kind of man was born from the idea that God was present in every man not only as compassion but as power, and so the country belonged to the people; for the will of the people—if the locks of their life could be given the art to turn—was then the will of God. Great and dangerous idea!" His peroration closes with the image of his country as a beautiful woman with leprous skin, heavy with child, fated to give birth either to "the most fearsome totalitarianism the world has ever known" or else "a babe of a new world, brave and tender, artful and wild." [22]

Irving Howe has found the social space between "the abstractions of ideology" and "the intimacies of the personal life" [23] barely present in our fiction, but these poles are connected by Henry James in his novels about feminists and anarchists. Our point of vantage in history enables us to see how *The Bostonians* makes an ironic and telling point about the hidden agreement between Basil Ransom's conservative idealizing of female "softness and docility" and Verena Terrant's feminist vision of women redeeming public life through their special qualities of tenderness and sympathy. We can see with contemporary eyes also James's Princess Casamassima as a devotee of radical chic, consumed by the illusion that political terrorism is somehow closer to "reality" than bourgeois life. Basil foreshadows the Southern agrarian, conservative intellectuals of our century, just as the Princess is a foretaste of some female terrorists of recent years. Even so, James was more fascinated with the characterological consequences of ideology than with the issues themselves, and the personal dramas in these novels tend to overwhelm the larger questions, politics being reduced to psychology.

There are more recent novelists who discover better the political meaning of cultural issues. They mingle psychological problems of identity with metaphysical issues about freedom and responsibility, yet at the same time their stories have much political insight and continuing pertinence. In this respect *The Middle of the Journey*, *All the King's Men*, and *Invisible Man* come to mind. All three can be assimilated to a typically modern pattern that the English critic Tony Tanner has found in Ellison's novel:

> The narrator has discovered what many American heroes

> have discovered, that he is not free to reorganize and order
> the world, but he can at least exercise the freedom to ar-
> range and name his perceptions of the world. He cannot
> perhaps assert and define himself in action, but sometimes
> at least he can assert and create himself in some private
> space not in the grip of historical forces. . . . His most im-
> portant affirmation may be, not of any pattern in the out-
> side world, but of the patterning power of his own mind. . . .
> What he has learned is that it is always dangerous to start to
> confuse your own particular patterning with reality itself.[24]

Tanner's reference to a "private space not in the grip of
historical forces" seems to give indirect support to another
critic's recent charge against the literary intellectuals of the
fifties that, in a time that cried out for radical attention to
political issues, they turned instead to the "intensities of the
isolated self or isolated personal relationships."[25] Morris Dickstein has thus turned Tanner's neutral description into an indictment of a decade. If true, this complaint would also tend to
validate the persisting relevance of Auden's original remark
about the peculiarly Ishmaelite character of our best books.

Certainly some such case can be made by a selective reading of Warren, Trilling, and Ellison. Robert Penn Warren's
novel fails to give any political content to the normative figure
of Hugh Miller, the decent politician, who resigns on principle
from Willie Stark's administration and reappears at the end as
someone with whom the narrator will have future political
associations, though of an unspecified kind. Furthermore, Warren has insisted that politics is only a framework for the deeper
concerns expressed through what the narrator makes out of the
politician's story in terms of his own problem of healing his self-
division and alienation from moral responsibility.[26] The hero of
*The Middle of the Journey*, set in the political mid-thirties and
published in 1947, is said to be "not really a political person"
who thinks of the world "as forces in struggle," and the only
thing we know about his political position at the end of the
book is that the fellow-traveling Crooms "no longer showed him
the right direction of moral and political development."[27]
Furthermore, the only depression visible is not the country's,
but the hero's. In panic fear, he remembers a disturbing en-

counter with his own death wish in a hospital; and death, as Hannah Arendt has said, "whether faced in actual dying or in the inner awareness of one's own mortality, is perhaps the most antipolitical experience there is," because it subtracts the individual from the communal effort to perpetuate common values.[28] Finally, the idea of a political future seems to vanish in Trilling's novel because the sign of the hero's maturation is said to be his awareness that he no longer distinguishes between what he is and what he expects himself to be. Similarly, one can read *Invisible Man* so as to conclude with one critic that the narrator, a "rabblerouser" who has become a writer, as Ellison once put it, has failed "to discover a guide to action in his own history" and "only finds himself locked more deeply into the confused ambivalence that has characterized his life."[29] I shall argue instead that in spite of these objections all three stories are important political novels.

*All the King's Men* is remarkably faithful to the larger pattern of Huey Long's life, and it also realistically comprehends the social divisions within Louisiana—the gap between the Delta gentry and the hill folk aggravated by a tradition of conservative government, which paved the way for a populistic dictator who provided the people with the valuable rudiments of a welfare state. Warren exploits the American fascination with political corruption, just as Adams, Twain, and Dos Passos do; but he goes beyond the convention to provide a historical basis for understanding Willie Stark's conversion of his own experience of having been gulled by cynical politicians into an emotional bond with poor whites whose interests he comes to serve. It is a part of the narrator's breaking out of his own passivity and cynicism to see that "the boss" in his own way was actually more than a clown or a vengeful hick, "Cousin Willie, a country boy with a Christmas tie," even though he "could not tell his greatness from his ungreatness and so mixed them together that what was adulterated was lost."[30]

Warren has spoken elsewhere about his own development by remarking how the Depression helped to destroy "a sense of entrapment" in history as being something "deeply engrained in the Southern mind" because in those years "you had to reorder society, and this meant you had to reorder all sorts of relationships." The idea that you could reorder them "opened the whole question psychologically." [31] *All the King's Men* still gains much of its power from its vital relation to this primary observation, rather than from the more philosophical dialectics of its argument about the modern split between idea and fact, which has its political correlative in Willie Stark's conflict between a populist idealism and an embittered Machiavellianism.

Like William James, whom Warren read while gestating his novel, the novelist was interested in the great-man theory of history and the role the hero plays in striking a new balance of forces, as James put it, by breaking "the old moral rules in a certain place" in order to usher in a new equilibrium of satisfactions. Willie's formulation of his own political pragmatism in the metaphor of a bottle of water thrown into a hot stove is a vernacular version of the philosopher's own theory. "The steam that blows the bottle and scares the teacher to wet her drawers," Willie explains, "is just the human business that is going to get done, and it will blow anything you put it in if you seal it tight, but you put it in the right place and let it get out in a certain way and it will run a freight engine." [32] Warren's embodiment of the populist demagogue is more impressive than the contrived manipulation of an intricate plot at the end of his story to illustrate a metaphysical argument about how a recognition of his guilt enables Jack Burden to assert responsibility and give up the alibi of his mechanistic view of the world.

Like Warren's novel, Trilling's ends with an analysis of a causal chain of personal relationships, guilts, and responsibilities, and its philosophizing about free will also tends to overshadow the political meanings in the story. Yet Trilling's reference to the middle of the journey, drawing on Dante's famous metaphor about being lost in a dark wood, points beyond an individual's mid-life crisis. The historian Charles Beard also used Dante's figure as an epigraph for his account of the New Deal years, *America in Midpassage*. In dramatizing the self-deceptions of fellow travelers, unable to face the grim realities of Stalinism, Trilling prophesies the response many liberals would have two years later when they could not accept the impressive amount of evidence that Alger Hiss was actually a duplicitous

Communist spy. Furthermore, the hero also opposes the opportunistic drift to a politically reactionary religiosity that both Whittaker Chambers in reality and Maxim Gifford in the novel express in their pretentious, pontifical way.

More than a decade ago Robert Warshow complained that Trilling had left out the "deeper layers of motivation" in the surrender to Stalinism among the middle class, especially the Jewish segment.[33] The objection is more applicable, however, to Warshow himself in his treatment of the Rosenbergs, whom he reduces to mere abstractions of the Party line, than it is to *The Middle of the Journey*. Warshow's complaint ignores the extent to which the real terrain of Trilling's novel is precisely the middle-class basis of the intellectual's relation to Stalinism. Maxim's hold on Laskell's imagination is that the Communist "brought the guilt into the open, the guilt of being what one was, the guilt one shared with others of one's comfortable class. There was a kind of relief in admitting the guilt to this huge dedicated man." And Laskell comes to see that Nancy Croom's willingness to provide a mail drop for Maxim's underground Party activities has something to do with her being "the well-loved child of the middle class," who is taught confidence in the future by the promises and presents of parents and so develops the vision of a future "always brighter and more spacious than the present." The novel also shows us that the New Deal economist Arthur Croom, a political realist and activist, responds to Maxim's defection by wondering what could be wrong with him, as if all deviation from the Party, with which Arthur has many differences, is inherently wrong. Thus he exposes his assumption that "a break with it was not an action in politics" but rather "an action in morals."[34] Arthur's response, I believe, is what Trilling meant when he spoke of his novel as exploring "the clandestine negation of the political life which Stalinist Communism had fostered among the intellectuals of the West."[35]

Trilling's novel also speaks politically to the sixties. Laskell's final argument with Maxim turns on the hero's concession that he may have been seeking forgiveness for his own guilt in his apparent charitableness to an accidental murderer. Nevertheless, Laskell decisively refuses to acquiesce in Maxim's religious systematizing of personal guilt into a universal theme. This seemingly personal problem has public implications, as Laskell intimates earlier in the story when he reflects on the German people's preoccupation with guilt and innocence: "so many words to explain the wrongs done to them, for the wronged and the weak are the innocent; so much cruelty to separate themselves from the guilty, for those who are punished are guilty and those who punish are innocent; so much adoration of strength, for the strong who once were weak are never guilty." [36] Laskell realizes in his final argument with Maxim and the Crooms that they share an illiberal tendency to accept myths of collective guilt and innocence that enable radicals to patronize members of the weaker class by absolving them, because of environmental deprivations, of any responsibility for anything, while enabling reactionaries to absolve members of the more powerful class of responsibility for injustices by the plea of original sin as a universal tendency.

What Laskell comes to see is that "if you don't know their names, if you don't know the color of their eyes, then you're talking about some metaphysical kind of guilt." [37] This criticism is relevant not only to the war-guilt debate about the Germans but also to the radical polemics about white racism in the 1960s and the reactionary defense of the Watergate conspiracy in the 1970s. The point of the political novel, after all, is not to define programs and policies, which is a politician's task, but to explore political ideas, and that is what *The Middle of the Journey* does with a subtlety that escapes those who reduce it to the question of Trilling's attitude toward Whittaker Chambers. Imaginatively, the book has its most vivid life in its psychological drama of Laskell's mid-life crisis, but as a novel of ideas, rather overschematized, its bearing is political.

For Ellison the "special province of the novel is time and social change." *Invisible Man* has an anonymous narrator whose experiences are symbolic and even surrealistic dramatizations of an interpretation of the social history of the American black as it bears upon his identity formation. That interpretation challenges Marxist and Black Nationalist views of the American racial problem. The narrator takes seriously the value of Southern elements in his identity as a defense against the standardizing impact of urban industrialism, and he comes to see that Marxists are blind in identifying his Southern tastes and folklore as mere backwardness, while also reducing the reality of color to class categories that ignore it by the pretension of rising to a more human level of universality. At the same time, he rejects the tribal racism of Ras as an archaism blind to the American elements in the black man's identity; and the narrator eventually sees that the radical Brotherhood he has joined has used him and Ras as pawns in a suicidal riot in Harlem, designed to create black victims for propaganda. Musing on unorganized black men in a Harlem subway, the narrator wonders if "the void of faceless faces, of soundless voices, lying outside history" might be "the true leaders, the bearers of something precious," especially if "history was a gambler, instead of a force in a laboratory experiment," [38] as the radical rationalism of the Brotherhood conceived of it. Looking at his world through the eyes of Rinehart, a trickster of many roles, the narrator sees that "freedom was not only the recognition of necessity," as Marxists believe, "it was the recognition of possibility" in the "beautiful absurdity" of an "American identity." None of these ideas was politically fashionable among Black Nationalists and their white fellow travelers in the late 1960s, but they had profound political implications for the civil rights movement that followed soon after the novel was published.

If *Invisible Man* seems to move its protagonist "outside of history," it is because Ellison puts Marxism, as a "science" of history, in the role of spokesman for the "inside" of history, and it is a rationalism that he rejects. But he does not acquiesce in the present. The novel begins and ends with the failure of a white man to recognize a black man, and the crucial point is made that "responsibility rests upon recognition, and recognition is a form of agreement." This statement defines the social conditions that are necessary before the hibernating narrator can emerge from his invisibility and play that "socially responsible role" he intends to take up in the future. He has come to see that slavery did not expunge his grandfather's humanity, that it constitutes an authentic black *and* American heritage because his grandfather's advice "to do 'em in with grins and yesses" is not a formula for simulated servility but rather an assertion of an ideal of equality and of the black man's need to find himself collectively by asserting "the principle on which the country was built and not the men, or at least not the men who did the violence."[39] This conclusion prophetically looks toward 1954, when the Supreme Court would take the crucial step of recognizing that racially segregated public schools could not be equal, and later when Martin Luther King would organize the Montgomery bus boycott that would initiate the civil rights movement. Only then could those "bearers of something precious," those "faceless faces" and "soundless voices," acquire faces and voices as players in the gamble of history.

In their emphasis on historical actualities, which idealists often ignore, Trilling, Warren, and Ellison deepen our political understanding rather than neglect it. Political positions of every color have to take account of human nature and historical circumstances or be doomed to futility. But it is possible to treat realism itself in such a way as to convert it into a specious substitute for political thinking or a disguised vehicle for conservatism. To illuminate both of these possibilities, it is useful to take a hard look at Ernest Hemingway's *For Whom the Bell Tolls* and James Gould Cozzens's *Guard of Honor*. Both of these can be classed with other novels that find political implications in war—such as John De Forest's *Miss Ravenel's Conversion* and Norman Mailer's *The Naked and the Dead*—and they also can be fitted into Tanner's design for contemporary fiction with its emphasis on the necessary but risky patterning power of one's own mind. What also link them, however, are the breadth of their canvases and their attraction to a tough-minded stoicism, in spite of all their differences in style and characterization.

Hemingway's novel makes a genuinely political point in its title by reminding readers (in 1940) of what the failure of the Spanish Republic meant to the West in terms of the coming struggle with fascism beyond the borders of Spain. But it is troubling as a political novel in that, despite the intentions of the title, the temper of it, as Warren has remarked, is "the old temper, the cast of characters is the old cast, and the assumptions lying far below the explicit intention are the old assumptions" of Hemingway's work. A psychically wounded hero finds his essential meaning in a romantically isolated love affair amid the violent ruins of civilization, cuts himself off from the confused world, and falls back upon "his private discipline and his private capacity to endure."[40]

Robert Jordan deliberately resists political thinking about the future because he wants to concentrate on winning the war; he values Maria's sexuality for disenthralling him from his political "bigotry"; and he is afflicted at the climax with a neurotic wish to kill himself, as his father had done. The politics of the situation emerge most clearly in Jordan's dialogues with the Russian journalist Karkov at Gaylord's Hotel, where the American professor is given disturbing and realistic glimpses of the ruthless brutality and duplicity of the Soviet operation in Spain. But in the name of "realism" Jordan typically half closes his eyes to what he learns, accepts Communist discipline as a practical necessity, and rationalizes the Soviet suppression of the anarchist P.O.U.M. group (to which George Orwell belonged) for the irrelevant reason that its members kept untidy campgrounds. Hemingway sees through some of the Popular Front's ideology, but he remains loyal to it.

Jordan nostalgically remembers the fighting in the Sierras when they had fought with the "true comradeship of the revolution," an experience he recalls in religious terms, as "a sort of state of grace," but his present in the novel is a fallen world in which that earlier mood seems to be "too naive."[41] Hannah Arendt noted that facing death under the circumstances of battle can have a political meaning when "the potential immortality of the group we belong to and, in the final analysis, of the species, moves into the center of our experience." But, as she also pointed out, these experiences, whose elementary force is beyond doubt, have never found an institutionalized political expression" and "the strong fraternal sentiments collective violence engenders have misled many good people into the hope that a new community together with a 'new man' will arise out of it," an illusion which can be actualized only under "conditions of immediate danger to life and limb."[42] We can see clearly now how the *putschist* versions of student politics in the

1960s, for example, destroyed themselves by feeding on this illusion, which Hemingway idealizes in memory.

But Arendt also justly observed that "to ask the impossible in order to attain the possible is not always counterproductive." As Max Weber noted, if it is unsuitable to recommend "Cato-like acts of courage from the comfortable heights of a university chair," so also is it inappropriate "to laud the opposite extreme and to declare that it is a duty to accommodate one's ideals to the opportunities which are rendered available by existing 'trends' and situations."[43] It is this latter conservative "realism" that emerges from Cozzens's *Guard of Honor*, which won a Pulitzer Prize in 1948.

Arthur Mizener rightly praised Cozzens as a man who "respects and, indeed, loves the actual world even though he knows its evils and inadequacies as well as those who cannot endure it."[44] Mizener took straight, however, the epigraph's quotation from *The Tempest* about "I and my fellows" being "ministers of Fate," though I think the novel's ironic point lies rather in the subversion of Ariel's boast that he and his fellow ministers are "invulnerable." Indeed, the strength of the novel's dramatization of wartime army life at a Florida air base is that it shows in such sharp and voluminous detail how the organization actually works through a process in which everyone has to cover for the "snafus" and vulnerabilities of their fellow soldiers. Everyone, in this sense, requires a guard of honor in someone else.

Cozzens's argument for politics as the "art of the possible" finds its occasion in a troubling incident of unauthorized racial discrimination to which black soldiers call attention by attempting to take over the officers' club, which has been segregated against Washington policy by a bumbling and prejudiced West Point colonel. Washington requires that the air-base general somehow repair injury to morale without undermining discipline or embarrassing the Air Force by leaving headquarters "*to stand on the front porch juggling a red hot poker while it squares enunciated theory with expedient practice.*" The source of wisdom in the story is a young general from headquarters who had been at the Quebec conference with Roosevelt and Churchill, and "those great personages showed General Nichols, the errand boy, the perhaps not-unartful nipper, how to make history." The point was not simply to find "the wisest and best course," but "to strike a bargain, a master bargain which was the congeries of a thousand small bargains wherein both high contracting parties had been trying, if possible, to get something for nothing; and if that were not possible, to give a little in order to gain a lot." Such agreement could ordinarily be obtained only "by a balance of disguised bribes and veiled threats." [45] The novel shows us in detail how the problems at the local air base are, in fact, under General Nichols's guidance, worked out in precisely this way by an artful combination of the carrot and the stick. Thus does political necessity bound the possible.

Cozzens's novel, with its panoramic and microscopic vision of a society at war, is a masterful example of old-fashioned literary realism, and his sense of the muddled workings of the military is much more credible than either left-wing stereotypes are about fascist militarism or right-wing stereotypes are about noble and efficient patriots. But what must trouble our response to General Nichols is that so much is made of his wisdom about means, for it takes for granted the ends of action—in his case, winning the war. We can sympathize with his pragmatism because of the extent to which the war against Hitler was a just one, but our sympathy is strained by Nichols's complacent discussion of his superior's advocacy of the strategic bombing of enemy cities. Even pragmatic realism, as later studies have shown, does not recommend this policy, and, morally, the loss of a distinction between civilian and military targets has been disastrous for limiting the use of violence to relatively rational ends. Judge Ross quite properly wonders at the end if he has not overestimated the subtlety of General Nichols, just as the judge's wife feared he would. Even so, the reader has the same doubt about the author, who sympathizes so clearly with the general's brusque dismissal of Marxists and Christians alike as men of merely "credulous faiths," which are mere substitutes for the "boy's eye views" he has long abandoned. We may even agree with Judge Ross that stubborn will has to impose "pattern" and "point" on "the Nature of

Things," which abhors "a drawn line and loves a hodgepodge, resists consistency and despises drama," but this stoical pragmatism is carried to extravagantly pseudorealistic lengths in Colonel Ross's reflections, in the wake of a drowning disaster, that the right disinterested response arises from seeing "the portentous truth" that "nothing, not the best you might hope, not the worst you might fear, would ever be very much, would ever be very anything." [46] Stubborn will then loses its point.

This exhausted conservatism forecasts the mood defined by Daniel Bell at the end of the 1950s. Bell notes that Freud, Tillich, and Niebuhr had provided his contemporaries with a stoical image of man, and he thinks it suitable to a political world in which not only millenarianism was archaic but even the use of ideas as "social levers." The exaggerated pseudo-"realism" of this view is exposed in Bell's unjustified conclusion that the passing of chiliastic politics has left nothing behind but a routine, day-to-day, "unheroic" life. He sees a world in which to invest issues with "moral color and high emotional charge is to invite conflicts which can only damage a society." [47] This position makes interest-group compromises the only legitimate form of political action.

The civil rights movement and the protest against the Vietnam War decisively made Bell's mood obsolete and expanded the range of political issues. Many protesters obviously had real and rational reasons for some causes, especially at a time when advocates of the Vietnam War often sounded like "crackpots" in their blindness to actual history, military realism, simple fact, and ordinary morality. But the New Left by 1969 had succumbed to a virulent anti-intellectual cult of action among SDS followers and, among its leaders, to internecine squabbles between doctrinaire and unhistorical ideologues who merely stood Bell's position on its head, as if questions of factual truth and moral principle could be resolved by simply substituting for them glib ideological stands. [48] Furthermore, in politics, unlike literature, apocalyptic views, so fashionable in the late 1960s, run the risk of relishing disaster as a necessary prelude to revolution and, by assuming that therefore "worse is better," only make bad worse.

The political novel cannot honestly disguise its politics on the pretext of attacking ideology, but it has nothing to do with agitprop's lust for action or with confirming our self-righteous satisfaction in having the "right" opinions—or "left" ones. I have argued that Auden's observation about our fiction's focus on timeless, unlocated, and internal conflicts seriously neglects the politically relevant informing ideas in many of our important books, just as Trilling's emphasis on the contempt for society itself in our novels minimizes their normative social orientation. I wish to conclude, however, on a note of strong agreement with Trilling's wise and eloquent reminder that "our fate, for better or worse, is political." The only way to endure it is to bring to bear on it all our subtlety, for "unless we insist that politics is imagination and mind we will learn that imagination and mind are politics, and of a kind that we will not like." [49] The political novel has been indispensable whenever it has been written out of this conviction that serious imagining and thinking are always necessary if we are to bear honorably what Auden called "the familiar weight of winter, conscience, and the State."

(1972, 1979)

Notes

1. Alexis de Tocqueville, *Democracy in America*, ed. J. P. Mayer and Max Lerner, trans. George Lawrence (New York, 1966), pp. 454–55, 439.

2. W. H. Auden, *New Year Letter* (London, 1942), p. 153.

3. Lionel Trilling, *The Liberal Imagination: Essays on Literature and Society* (New York, 1949), p. 212; Richard Chase, "The Classic Literature: Art and Idea," in *Paths of American Thought*, ed. Arthur M. Schlesinger, Jr. and Morton G. White (Boston, 1963), p. 54; Marius Bewley, *The Eccentric Design* (New York, 1963), pp. 292–93; Joel Porte, *The Romance in America: Studies in Cooper, Poe, Hawthorne, Melville, and James* (Middletown, Conn., 1969), p. ix; Quentin Anderson, *The Imperial Self: An Essay in American Literary and Cultural History* (New York, 1971), pp. 39, 233.

4. Auden, *New Year Letter*, p. 153; Richard Chase, *The American Novel and Its Tradition* (Garden City, N.Y., 1957), p. 135; Anderson, *Imperial Self*, pp. 77, 170, 192.

5. A. N. Kaul, *The American Vision: Actual and Ideal Society in Nineteenth-Century Fiction* (New Haven, Conn., 1964), p. 60; Nicholaus Mills, *American and English Fiction in the Nineteenth Century: An Antigenre Critique and Comparison* (Bloomington, Ind., 1974), p. 111. Before Mills published his book in 1974 I had challenged this critical tradition and traced it back to Tocqueville (whom Mills also mentions) and Auden in Strout, "From Trilling to Anderson: The Strange History of Tocqueville's Idea of a Democratic Poetry," *American Quarterly* 24 (1972):601–6.

6. Irving Howe, *Politics and the Novel* (New York, 1957), p. 162; Quentin Anderson, "Practical and Visionary Americans," *American Scholar* 45 (Summer 1976):408.

7. Trilling, "Dreiser, Anderson, Lewis, and the Riddle of Society," *Reporter*, 5(November 13, 1951):39; Kaul, *American Vision*, p. 312.

8. Bernard DeVoto, ed., *The Viking Portable Mark Twain* (New York, 1946), p. 15.

9. Mark Twain and Charles Dudley Warner, *The Gilded Age* (Seattle, 1968), p. 358.

10. *"Democracy" and "Esther": Two Novels by Henry Adams*, introduction by Ernest Samuels (Garden City, N.Y., 1961), p. 42; idem, *The Education of Henry Adams*, (New York, 1931), p. 47.

11. J. G. A. Pocock, "Civic Humanism and Its Role in Anglo-American Thought," in Pocock, *Politics, Language, and Time: Essays on Political Thought and History* (New York, 1971), pp. 100–101.

12. Quoted in Ernest Samuels, *Henry Adams, The Middle Years* (Cambridge, Mass., 1965), pp. 331, 353, 363.

13. Trilling, "Dreiser, Anderson, Lewis," p. 37.

14. John Dos Passos, "Whither the American Writer?" *Modern Quarterly* 6 (Summer 1932):12; idem, *U.S.A.* (New York, 1937), pp. 431, 437.

15. Jean-Paul Sartre, "John Dos Passos and *1919*," in J.-P. Sartre, *Literary Essays* (New York, 1957), p. 89.

16. Townsend Ludington, ed., *The Fourteenth Chronicle* (Boston, 1973), pp. 383, 460.

17. Erich Auerbach, *Mimesis: The Representation of Reality in Western Literature*, trans. Willard R. Trask (Princeton, N.J., 1974), pp. 43, 554. On the contemporaneity of the biblical "type," cf. Frank Kermode, "Novel, History, and Type," *Novel* 1 (Spring 1968):231–38.

18. See chapter 5.

19. Adams, *Education*, p. 498.

20. Norman Mailer, *The Armies of the Night: History as a Novel, the Novel as History* (New York, 1968), pp. 67–68, 208, 211–12.

21. Sacvan Bercovitch notes the Mather–Adams–Mailer connection in his *The Puritan Origins of the American Self* (New Haven, Conn., 1975), p. 243, n.62.

22. Mailer, *Armies of the Night*, pp. 311, 319, 320.

23. Howe, *Politics and the Novel*, p. 163.

24. Tony Tanner, *City of Words: American Fiction 1950–1970* (New York, 1971), pp. 58–60.

25. Morris Dickstein, "The Cold War Blues," *Partisan Review* 41, no. 1 (1974):44.

26. Malcolm Cowley, ed., *Writers at Work: The Paris Review Interviews* (New York, 1959), "Robert Penn Warren," p. 203.

27. Lionel Trilling, *The Middle of the Journey* (New York, 1949), pp. 34, 235.

28. Hannah Arendt, "On Violence," in H. Arendt, *Crises of the Republic* (New York, 1972), p. 164.

29. Harry B. Henderson III, *Versions of the Past: The Historical Imagination in American Fiction* (New York, 1974), p. 298.

30. Robert Penn Warren, *All the King's Men* (New York, 1946), p. 452.

31. Marshall Walker, "Robert Penn Warren: An Interview," *Journal of American Studies* 8 (August 1974):232, 238.

32. Quoted in Cushing Strout, "*All the King's Men* and the Shadow of William James," *Southern Review* 6, no. 4 (October 1970):922–23.

33. Robert Warshow, "The Legacy of the 30's," in R. Warshow, *The Immediate Experience* (New York, 1962), p. 45.

34. Trilling, *Middle of the Journey*, p. 145.

35. Trilling, "Whittaker Chambers and *The Middle of the Journey*," *New York Review of Books* 22 (17 April 1975):23.

36. Trilling, *Middle of the Journey*, p. 145.

37. Ibid., p. 271.

38. Ralph Ellison, *Invisible Man* (New York, 1952), pp. 331, 333, 377, 422.

39. Ibid., pp. 11, 433.

40. Robert Penn Warren, "Hemingway," in *Literary Opinion in America*, 3d ed. rev., Morton Dauwen Zabel, ed. (New York, 1962), 2:455, 460.

41. Ernest Hemingway, *For Whom the Bell Tolls* (New York, 1940), pp. 235, 237.

42. Arendt, "On Violence," pp. 165–66.

43. Max Weber, *The Methodology of the Social Sciences*, trans. and ed. Edward A. Shils and Henry A. Finch (Glencoe, Ill., 1949), p. 25.

44. Arthur Mizener, "The Undistorted Mirror," *Kenyon Review* 28(November 1966):611.

45. James Gould Cozzens, *Guard of Honor* (New York, 1948), pp. 222, 395. Italics in original.

46. Ibid., pp. 397, 572, 573.

47. Daniel Bell, *The End of Ideology* (Glencoe, Ill., 1960), pp. 110, 288–89.

48. Edward J. Bacciocco, Jr., *The New Left in America: Reform to Revolution, 1956–1970* (Stanford, Calif., 1974), pp. 183–84, 223.

49. Trilling, *Liberal Imagination* (New York, 1949), p. 100.

# PART 3
# The Veracious and the Voracious Imaginations

Poetry and history are, then, the two wings
of the same breathing creature, the two linked
moments of the knowing mind.
—Benedetto Croce, *History as the Story of Liberty*

# 7 / The Rediscovery of the Documentary

Modern Americans, Dwight Macdonald complained in 1957, tend to value facts in themselves, "treating them, in short, as objects of consumption rather than as productive tools." They thus devalue the intellectual, the aesthetic, and the ethical, and overestimate the importance of information. Yet Macdonald himself believed that the whole middle section of *Moby Dick*, in its encyclopedic treatment of information about whaling, is "a happy Triumph of the Fact: from an intense concern with the exact 'way it is,' a concentration on the minutiae of whaling that reminds one of a mystic centering his whole consciousness on one object, Melville draws a noble poetry."[1] Moreover, in *Benito Cereno* and *Billy Budd* documentary reports enter directly into his stories as such, where they function as alternate and suspect versions of an elusive truth. For Melville, the imagined and the documentary cohabit between the covers of the same book. In the 1960s facts acquired aesthetic status in the so-called "nonfiction novel" and documentary dramas. One critic, who holds that man can find in the making of forms a power "to free him from history by allowing him to reshape it as he will," concedes that "today, however, we can perhaps feel the cogency of an attempt to merge fact and art—even to surrender art to fact."[2] This merger of history and art, he acknowledges, now takes place both on history's side and on art's side, modifying Aristotle's separation of them.

What makes this merger of art and history seem to be novel is the persisting influence of literary modernism with its rejection of "realism" and preference for self-conscious artifice. Virginia Woolf, for example, believed that the authenticity of the artist's facts "lies in the truth of his own vision" and its world is "rarer, intenser, and more wholly of a piece than the world that is largely made of authentic information supplied by other people." For her, "sober fact," from which good biography is made, is the proper "rest and refreshment" for "a tired imagination."[3] From this point of view the turn to documentary fact is only a weakness that the strong imagination would ordinarily be able to resist. The bias of this position emerges in her complaint that E. M. Forster had a strong impulse to belong both to the camp of "teachers" like Tolstoy and Dickens as well as to the camp of "pure artists" like Jane Austen and Turgenev. Forster failed to unify the camps because "that admirable gift of his for observation has served him too well." It hobbles his flights of fantasy and poetry. Woolf complains that Forster's novels too often fail "to connect the actual thing with the meaning of the thing and to carry the reader's mind across the chasm which divides the two without spilling a single drop of its belief."[4]

The metaphor is telling: art is a suspension bridge flung over the gulf dividing the actual from its meaning. But neither Mark Twain in *Life on the Mississippi*, George Orwell in *Homage to Catalonia*, James Agee in *Let Us Now Praise Famous Men*, or Norman Mailer in *The Armies of the Night*, for example, would concede that they had sacrificed their vision of things to their talent for observation, or that the actual and the meaningful were sundered from each other. Their whole point would be that only by close observation could they search out, discover, and evoke the latent meaning of things. Though they believed, as a passenger on Twain's steamboat put it, that one should "always dress a fact in tights, never in an ulster," their empiricism did not preclude extensive reflection on moral and ideological issues. Even Truman Capote's *In Cold Blood*, which "leaves to the reader the attribution of value and the responsibility of moral interpretation" and "resists the temptation to impose meaning or to moralize upon fundamentally inexplicable events," as John Hollowell has remarked, has a mythic significance achieved by its poeticized prose and dramatic arrangement of the telling: "The destiny of an archetypal American family crosses paths with warped killers whose vengeance is portrayed more as the result of fate than of human motivation."[5] This documentary story was widely perceived as emblematic for a decade of assassinations, war, and racial violence, yet its questions are psychological, not political, moral, or ideological. Mailer's memoir is more to my point because his search for meaning in what happened at the march on the Pentagon is explicit and its issues are historical.

Investigatory hearings, dominating the McCarthy period, are a ritual form of politics with their own drama, usually tediously told. Even so, a scientist at the 1954 Oppenheimer security hearing saw that it was in a way "what novels are about" because its real subject was Oppenheimer's character: "There is a dramatic moment and the history of the man, what made him act, what he did, and what sort of person he was." Dr. Isadore I. Rabi told the Personnel Security Board: "That is what you are really doing here. You are writing a man's life."[6] Heinar Kipphardt saw Rabi's point by turning the hearing into a documentary drama, resembling Brecht's *Galileo* in its image of the hero. Similarly, William Gibson saw in the actual letters exchanged between John and Abigail Adams a drama of enforced separation, documenting their sober, civic, and tender fidelity to each other and the American Revolution, a counterpoint to an America divided in 1969 by throes of agony over racial conflict, the Vietnam War, and campus rebellions. "I am ashamed of the age I live in"—John Adams's lament was also Gibson's who used it as his motto for *American Primitive*, a play that celebrates an American past without sentimentalizing or vulgarizing it.

Artists can become historians when they look into their own families, as we all do. The most dramatic and publicized recent example is Alex Haley's fictionalized record of his search for his ancestors in *Roots*, which has stimulated a widespread resurgence of genealogical passion. Earlier the same impulse was at work in John Updike when he surprised everybody by writing a closet drama about President James Buchanan. Updike had felt "a mystery" in his own family about the man for whom he was named, a grandfather who had been a Democrat, not a Lincoln Republican, and who shared many traits with Buchanan. What sort of values had they represented? Even older than his grandfather was the husband of his grandfather's sister, a man who spoke to the novelist's imagination like a whisper from a green world of "a Pennsylvania dying about us, though its buildings like bones remained." [7] Trying to make sense out of his personal heritage, Updike read history and worked on a historical novel; failing to see his way into it, he turned instead to using the documents he had studied by converting them into a closet drama, *Buchanan Dying*. By then he was not only an artist; he was also a historian of a public man. Writing a historical play was his way of taking into account the presence in himself not only of his personal past, but of a collective historical past, constructed and debated by critical intelligences. Like them, Updike fed his imagination with documents as well as memories.

Much modern art has privatized its characters, shrinking their world to the dimensions of intrapsychic conflict, whose boundary is the family, or cosmically expanding it to the metaphysical anguish of the Absurd. What is routinely neglected is the image of man in history. These examples of the memoir and the drama have corrected this deficiency by connecting actual private troubles with actual public issues. Sometimes, as in the agitprop theater of the 1960s, the results can be disastrous; Paul Foster's *Tom Paine*, for example, reduces history to the spectacle of a self-righteous lambasting of caricatured enemies of right-thinking leftists, "something of a charade conceived in surrealistic terms . . . peppered with four-letter words," as described by a reviewer who perversely praised it for not resembling anything having to do with history. [8] But at their best fact-oriented works imaginatively engage the mind and move the feelings about an intellectually credible world and, through a reliance on speech actually spoken and deeds actually done, open doors on a wider world. Only specific analysis can show where such works fall in relation to the possible extremes—the prosaic inhibition of the imagination or the distortion of historical consciousness. A closer look at Mailer, Kipphardt, Gibson, and Updike will clarify the issues at stake in this recent literary emphasis on the documentary as an aesthetic resource. They constitute a spectrum in terms of a mixture of language from the single voice of Mailer to the edited documentary speech of Kipphardt and the plays of Gibson and Updike, where the element of artifice is more evident in the arrangement of actual speech and authorial commentary. Whatever their limitations, these examples transcend those corruptions of both art and history in a spate of popular films and novels, where a simplistic version of the facts is matched by an aesthetic of crude melodrama. In such cases Virginia Woolf's argument that "fact" and "fiction" destroy each other is all too true because each side of the polarity has become infected.

In his struggle with the problem of designating a genre for *The Armies of the Night* Norman Mailer oscillates between calling parts of it "novel" and parts of it "history." Reversing himself as he tells his story, he eventually concludes that the more personal part of the book is historical because it documents events that he witnessed, while the more public part of the book, which he had to construct from newspapers and testimony, since he was in jail for civil disobedience while "the battle of the Pentagon" took place, is "a condensation of a collective novel," because it relies on his talents as a novelist for dealing with "emotional, spiritual, psychical, moral, existential, or supernatural" matters.[9] The trouble with this nomenclature is that historians normally do not witness the events they talk about, while they do often deal with emotional, psychic, and moral issues.

Actually, neither "novel" nor "history," nor the "new journalism" is an appropriate term for the genre of *The Armies of the Night*. It is a confessional memoir, and it necessarily forces the author to struggle with three different elements: the intellectual themes of the account, the artistic shape of the story, and the historical identity of the writer.[10] Like St. Augustine, the founder of the form, Mailer looks back from the perspective of a theory of history that transcends political struggles by investing them with a metaphysical meaning.

A recent theoretician of the "nonfiction novel" interprets Mailer as a "Merry Prankster of neo-politics," acting out a schizophrenic divorce of fact from meaning that characteristically afflicts contemporary experience. There is grist for this mill: Mailer despises legally oriented reformers, but gets himself out of a short jail sentence on a ridiculous technicality; he issues diatribes against the media, but arranges to have himself filmed during the demonstration. Yet far from being supposedly aware of the futility of imposing "grand patterns of meaning on the actual," [11] he organizes his account by metaphors that borrow grand meanings from Matthew Arnold, Hemingway, Lincoln, and Henry Adams.

Mailer's egotism can express itself empirically enough, as it does in the first book of his memoir; but his metahistorical overbeliefs emerge in the second book when he moves beyond his own adventure to describe the battle of the Pentagon, which he did not witness. As a romantic antirationalist, Mailer celebrates action not according to principle, but on behalf of a revolution whose nature is discoverable only in the making of it. His antirationalism makes him a kind of Robert Jordan of this second civil war, and like Hemingway, Mailer is searching for a hero's code. Paradoxically, he finds what Justice Oliver Wendell Holmes once called "the soldier's faith" in the actions of youthful protesters who intentionally provoke the excesses of retaliating authority and thus, by suffering bravely under fire, win Mailer's accolade of a manhood earned through "a rite of passage" that echoes Valley Forge, Gettysburg, and Normandy. It is more romantic than any of these military engagements because the march on the Pentagon being "a symbolic war, victory had no tangible fruit." [12] As he knows, the immediate beneficiary of the march was the President of the United States, whose popularity shot up in the polls. Mailer is not interested in political results, however, but in the larger implications of heroism.

His account mingles the reporter with the prophet, producing a contemporary jeremiad, lamenting moral decline, calling for heroic idealism, and prophesying an apocalyptic issue of national redemption or damnation. His title echoes Matthew Arnold's metaphor about ignorant armies "on a darkling plain," and his conclusion borrows Arnold's metaphor of "wandering between two worlds, one dead, the other powerless to be born." Mailer's peroration carries out this idiom in an anthropomorphic image of America as a "tormented lovely girl," feeling labor pains, who may give birth to either "a babe of a new world" or "the most fearsome totalitarianism the world has ever known." His rhetoric also echoes Lincoln's Gettysburg Address, not only in identifying the meaning of America with the idea of democracy ("for the will of the people—if the locks of their life could be given the art to turn—was then the will of God"), but in reviving Lincoln's metaphor of a nation "conceived in liberty" and requiring a "new birth of liberty." In this light Mailer sees the Quaker "saints" of civil disobedience as redeemers of the sins of America, a saving remnant. For Mailer "the whole crisis of Christianity in America" is the separation of military heroes and protesting saints.[13] In prescribing their union Mailer is also reminiscent of *The Education of Henry Adams*, where the historian pictures Theodore Roosevelt "training Constantines and battling Trusts" to make Christian soldiers, while Adams prophesies a new man to be born of the "contact between the new and the old energies," before history, like a comet approaching perihelion, achieves its maximum speed and disintegrates.[14]

Mailer thinks that conflicting testimony must frustrate any attempt to be fair or dependable in narrating the history of the march, but his uneasiness about being a novelist writing history as a participant observer reflects a confusion about his genre. It is his devotion to the sermonic metaphors of the jeremiad that transforms his testimonial memoir into something other than history. Using literary methods to imagine a historical situation is not necessarily moving beyond the bounds of a historian. In the 1920s the historian Carl Becker spoke of his *Eve of the Revolution* as an effort to communicate the "quality of the thought and feelings of those days" by enabling the reader "to enter into such states of mind and feeling," a method which did not depend upon "a mere verification of references."[15] Like Thucydides, he used paraphrases of the sort of thing that representative members of social groups would have said; given his own extensive knowledge of the sources, the inventions were never merely fanciful. In "The Spirit of '76" Becker even invented the edited fragments of an imaginary memoir by a fictional colonial New Yorker in order to dramatize three different political perspectives (the editor's, the memoir writer's, and the latter's father-in-law) on the coming of the Revolution.[16] But Becker's tongue-in-cheek presentation made it evident that his "documentation" is typically or symbolically, rather than literally, true to the actual situation.

Marguerite Yourcenar in the *Memoirs of Hadrian* went even further than Becker by inventing an entire memoir by an actual historical person. Her critical bibliography, a wide-ranging, learned exercise of historical scholarship, testifies to her scrupulous sense of historical responsibility, her method of making changes and additions that would "in no way change the spirit or the significance of the incident of the fact in question," that would choose between historians' hypotheses "only with good reason," and that would otherwise try to leave "that very incertitude which before it existed in history doubtless existed in life itself."[17] Creating a memoir for the historical purpose of reconstructing "what a man has believed himself to be, what he wished to be, and what he was" inevitably "borders on the domain of fiction, and sometimes of poetry," she concedes, but her bibliographic note is impressive evidence of her ambition "to approach inner reality, if possible, through careful examination of what the documents themselves afford," because the "human significance" of her work would be "greatly enriched" by "close adherence" to historical facts.[18] Her book testifies to how a profound historical consciousness can coexist with a novelist's imagination, even though her reconstruction dispenses with the footnoted formal statement of evidence. In such a work, as she remarks, "one always rebuilds the monument after one's own fashion, but it is already something accomplished to employ only authentic stones." Her spiritual preparation for the task of historical empathy was the long discipline of learning "to calculate exactly" the distance between the emperor and herself.[19] Both Becker and Yourcenar refute the claims of the nonfiction novel to achieving some radical novelty in merging fictional means with historical purposes and subjects.

Selection and organization of facts are essential to history as well as to art; but the element of invention, which is intrinsic to art, has to come to terms in historical dramas, especially when they are documentary in form, with the problem posed by the existence of historical evidence and the need for critical treatment of it. A recent thoughtful study of historical drama, however, sees the dramatists' "pretense" to render an actual world belied by their acknowledgment that a play "creates its own world with a closed, internal system of references." The dramatist's vision of history is thus seen as "a fiction which the reader can experience like any other," even though dramas, unlike historical novels, tend to make public persons central characters.[20] Given these assumptions, no historical criticism is possible.

Yet even if we grant the force of the aphorism Herbert Lindenberger quotes from Schiller that, unlike narratives, "all *dramatic* forms turn the past into present," creating an effect of immediacy, we still respond, as Lindenberger notes, to the comic effects in Shaw's *Caesar and Cleopatra* because of our awareness of its deliberate anachronisms.[21] They presuppose a critical historical sense both in the dramatist and the audience. Lindenberger, furthermore, believes that drama is even better suited than prose fiction or narrative history to expose the motives of political acts and to "portray a person's role in intricate ways in which the private self becomes a part of the roles it is forced to play in public situations," and in this sense drama is "the ideal medium for the understanding of politics."[22] But his persuasive case for drama thus gives it an intellectual cognitive role, and when political matters are embedded in an actual historical context, how can either dramatist or audience escape from a reckoning with the demands made on us by our modern historical conscience and imagination? To subordinate them entirely to the power of the theater to enchant with eloquence, music, and spectacle would be to reduce historical drama to the level of a pretentious circus or street-theater agitprop.

Lindenberger champions the Epic theater conventions of Brecht for modern historical drama because they enable us to look openly at the past from the "unashamedly present-day vantage point."[23] But, while it is true that as a Marxist Brecht was concerned to understand reality in order to change it for the sake of the future, he also wished moderns to exercise a historical sense. It would not "annihilate distance, fill in the gap, gloss over the differences" between old plays and new, but instead take a "delight in comparisons, in distance, in dissimilarity—whch is at the same time a delight in what is close and proper to ourselves."[24] It was also part of his Marxism to insist on seeing past social structures as different because "we must leave them their distinguishing marks and keep their impermanence always before our eyes, so that our own period can be seen to be impermanent too."[25] These postulates provide no warrant for projecting the present into the past. If Brecht does so, it is because they are in tension with his technique of presenting parables about typical social attitudes, a technique revealed by his suggestion that "the poetic approach to history can be studied in the so-called panoramas at sideshows in fairs."[26] This style of deliberate simplification, designed to influence people to act, is not appropriate to a complex and concrete historical sense but rather to his pedagogical political interest: "Once I've found out what modes of behavior are most useful to the human race I show them to people and underline them."[27]

Lindenberger quite rightly notes that "despite its pretensions about apprehending reality directly, documentary drama, like any form of drama, offers a very selective view of history. Indeed, the documentary plays of the 1960s are notable for the high degree of manipulation which their authors—or "arrangers"—have applied to the documents from which the plays are drawn."[28] He notes in Heinar Kipphardt's *In the Matter of J. Robert Oppenheimer*, for example, that its carefully paired witnesses are arranged with a symmetry that suggests "the virtues and vices in morality plays." Lindenberger's position on the historical drama in general, however, does not permit him to criticize any manipulation, and he assimilates the documentary dramas of the 1960s to the category of inspirational martyr plays, which are as old as the Middle Ages. Brecht, as he points out, rewrote his *Life of Galileo* in response to the dropping of the first atomic bomb, only a more memorable example of the historical dramatist's traditional shamelessness "in reading the present into the past." [29] The example, however, ought to unsettle us about that shamelessness. Brecht claimed that the control of government over American nuclear scientists had put Galileo in a new light, very different from the heroic aura of his first version, written in 1938–39, which was historically grounded. But in making Galileo accuse himself of failure for not having "provoked a major upheaval" by carrying out the social implications of the new science, Brecht is blatantly anachronistic and implausible, unable to dramatize persuasively what he takes to be the hero's social crime. [30] The point is not that Galileo's dilemma has no resonance at all with, say, the Oppenheimer case. A historian of science has even drawn up a tally of the correspondences, and he finds that the representatives of authority in both cases "are remarkably similar in their complex motivations." [31] But Brecht's *Galileo* makes no contact with Galileo's Christianity and his maintenance to the end of his science and his faith, despite his willingness to submit out of obedience to clerical authority.

Kipphardt's *In the Matter of J. Robert Oppenheimer* responds to the same contemporary political situation of nuclear science, but it encourages the audience's sense that history is being performed in an unmediated way directly out of the documents, much as the Watergate hearings later did. While Kipphardt's preface claims that his use of the government transcript of the security hearing "adheres strictly to the facts," it also equivocally concedes that he has "freely" adapted the record. [32] Justifiably, he had to be very selective in using such a lengthy document, but he went much further than selection in modifying the actual transcript, even to the extent, as he explains, of reformulating speeches and inventing lengthy monologues for his witnesses and his protagonist. The play reflects not only the main issues of the hearing, but also the implicit influence of Brecht's revisionist play, *Galileo*, with its scientist-hero who at first seems to be a martyred victim of reactionary forces and ultimately is shown to be a tragic hero, a remorseful betrayer of the humanistic, libertarian ideology of science. Kipphardt's true hero briefly appears as the Danish scientist, Niels Bohr, who unsuccessfully tried to persuade Roosevelt and Churchill to internationalize the atomic bomb before the end of the war, in contrast to Oppenheimer's advisory role in supporting the decision to drop the bomb on Japan. Kipphardt's play contributes provocatively to an argument about the political role of nuclear scientists, and its major dramatic value lies in its transcendence of a simple melodrama about Oppenheimer's victimization by chauvinistic "red-baiting" prosecutors and one-eyed judges.

Kipphardt's *Oppenheimer* overlaps the historical figure who appears in the transcript but also contradicts it in the final monologue, a self-accusing refusal to use science any longer for purposes of national defense. In documentary fact, Oppenheimer's only comment on this matter in 1954 after the hearing was to say: "I know that they [scientists] will work faithfully to preserve and strengthen this country. I hope that the fruit of their work will be used with humanity, with wisdom and with courage. I know that their counsel when sought will be given honestly and freely. I hope that it will be heard." [33] In the play he is, as his enemies charged in a different sense, a betrayer, an "ideological traitor," who informed on his left-wing friends and deserted a supranational "spirit of science." [34] In this reversal the protagonist comes to conclude that the actions the security board held against him were closer to the true idea of science than the services to the government for which he was praised.

Kipphardt uses Oppenheimer as a ventriloquist's dummy to pass judgment on all those scientists who have worked on war projects, doing "the work of the Devil," while he permits the audience to think that his own point of view is mirrored in the documentary evidence. Unless the spectators happen to have read nearly a thousand pages of testimony, they cannot tell where the author's "tragic hero" (Brecht's Galileo in modern dress) and the historical Oppenheimer part company. The play's genuine dramatic interest is purchased at the price of historical distortion. The documentary record of the hearing provides evidence enough of tragic elements of hubris in Op-

penheimer's career, but not of his awareness of it as a sub-
servience to authority.[35]

A scrupulous and effective example of a documentary
drama is William Gibson's *American Primitive*. It dramatizes
the letters exchanged between John Adams and his wife Abigail
in the years of the American Revolution when they were
separated by the demands of politics and war. Gibson's method
uses a chorus for comment, but the letters (spoken as if being
written or read at the moment) exploit the actual phrases of
their writers, though they are abstracted from the documents
and combined by Gibson's editing. When Abigail learns that
her husband must be sent to France, for example, her response,
bewailing her sense of loss in seeing his honors as the badges of
her unhappiness, is expressed in terms derived from three different letters written over a period of a year at the end of the
war, four years after he left for France.[36] But because this theme
of loss continually recurs in the course of their correspondence,
the violation of the chronology makes emotional and dramatic
sense without distorting the essential truth about their relationship.

The moving quality of the play lies in its counterpoint
between the demands of public life on the Adamses and the
deep affections and sorrows of their private life. What makes
them remarkable is not the mere fact of this conflict in their
lives, but their principled commitment to the sacrifice of their
private happiness for the sake of the public good, in keeping
with their sense of religious obligation. It is this extraordinary
fidelity on both private and public levels that implicitly comments on the contemporary world: "What kind of people not
like us did it take?" If people like John and Abigail Adams
began the country, comments the chorus, "We are the kind who
end a dream."[37]

Gibson did not think of his text as a play but as "eyewit-
ness history," lending itself to recital, projections, music, and
dance. He emphasized the need for a battle map, recording
changes in the military peril threatening the colonists, because
"the psychological progression in the text is minimal."[38]
Though *American Primitive* has been performed a few times, it
is essentially a reading of letters. As drama, however, it de-

serves to be put in the company of Robert Lowell's reworking of Hawthorne's story of the Revolution, "My Kinsman, Major Molineux," rather than with the slick and vulgarized musical "1776." (In *Golda* Gibson unfortunately tried to repeat the same idea, this time with a stay-at-home husband and a wife separated from private life by the demands of politics and war, a reversal politically tuned to the new feminism, but he did not have the eighteenth-century eloquent dialogue of the Adamses to make listening memorable.)

John Updike's historical play, though it shares a common interest with Gibson in the language of a real person as a source for drama, is even more of a reader's text than *American Primitive*, for *Buchanan Dying* was written as closet drama and contains an eighty-page commentary, which is a necessary adjunct to the play. The tension it records between Updike's historical conscience and his novelist's imagination is itself a quiet drama about his struggle with his unfulfilled plan of making a novel out of Buchanan's story. Updike's problem with his subject is not so much the challenge of dealing with a prosaic protagonist, a difficulty the play imaginatively faces, but rather the weighty burden of Updike's historical awareness of how much was known about the protagonist. Scrupulously respectful of historical reality, Updike was very much aware that "an actual man, Buchanan, had done this and this, exactly so, once: and no other way. There was no air." As a novelist, he needed "a palpable medium of the half-remembered in which to swim" and found that in this case his imagination was "frozen by the theoretical discoverability of *everything*." Only a play seemed possible in which speech, "which is all impalpable that remains to us of the dead," could then "be all." [39] Updike accepted his burden but shifted to another medium to lessen its weight and find the necessary aesthetic distance. His sense of artistic and historical responsibility is exemplary for refusing simple solutions to a complex problem.

Updike's relation to his material is a story behind the story. Indeed, the two reinforce each other by linking two dramas, his own and Buchanan's. He candidly confessed that he was partly balked from following his long-standing plan of completing a tetralogy about Pennsylvania with a historical novel because of

"the many novelistic touches" in the best biography of
Buchanan, upon which he closely relied for "main text, source,
and guide."[40] Updike's pursuit of his project had its own moments of excitement and frustration. He felt he had "touched
something live" when in the British Museum's great round
reading room he sliced the uncut pages of an 1864 book about
Henry Clay, making "startled British faces" look around; or
when, at the Historical Society of Pennsylvania, he held the
very sheets of paper emending Buchanan's proposed reply to
the South Carolina commissioners, signifying that "a tide had
turned" with the passing of the possibility of a negotiated
peaceful secession," and felt American history flowing through
the "furious hatchings of ink" in his hands; and again, when,
one winter, unable to make his novel move, he flew to
Buchanan's home and looking in the window, "solitary as a
burglar, as a lover," felt that coming closer had only put him
farther away.[41] The closed house was a portent that the author
was barred from getting inside his novel. In accumulating the
pages of his play, he broke his leg, turned forty, and buried his
father. Through these episodes the historical dramatist must
have felt an emotional link with Buchanan's agonized wrestlings with an intractable problem.

Much of Updike's story is historically determined by the
political issues involving slavery and the Union, where "the sun
of history beats glaringly down."[42] But he found an opening for
his imagination in the biographical ambiguity surrounding the
girl who broke her engagement to Buchanan and soon died
under mysterious circumstances. Acknowledging that other
possible explanations exist, Updike chose the one suggested in
an actual letter—that she "committed suicide in a fit of
jealousy, believing he had ceased to love her."[43] Appropriately,
the most dramatic moment of the play turns on two lost documents, her letter breaking off the engagement and the in-
dignant reply of the South Carolina commissioners to the
president's stated intention to defend Fort Sumter against
hostile attacks. Buchanan's dying reveries and deliriums
provide the structure for the play, and Updike fuses the story of
the private man with the story of the public statesman by dramatically substituting an invented version of the lost letter

from Anne Coleman for the lost reply of the commissioners from secessionist South Carolina. This substitution sets up a resonance between the president's personal and political failures. In the play he speaks of the South as "our wife, fair yet willful, delicate yet proud," but the South Carolina commissioners reject him just as his fiancée had done, an alarming aggressive action following in both cases.

The play also creates another resonance between biography and history by suggesting a psychological basis, as well as a familiar political one, for Buchanan's hostility to Stephen A. Douglas. Their falling out over the Kansas Lecompton constitution was historically crucial for the later failure of the Democratic party to present a united front in 1860, an event paving the way for Lincoln's election as a minority president. In the play the same marital metaphor of the South as a wife, which Buchanan uses to endorse a policy of forbearance and Douglas uses to justify a rebuke of the South, reappears in the mouth of the shade of Buchanan's father, who once too severely and unfairly rebuked his son for a minor collegiate insubordination.[44] This subterranean connection suggests that "the little giant from Peoria" reminded Buchanan of his father and so led the president, as he later fears, to have "harried him too hard over Lecompton."[45] Whether or not Buchanan's hostility to Douglas had in it something irrational, Updike rightly saw it as a crucial exchange; the most searching recent history of the coming of the war concludes that Buchanan's "narrow legalistic defense of Lecompton," when he might instead have given his support to a referendum which would show Congress whether the people of Kansas wanted the Lecompton constitution, represented a "basic mistake," a failure to see how badly the northern wing of the Democratic party would be damaged even by a victory for the administration's position.[46]

Updike's sympathetic portrayal of a president conventionally regarded as weak and ineffective reflects his own shrewd historical judgment that Buchanan's forbearing, delaying tactics helped to give "defensive coloring to the dubious cause of putting down secession with force."[47] Updike sees in our indignation over contemporary corrupting presidential power a basis for sympathy with Buchanan's cautious constitu-

tionalism, but historical judgment can even more convincingly
sustain the view taken in the play that, at least with respect to
his policy over the forts in South Carolina, Buchanan had "a
justifiable fear" of "delivering a fatal blow to compromise at a
time when, on both fronts, there appeared to be some grounds
for renewed hope." [48] Lincoln's own announced policy for the
forts did not much differ from Buchanan's.

Updike's portrait of Buchanan is thoroughly based on historical knowledge, but his device of dramatizing the president's
sometimes delirious dying memories is a useful one, for it gains
the author a limited justified freedom from the limits of documentation. This liberty allows him, for example, to imagine
that a dying Buchanan might confusedly have thought for a
moment of suggesting to the justices of the Supreme Court that
"a person can't be property," an opinion the Court had decisively rejected in the Dred Scott Case. [49] Focused on a dying
man, the play can also create suspense about Buchanan's success in coming to terms with his own inner peace, as war looms.
Updike juxtaposes Buchanan's efforts to save the Union with
his personal wrestlings with religious doubts in a Presbyterian
tradition stressing a saving experience of faith. "Have you
secured our eternal union?" asks the wife of a politician. "No, I
have been talking idly, with a very worldly man," replies
Buchanan, after the reassuring clergyman has told him he is
entitled to hope that he has had an experience of saving grace.
Buchanan's actual last words were an appeal to God to do with
him as He would, and Updike supplements them with a more
poetic and less conventional penultimate statement, made by a
practicing Christian and teacher who was executed by the
Nazis: "'All that is heavy is fallen away.'" [50] This dimension of
Buchanan's consciousness gives depth to a conservative mind,
characteristic of Updike's native state in exhibiting a "mild
misty doughy middleness, between immoderate norths and
souths," the author's own "first taste of life." [51]

Updike's play faced the challenge of having a protagonist
who is one of the least admired and least exciting of historical
figures. While it cannot come close to turning Buchanan into a
personality as appealing as Lincoln is to both the literary and
historical imagination, it performs a valuable service in rescu-

ing Buchanan from the historical limbo where "a cloud of disgrace" has hung over him for over a century. The psychological link of author and subject is perhaps unconsciously revealed when the novelist quotes the injunction "*sufficient to the day is the evil thereof*" in the context of mentioning his vulnerability to three personal crises attending the "accumulation" of his pages about Buchanan. Significantly, he puts the same passage in the mouth of the president when he was defending himself from criticism of the most vulnerable elements of his policies—acquiescence in the expansionist aim to acquire Cuba, the conquest of Mexico, and a willingness to draw the Missouri Compromise line out to the Pacific so as to preserve slavery below the line.[52] Updike's experience of limitation as a person and an artist gave him a basis for sympathy with the president, but Buchanan did not understand that the Union would have to change in order to survive. Updike realized, however, that his project of four novels had to undergo revision in order to be fulfilled. His scrupulosity about historical knowledge and his artistic imagination could be reconciled only by his moving to another medium. But for a widely read novelist the decision to write a closet drama, however brilliant, must have the flavor of a necessary evil.

# Notes

1. Dwight Macdonald, "The Triumph of Fact," *Anchor Review* 2 (1957):117.

2. Murray Krieger, "Fiction, History, and Empirical Reality," *Critical Inquiry*, 1, no. 2 (December 1974):347, 345.

3. Virginia Woolf, "The Art of Biography," in Woolf, *The Death of the Moth* (New York, 1943), pp. 193–94, 196.

4. Virginia Woolf "The Novels of E. M. Forster," in *Death of the Moth*, p. 166.

5. John Hollowell, *Fact and Fiction: The New Journalism and the Nonfiction Novel* (Chapel Hill, N.C., 1977), p. 79.

6. Isadore I. Rabi, quoted in Cushing Strout, ed., *Conscience, Science, and Security: The Case of Dr. J. Robert Oppenheimer* (Chicago, 1963), p. 1. Using

this selection from the documentary record "In the Matter of J. Robert Oppenheimer," transcript of a hearing before the Personnel Security Board (Washington, 1954), I directed a playreading (before Kipphardt's version had appeared) at the California Institute of Technology.

7. John Updike, *Buchanan Dying* (New York, 1974), p. 256.

8. Quoted in David Caute, *The Illusion: An Essay on Politics, Theater, and the Novel* (New York, 1971), pp. 231–32.

9. Norman Mailer, *The Armies of the Night: History as a Novel, the Novel as History* (New York, 1968), p. 284.

10. On autobiography see Francis R. Hart, "Notes for an Anatomy of Modern Autobiography," *New Literary History* 1, no. 3 (Spring 1970):485–511.

11. Mas'ud Zavarzadeh, *The Mythopoeic Reality: The Postwar American Nonfiction Novel* (Urbana, Ill, 1976), pp. 157, 163.

12. Mailer, *Armies of the Night*, pp. 224, 311.

13. Ibid., pp. 319, 320.

14. Henry Adams, *The Education of Henry Adams*, ed. Ernest Samuels (Boston, 1974), p. 500.

15. Carl Becker, *The Eve of the Revolution* (New Haven, 1918), pp. vii–viii.

16. Carl Becker, "The Spirit of '76," in Becker, *Everyman His Own Historian: Essays on History and Politics* (New York, 1935), pp. 47–80.

17. Marguerite Yourcenar, "Notebooks on *Memoirs of Hadrian*," trans. Grace Frick (London, 1955), pp. 318–19.

18. Ibid., p. 307.

19. Yourcenar, "Notebooks on *Memoirs of Hadrian*," *Anchor Review* 2 (1957):176, 163.

20. Herbert Lindenberger, *Historical Drama: The Relation of Literature to Reality* (Chicago, 1975), pp. 4, 27.

21. Ibid., pp. 70, 72.

22. Ibid., p. 101.

23. Ibid., p. 18.

24. Bertolt Brecht, "Appendices to the Short Organum," in *Brecht on Theater: The Development of an Aesthetic*, trans. John Willett (New York, 1964), p. 276.

25. "Brecht, A Short Organum for the Theatre," in *Brecht on Theater*, p. 190.

26. Ibid., p. 201.

27. Brecht, "Interview with an Exile," in *Brecht on Theater*, p. 67.

28. Lindenberger, *Historical Drama*, p. 20.

29. Ibid., p. 6.

30. Gerhard Szczesny, *The Case against Bertolt Brecht with Arguments Drawn from His Life of Galileo*, trans. Alexander Gode (New York, 1969), p. 26.

31. Georgio De Santillana, *The Crime of Galileo* (Chicago, 1955), p. ix.

32. Heinar Kipphardt, *In the Matter of J. Robert Oppenheimer*, trans. Ruth Speirs (New York, 1968), p. 5.

33. *Science News Letter* 66 (10 July 1954):21.

34. Kipphardt, *Oppenheimer*, p. 126.

35. On the tragic and ironic elements of the case see Strout, "The Oppenheimer Case: Melodrama, Tragedy, and Irony," *Virginia Quarterly Review* 40 (Spring 1964):268–80.

36. Cf. William Gibson, *American Primitive* (New York, 1972), p. 112 and Charles Francis Adams, ed., *Familiar Letters of John Adams* (Boston, 1975), Abigail Adams to John Adams, 9 December 1781, 25 October 1782, 23 December 1782, pp. 401, 406, 411.

37. Gibson, *American Primitive*, p. 7.

38. Ibid., preface.

39. Updike, *Buchanan Dying*, p. 259.

40. Ibid., p. 183.

41. Ibid., pp. 256, 258.

42. Ibid., p. 192.

43. Ibid., p. 190.

44. Ibid., pp. 90, 160.

45. Ibid., p. 103.

46. David M. Potter, *The Impending Crisis 1848–1861*, ed. Don. E. Fehrenbacher (New York, 1976), p. 319.

47. Updike, *Buchanan Dying*, p. 205.

48. Potter, *Impending Crisis*, p. 545.

49. Updike, *Buchanan Dying*, p. 161.

50. Ibid., pp. 169, 180.

51. Ibid., p. 259.

52. Ibid., cf. pp. 26 and 259.

# 8/Analogical History:
## *The Crucible*

The historical play has one eye on the milieu of the audience, and the question is whether or not its other eye can focus on the past without astigmatism. The dramatist can find one credible solution when there is, in some important respect, a genuine analogy between past and present. A widely performed and controversial example of this use of history in the theater is Arthur Miller's *The Crucible*. Miller has argued for its historical truth, pointed to its contemporary parallels, and defined its transhistorical subject as a social process that includes, but also transcends, the Salem witchcraft trials and the anticommunist investigations of the 1950s, symbolized by Senator Joseph McCarthy.

Miller's harshest critic, however, has condemned him for putting a rationalistic skeptic at the center of a Puritan episode and for using the hero's refusal to confess or inform on others as a specious plea on behalf of Alger Hiss and the Rosenbergs, accused of being Soviet spies. Robert Warshow's bill of indictment faults both Miller's historical and political intelligence, reducing the play to a fellow-traveling tendency to assume that "the Rosenbergs are innocent, one might say, by definition," their sympathizers being "right" without having to prove themselves in the world of experience by testing specific beliefs against concrete circumstances.[1] Except for defining witchcraft as a theological rather than a political issue, Warshow made no analysis of the Salem trials or the social origins of witchcraft. If we look at what recent historians have said about these topics, however, we can find an illuminating way to appraise *The Crucible*, Miller's defense of it, and Warshow's objections to Miller's strategy.

The validity of *The Crucible* depends upon its ability to do three things at once—to interpret the Salem trials, to imply a contemporary parallel, and to dramatize a social process that is not necessarily restricted to American history. In his own view of the play Miller has moved from stressing its historical meaning to emphasizing its concern for a recurring process of social paranoia. The irony of his attempt to carry out this demanding project is that where Miller believes he is being most documentary, he is least historically convincing and where he is most inventive, he also is in touch with the most important psychological dimension of the witchcraft panic, though he curtails its application too narrowly. Miller's comments on the play are much less reliable than they appear to be on matters of fact, but the drama itself deserves much more respect than Warshow was prepared to grant it in the 1950s.

Warshow would not have been surprised by recent historical arguments for the guilt of Alger Hiss and Julius Rosenberg. But these historians do not absolve Congress, the FBI, and American presidents of their guilt in heresy-hunting distortions of the investigatory and legal process.[2] Miller's exploitation of the witch-hunt metaphor can still stand. In discussing his play Miller mentioned the Rosenberg trial in order to criticize the judge and defense attorney for not taking expert testimony on the scientific value of the bomb-lens diagram supposedly transmitted to the Russians, and the point is well taken, whatever the truth may be about the guilt of the Rosenbergs. Miller admitted that he had been "caught up" in anti-McCarthyism, but he also insisted that the artistic side of him was drawn to a "tragic process underlying the political manifestations" whenever "irrational terror takes to itself the fiat of moral goodness." Nothing in these remarks contradicts his earlier remarks about the play, made a month after its first production, when he emphasized his deep admiration for those hanged at Salem, people who "could have such a belief in themselves and in the rightness of their consciences as to give their lives rather than say what they thought was false."[3] But Miller's shift in emphasis does point to the problem of his play because there are some crucial differences between the dilemma of an accused witch and the plight of someone accused of being a Communist, just as there are some similarities as well. Miller could take it for granted that his audience in 1953 would treat any accusation of witchcraft as a false one, but he could not rightly take it for granted that any accusation of Communist party membership, public or secret, was necessarily mistaken. Warshow may have been right to detect this specious assumption in some of the play's enthusiasts, but Miller's commentary on the play has tried explicitly to meet Warshow's objection.

The political catchphrase "witch-hunt" has always been a liberal slogan with a built-in historical assumption that what happened at Salem in 1692 was a disastrous miscarriage of justice. The Puritans and the state authorities eventually came to the same conclusion. Senator McCarthy has become a synonym for demagoguery now for most Americans. Miller's use of the implied analogy between the two periods is likely to win immediate assent from current audiences. The risk is that the assumption will be made all too easily and too vaguely, making the play's protest conventional and complacent. The problem does not lie in analogy itself as a dramatist's way of using historical material. All analogies risk blurring the nuances of difference among various attitudes, but the social processes at work in conflicts over them are not unique. If they were, we would not be able to provide explanations that turn on generalizations derived from comparing social situations. Part of our human interest in history is in recognizing analogies; it is a crucial part of the historian's wisdom to know how to keep them in their place so that they do not become either too literal or too sweeping. Miller's play cannot be faulted because it suggests analogies to other times. The question rather is whether we can identify the working and limits of the play's analogical power without begging too many questions about specific events or rising to an abstract level of fatal vagueness.

Warshow rightly pointed out that accused witches did not die for a cause, as Sacco and Vanzetti did; they were instead upholding their integrity against "an insanely mistaken community."[4] That is Miller's point as well, but he recognizes that there was an aura of treason to witchcraft. In Puritan theory to become a witch was to join an undergound conspiracy to subvert the community. Just as spies have sometimes been disarmingly respectable scientists or government servants, whose ideological commitments have led them into treason, so also Puritans could never be sure that the Devil had not ideologically persuaded some of the community's most respected citizens into becoming spies for the infernal region. In trying both kinds of crime the courts have depended heavily on evidence about internal matters of intention and belief. For Puritans repentance was always available as a remedy for the guilt of being a witch, and in our secular society the repentant ex-Communist witness has often been acclaimed by congressional investigating committees. Moreover, the temptation to make alleged witches scapegoats for Puritan anxieties about British imperial curtailments of their colonial independence has its counterpart in the 1950s when the public and politicians were distressed to find themselves without a monopoly of nuclear weapons and without the luxury of returning to a traditional continental isolationism after victory in World War II. It was useful to believe that "softness on communism" was to blame.

At the same time the political cult of religion was evident in the Eisenhower administration's official piety; Dr. Norman Vincent Peale, the Reverend Billy Graham, and Bishop Fulton J. Sheen were popular on radio and television, and the pledge of allegiance to the flag was revised to include reference to God. Miller later spoke of being appalled by the "new religiosity in the air" and "official piety,"[5] and above all, a mood in which men were "handing conscience to other men and thanking other men for the opportunity of doing so." In these terms the Salem trials spoke to the McCarthy era.

If the witch-hunts spoke to this atmosphere, Miller himself had something to say to it when he later was called before the House Committee on Un-American Activities. Earlier he had been denied a passport under regulations refusing the privilege to citizens believed to be supporting the Communist movement, whether they were members of the Party or not. He chose to challenge the committee to show that its question, demanding that he name a writer he had seen nearly a decade ago at a meeting of Communist writers, was pertinent to some legislative end; and he won on appeal a reversal of his contempt citation for refusing to name others. McCarthy's political attack on Communism always was irrelevant to the real problem of espionage. "The Broadway–Hollywood celebrities who were the victims in these American purge trials," as Alfred Kazin has observed, "were picked because they were 'names.' *They* were not spies but veterans of the 1930s, people of commonplace political reflexes who had been frightened by Hitler and the Depression into the usual delusion that the Soviet Union was 'Socialist' and offered a way out." The victims were not dedicated Stalinists, who had no compunctions about lying, but those "who could not confess their now shameful past without betraying others whom they still identified with themselves."[6] Obviously, Miller's stance would not have been admirable if (contrary to fact) his refusal to name others concealed information helpful in the detection and prevention of espionage.

*The Crucible* calls attention to the way in which the seriousness of treason (or witchcraft) can lead a panicked community to a paranoid fear of its pervasiveness. Miller's focus is on the process of demonizing, a trait to be found not only in McCarthy's America, he noted, but also in Communist countries where "all resistance of any import is linked to the totally malign capitalist succubi."[7] The crucial point for him is the "political paranoia, whichever side makes use of that source of power."[8]

Miller's internal commentary on his play tried to answer the objection that more than diabolism must be involved when there is "certain proof" that spies are at work in both America and Russia. "I have no doubt that people *were* communing with, and even worshiping, the Devil in Salem," he wrote, "and if the whole truth could be known in this case, as it is in others, we should discover a regular and conventionalized propitiation of the dark spirit."[9] Chadwick Hansen made much the same argument in *Witchcraft at Salem* (1969). Yet, although some of the girls were playing around with Tituba's voodoo conjuring, as the play recognizes, there is no evidence for William Barker's sensational confession that he attended a meeting of over a hundred witches at Salem, conspiring "to destroy the Church of God, and to set up Satan's Kingdom."[10] As Keith Thomas in his study of English and European witchcraft points out, though individuals certainly have tried to use occult means to hurt people, there is no convincing historical evidence for witchcraft as a collectively organized, counterreligion of paganism.[11] Anyway, by putting the skeptical John Proctor at the center of his play, Miller, in fact, gives more weight to denials of the existence of witchcraft, and the play's version of the Reverend Mr. Hale eventually concludes with Proctor that the whole panic is a fraud.

The major objection to Miller's conception of the Salem trials is that he purchases contemporary relevance at the price of falling into diabolism himself. The point has greatest force with respect to his treatment of the Puritan authorities, who appear to be so malevolent as to lend credence to the charge that his play turns the prosecution into witches, dedicated to malevolence with the sort of depravity Puritans attributed to them. *The Crucible* neglects the historical role of the ministers, who warned the court against reliance on "spectral evidence," rather than on the traditional tests of voluntary confession and the testimony of two credible witnesses. Puritan theologians knew very well that the Devil's minions were able, as Cotton Mather put it, to "personate the Children of Light in their Delusions," to appear "in the shapes of persons not only innocent, but also very virtuous."[12] For this reason none of the evidence given by the accusing girls about their affliction by the spectral shapes of good Salem citizens should have been taken as pointing to their guilt. The clergy were clear on this point.

The clergy did accept the reality of the danger and warned that "murmuring frenzies of late prevailing in the country," expressed in discontent at poverty or misery, were sources of the temptation to sign pacts with the Devil.[13] The collective advice of the ministers to the court in 1692 properly emphasized the fallibility of specter evidence and of the "afflictions" by look or touch, favored by the young girls, but it also recommended "speedy and vigorous prosecution" of the guilty.[14] Miller spoke of always having in mind the image of Cotton Mather on horseback, calming a crowd that was becoming rebellious against the punishment of a condemned witch, George Burroughs; he had aroused sympathy by ending his last speech with a perfect rendition of the Lord's Prayer, as witches were supposedly incapable of doing.[15] This anecdote, however, comes from one of Mather's enemies, and even if it happened, Mather might defend himself on the ground that Burroughs was the only person executed about whom there was much nonspectral testimony of his supposedly supernatural strength.[16]

Miller's Reverend Mr. Hale is at least based on the reality of the actual Hale's initial support and later criticism of the trials, but even he thought that the judges were animated by "a conscientious endeavor to do the thing that was right."[17] The worst distortion in the play is Miller's Deputy Governor Danforth, a crudely bigoted and blinded character. One would never imagine from the play that Governor Phips put a stop to the trials and issued a general pardon of the remaining victims. One of the hazards of his analogical method is that Miller's anger at the authorities in his own day is projected onto his treatment of the Puritan officials. Ironically, he is most historically misleading where he thinks he is being accurate, the evil of the prosecutors being for him a matter of "immutable" facts, their "absolute dedication to evil" supposedly being a documentary matter. Miller even believes he failed to make the judge evil enough, because he is convinced that the judges "cooked up" the hysteria.[18] Miller never explains how this conspiracy thesis jibes with his assertion that "the central impulse for writing at all was not the social but the interior psychological question, which was the question of that guilt residing in Salem which the hysteria merely unleashed, but did not create." This confusion is part of Miller's failure to grasp David Levin's observation on the trials that injustice is more terrifying "because the cruel and unjust people are not vicious or stupid; they are predestined to cruelty and injustice by all the circumstances of their intellectual environment."[19] Miller in his preface appeals to pity for all of Salem, but nothing in his portraits of accusers and judges moves us to feel it for them. The deficiency is both aesthetic and historical.

Despite his commentary on guilt as a creator of social paranoia, Miller's critics argue that his actual treatment of the accusers is reductively rationalistic, the accusers' motives being too simple and clear. Moreover, Warshow found it significant that Miller chose John Proctor as a leading character, "one of the more 'modern' figures in the trials, hardheaded, skeptical, a voice of common sense." Warshow complained: "You will never learn from this John Proctor that Salem was a religious community, quite as ready to hang a Quaker as a witch." He protested also that by inventing an adulterous relation between Abigail Williams and Proctor as an explanation, Miller cast away "the element of religious and psychological complexity which gives the Salem trials their dramatic interest in the first place." [20] One could add to Warshow's list the item that Miller claims to have conceived the play when he saw in the records at Salem how Abigail Williams, a former servant girl to the Proctors, had accused the wife, but not the husband. This explanation garbles the facts: Abigail did unhesitatingly name both husband and wife on two occasions; and since she was not yet an adolescent, it is unlikely that she had sexual relations with a man who was then sixty. (Perhaps Miller confused her with the Proctors' current servant, Mary Warren, aged twenty, who confessed that the girls were dissembling and held off from implicating John Proctor until she finally succumbed to her own confusion under pressure in prison and confessed to her master's apparition having come to her lap. [21])

Miller *can* cite testimony, however, to show some conscious malice of a simple kind in Salem. A witness for Elizabeth Proctor testified to hearing one of the "afflicted" girls confess that they named Elizabeth "for sport, they must have some sport," and Miller is right that the Putnams prompted the girls; at least they told Mercy Lewis that she had named Elizabeth Proctor in a fit, even though Mercy stoutly denied ever having done so. [22] More important, the actual Proctor, who dismissed the girls' charges as a "delusion of the devil," was not at all unrepresentative in his status as a victim, being a prosperous farmer and tavern keeper, better appreciated in Ipswich and Salem Town than in Salem Village. Miller's view of the accused and accusers constituting factions in the village's social life is much truer to recent historiography than Warshow's abstract reduction of witchcraft to a mere "metaphysical error." [23]

It is illuminating to look at the strengths and weaknesses of *The Crucible* in the light of contemporary sophisticated historical accounts of witchcraft. Miller's small facts are often wrong, but his sense of the large ones in the social conflict at work points us in the right direction. His editorial commentary on the Putnam family's alleged support of the minister, James Bayley, for example, is contradicted by the historians in *Salem Possessed: The Social Origins of Witchcraft*, who find him supported instead by those who favored George Burroughs, [24] later to be executed as a witch; but the playwright and the two social historians do agree in focusing their explanations on rivalry over ministers, land claims, village boundaries, and family ambitions. In *Salem Possessed* the Putnam family is also the major source of the witchcraft slander. Miller's rationalism in this respect has solid historical foundation, and he adds depth to it in his preface by citing the panic's role in providing the opportunity not only for repression, but for confession as a venting of guilt in displaced form. The social historians go even further in their provocative suggestion that "if the first half-dozen witches had confessed and taken upon themselves the collective guilt of the community, it is just possible that the outbreak would have come to a stop right there, fulfilled in its purpose." [25]

Recent historical understanding of witchcraft is subtle in its treatment of the role of guilt, taking a leaf from Freud's notebook on defense mechanisms. Keith Thomas, in a study of English and European witchcraft, notes that in Essex County it was the accusers' sense of guilt over their own failures of neighborliness that generated the charges against others. The accusers felt that the witches were justified in holding a grudge and taking revenge through occult means. In a society in transition from a village ethos to a more individualistic economy it was easy to feel that one had lost and betrayed older norms of community life. Miller makes an analogous point in his internal commentary on the play by seeing the panic as marking a shift in balance toward a "greater individual freedom."[26] Unfortunately, however, he does not show us this process at work in the lives of the adult accusers. The adultery of John Proctor with Abigail Williams in the play is an appropriate invention for introducing the idea of guilt, but neither of them is under any illusion about the charges of witchcraft; neither believes in the charges. In this respect the historians are more psychologically sophisticated than the playwright.

Turning this English light on the Salem case, Paul Boyer and Stephen Nissenbaum in *Salem Possessed* see the victims as representing a recent "emergent merchant capitalism," opposed by spokesmen for an older village order of life, a theme partially hinted at in Miller's comment that Francis Nurse may have created resentment by rising in his social status.[27] It suits the historians' thesis that John Proctor was richer than any of his accusers. It used to be historically fashionable to explain the Radical Right's McCarthyism as a reflex of its uncertain status as nouveau riche, resentful of more established, more cosmopolitan, and better-educated Americans. Today, this sociological thesis of rising has been reversed to explain the victims of slander in Salem. In this sense the two eras are mirror images for historians.

Miller's departures from the historical record are intentional with respect to Proctor's adultery and resulting ambivalence about how to plead when charged. Some critics have felt that this fictionalized relationship is too shallow and pulls the spectator's attention away from the public issues.[28] These inventions are, however, dramatically useful in balancing against the tendency of the play to move in the direction of a social melodrama in which villainy defeats simple innocence. But they also have a historical appropriateness. Miller argues that "sex, sin, and the Devil" are always linked and were in Salem imaginations.[29] Though historians have seen more signs of aggressiveness and cupidity in the records, Miller could make a stronger case by citing the laws, for fornication and adultery were public crimes, not mere private vices. Warshow cited Hawthorne against Miller in terms of taking Puritan problems seriously in his work,[30] yet *The Crucible* follows Hawthorne in its use of sexual infidelity as a theme, whether in *The Scarlet*

*Letter* or "Young Goodman Brown." In the short story the un-
fortunate protagonist accepts mere spectral evidence for the depravity of his fellow citizens, as the Salem judges did, and
projects onto his young wife his own faithlessness in concealing
from her the purpose of his journey into the forest to attend a
witches' sabbath on the very night she has urged him to stay
with her. Hawthorne in "Main Street" saw in the mutual suspicion between husband and wife a proof of the "Universal Mad-
ness" generated by the witchcraft panic. The question of trust
is both a private and public issue for Hawthorne and the community of Salem Village.

For Warshow *The Crucible* has "nothing to say about the
Salem trials" and only makes "the flimsiest pretense" that it
has.[31] But in his absorption with the contemporary pertinence
of the play, Warshow misses the crucial historical point that the
issue of truth telling, which is at the heart of the play, is a profoundly Puritan one. "Our seventeenth-century ancestors dif-
fered from us in most ways," Chadwick Hansen has pointed
out, "but in nothing did they differ more in their attitude
toward the truth. In this they were closer to the Middle Ages
than to us. For them a lie—a breaking of one's faith—was the
worst of sins."[32] Like Dante, they believed that the sins of fraud
were worse than the sins of lust or violence. Miller's John Proctor, in his concern for his good name in the eyes of others, in his
sense of sin in betraying his wife, and in his final refusal to falsify his experience or lie about others in order to save his life, is
a good Puritan man of his time. When the Reverend Mr. Hale
makes the argument that no principle may justify the loss of
life, Proctor's wife rightly condemns it as "the Devil's argument." In the last act the suspense of the climax is tautly
strung out when Proctor, with the consent of his wife, rescues
his sense of himself as a good and truthful man at the tragic
price of being hanged.

This feature of the play is more sound historically than
analogically because refusing to lie and refusing to inform on
others are different virtues. To refuse to tell the truth about
one's associations to Congressional investigators had its own de-
cency when the investigators had recklessly disregarded the
protections of the First Amendment as a shield for free speech

and freedom of association. But the refusal of the charged witches to lie about their associations in order to save their lives was the passing of a much greater ordeal. *The Crucible* points to the "terrible marvel" that a score of people, at a time when no confessed witches were executed, chose to die rather than to falsify their own integrity. That is what had impressed Miller the most on his visit to Salem, and in this respect his play is an appropriate memorial to their valor: "The form, the shape, the meaning of *The Crucible* were all compounded out of the faith of those who were hanged,"[33] he wrote when the much more successful revival of the play was about to open in March 1958, with the McCarthy climate receding into the past.

The play's unforeseen and inexact analogy between Miller's hero and the author himself may mislead us into overlooking his heroine. Elizabeth Proctor has a crucial role in the play, for she too has a problem about truth. She confesses to her husband that her own coldness, her sense of her own unworthiness to be loved, helped prompt his lechery: "Suspicion kissed you when I did; I never knew how I should say my love. It were a cold house I kept!" By an ironic turn of the plot, she has tried to protect her husband's reputation by refusing to admit the truth about his lechery, only to learn from him that he has already confessed it in order to establish the motive for Abigail's accusations and thus to discredit them. Her silence has not helped but hurt him. Her husband crucially knows that, even if fire were singeing her, she would not make a false confession of witchcraft, and she is saved only because she is pregnant, as the actual Elizabeth was. At the climax she rejects Hale's plea to urge her husband to save his life by lying, because she knows that he has at last found a way to restore his integrity, and she will not take his goodness from him. The curtain falls on the sun's pouring in upon her face, as "the drums rattle like bones in the morning air." The theatrical power of this final scene is not a matter of Miller's stagecraft blotting out the deficiencies of his historical understanding. Given the importance of lying as a Puritan sin, the scene has the power to move us on several levels—aesthetic, moral, and historical.

For Warshow the play "cannot be caught" saying anything precise about the McCarthy era it was really about because it begs all the questions one needs to ask about particular cases. As a result, *The Crucible* is vulnerable to simplistic responses in any "liberal" audience wishing to read its own political or historical prejudices into the play. But Miller the dramatist is interested in a process. As a study of a social panic about fears of subversion, when the evidence is largely a matter of intention and belief, *The Crucible* earns its analogical power by focusing on the process of scapegoating, with its attendant impulses to censor and confess in a climate of increasingly paranoid fears of conspiracies. In this context, individuals are hard pressed to steer by truth and charity, and authorities are tempted to compromise their best principles. *The Crucible* anatomizes this paradigm without confronting the crucial factual questions in the cases of Alger Hiss or Julius Rosenberg. Warshow's reading of the play reductively caricatures its possible political meaning as much as Miller's dramaturgy reductively caricatures Puritan authority in Salem. Warshow's disdain for sentimental liberalism in the theater distorts his response to the play itself. *The Crucible* suffers from serious flaws, as Warshow insisted; they can be summed up as the failure to withstand all the temptations of melodrama, aesthetic and historical. Miller's creation of tragic conflict in the Proctors is, however, an artist's version of the historian's sensitivity to social complexities because both represent a reaching out for an objectivity that refuses to accept the Manichean perspective of melodrama, where there are only sheep and goats.

For this reason the mutual guilt of the Proctors, which Miller invented, suggests more about the dynamics of the panic than his portraits of the accusers and judges do. Aesthetic and historical considerations merge at this point. Proctor was vulnerable to confessing falsely because he felt himself already tainted with guilt: "Let Rebecca go like a saint; for me it is a fraud!" On what other basis can we explain the detailed confession and repentance of William Barker of Andover, where there were more arrests than in Salem. For that matter, to respond to the play's analogical power, how else can we explain Robert Oppenheimer's surprisingly passive response in 1954 to his inquisitors, except on the basis of the guilt he must have felt, not for the policy "crimes" he was charged with by his political opponents, but for the inept lie he had told years ago, which had damged his friend, Haakon Chevalier, in trying to protect him? *Salem Possessed* makes the point, however, about the accusers of witches and their judges: the confession drawn by them from the mouths of the accused "was surely one that on some level they themselves longed to make."[34]

*The Crucible* overlaps *Salem Possessed* in attributing motivation, more consciously in the play and more unconsciously in the history, to worldly fears, hopes, and enmities. They overlap as well in associating the tragedy, at a deeper level, with the theme of guilt. Miller's invented moral dilemma is comparable in this respect to the social historians' grasp of guilt as a social reality, but his contemporary eye blinds him to their sense of its scope. Liberal and radical tradition, which has always condemned witchcraft trials, is often favorable to historical materialism. Lionel Trilling's protagonist in *The Middle of the Journey* reflects on the paradox, however, that "educated people more and more accounted for human action by the influence of environment and the necessities and habits imposed by society. Yet innocence and guilt were more earnestly spoken of than ever before."[35] It is this tendency in our political life that keeps *The Crucible*, for all its lapses, alive for us in an age that continues to be familiar with public confessions, political paranoia, and the breakdown of public trust.

It is not witchcraft itself that stand in the way of our modern understanding of the Salem trials, nor is Miller's rationalism about it far removed from their contemporary critics. Miller's Proctor never commits himself about the reality of withcraft in principle, and the actual Proctor also wanted to thrash the accusing girls and knock some sense into their heads. His petition to the ministers of Boston (on behalf of himself, his son, and others) that they witness the proceedings, move the trials to Boston, or change the magistrates, who were credulous or prejudiced, spoke of the panic as a "Delusion of the Devil."[36] Thomas Brattle, a Boston merchant, also trenchantly criticized the court's reliance on spectral evidence and other specious forms of testimony. Skepticism about the Salem hysteria is not a modern projection of our secular age. Nor is the heroism of

Miller's Proctor in meeting his doom a literary invention. Brattle speaks of Proctor being one of those whose exemplary conduct from the jail to Gallows Hill and on the gallows itself was "very affecting and melting to the hearts of some considerable spectators." [37]

But there is one notable feature of Brattle's report about the hanged innocents that neither Miller nor the historians have taken into account. (Miller's version of Proctor as a skeptic is shared by Marion Starkey, whose *The Devil in Massachusetts* was available to him.) The trials did take place at a time when traditional Puritanism was no longer the sovereign power in Church and State; and Proctor's angry question in the play "Is there no good penitence but it be public?" can be seen as a mark of the waning of Puritan belief in public confession for church membership and in public forms of penance. Miller's Proctor is finally concerned, however, not to be used, not to have his signature exploited by his enemies. We never glimpse him on the gallows, but if we did, the contrast between him and the historical Proctor would become evident. Miller remains adamantly opposed to his inquisitors; his only regret as a dramatist is that he did not portray Salem authority in even darker colors. The actual John Proctor, however, though he charged the authorities with such "Popish Cruelties" as torturing his son, was not defiant on the gallows. On the contrary, according to Brattle's testimony about the victims:

> With great affection they entreated Mr. C. M. [Cotton Mather] to pray with them: they prayed that God would discover what witchcrafts were among us; they forgave their accusers; they spoke without reflection on Jury and Judges, for bringing them in guilty, and condemning them: they prayed earnestly for pardon for all other sins, and for an interest in the precious blood of our dear Redeemer; and seemed to be very sincere, upright, and sensible of their circumstances on all accounts; especially Proctor and Willard. . . . [38]

If Miller had responded to this tie between victim and executioner, he would not have been denied modern parallels merely by taking account of this Puritan behavior on the part of his hero. But his play would then suggest analogies with more weighty trials, having more complex dynamics, than the sort of congressional hearing in which he himself would appear as a witness. The identification of accused persons with the ideology of their judges is what Arthur Koestler saw as the most dramatic feature of the Moscow trials in *Darkness at Noon*, and one could make a similar point about Galileo's Catholicism, Oppenheimer's commitment to using the atomic bomb, or Julius Rosenberg's confidence that the American legal system would come to his rescue. Miller could not move beyond the modern idea of the need (which Elizabeth expresses) for John Proctor to forgive himself. What is unimaginable from *The Crucible* is a John Proctor who finally forgave his enemies. In this respect Miller's imagination was not adequate to grasp historical reality, and our historians themselves, for all their shrewdness about sociology and psychology in Salem, have given us no glimpse of the extraordinary scene that melted the hearts of "some considerable spectators."

## Notes

1. Robert Warshow, "The Liberal Conscience in *The Crucible*," in Warshow, *The Immediate Experience* (New York, 1962), pp. 192, 200.

2. See Allen Weinstein, *Perjury: The Hiss–Chambers Case* (New York, 1978); Sol Stern and Ronald Radosh, "The Hidden Rosenberg Case," *New Republic* 180, no. 25 (23 June 1979):13–25; and Arthur Miller, "It Could Happen Here—And Did," in *The Theater Essays of Arthur Miller*, ed. Robert A. Martin (New York, 1978), pp. 298–99.

3. Miller, "It Could Happen Here," p. 295; Miller, "Journey to *The Crucible*," in *Theater Essays*, p. 29.

4. Warshow, *Immediate Experience*, p. 200.

5. Miller, "Introduction to the *Collected Plays*," in *Theater Essays*, pp. 154–55.

6. Alfred Kazin, *New York Jew* (New York, 1978), p. 189. For Miller's role see "Arthur Miller: An Interview," in *Theater Essays*, p. 291.

7. Arthur Miller, *The Crucible* (Clinton, Mass., Penguin ed., 1976), p. 34.

8. Miller, "It Could Happen Here," p. 296.

9. Miller, *The Crucible*, p. 35.

10. David Levin, ed., *What Happened in Salem? Documents Pertaining to the Seventeenth Century Witchcraft Trials* (New York, 1952), "Confession of William Barker," p. 139.

11. Keith Thomas, *Religion and the Decline of Magic* (New York, 1971), p. 514.

12. Cotton Mather, "A Discourse on Witchcraft," in Levin, *What Happened in Salem?*, p. 151; Cotton Mather to John Richards, ibid., p. 155.

13. Cotton Mather to John Richards, ibid., p. 159.

14. The Return of Several Ministers etc.," ibid., p. 161.

15. Miller, Introduction to the *Collected Plays*," in *Theater Essays*, p. 157.

16. Paul Boyer and Stephen Nissenbaum, *Salem Possessed: The Social Origins of Witchcraft* (Cambridge, Mass., 1974), p. 13, n. 32.

17. Quoted in Boyer and Nissenbaum, *Salem Possessed*, p. 19.

18. Miller, "Introduction to the *Collected Plays*," in *Theater Essays*, p. 157; "Morality and Modern Drama," ibid., p. 211.

19. Miller, "Introduction to the *Collected Plays*," in *Theater Essays*, pp. 156–57; David Levin, "Historical Fact in Fiction and Drama: The Salem Witchcraft Trials," in D. Levin *In Defense of Historical Literature: Essays on American History, Autobiography, Drama, and Fiction* (New York, 1967), p. 97.

20. Warshow, *Immediate Experience*, p. 193.

21. See W. E. Woodard, ed., *Records of Salem Witchcraft* (Roxbury, Mass., 1864), 1:64–65, 70–71 (Abigail Williams) and 128–33 (Mary Warren).

22. Samuel Barton and John Houghton for Elizabeth Proctor, in Levin, *What Happened in Salem?*, p. 102; Daniel Elliott for Elizabeth Proctor, ibid., p. 103.

23. Warshow, *Immediate Experience*, p. 191.

24. Cf. Miller, *The Crucible*, p. 14, and Boyer and Nissenbaum, *Salem Possessed*, pp. 54–56.

25. Cf. Miller, *The Crucible*, p. 7, and Boyer and Nissenbaum, *Salem Possessed*, p. 215.

26. Cf. Thomas, *Religion and the Decline of Magic*, pp. 552–53, 566, and Miller, *The Crucible*, p. 7.

27. Cf. Boyer and Nissenbaum, *Salem Possessed*, p. 209, and Miller, *The Crucible*, p. 26.

28. See Herbert Blau, "No Play Is Deeper than Its Witches," in *Twentieth Century Interpretations of "The Crucible*," ed. John H. Ferres (New York, 1972), p. 63.

29. Miller, *The Crucible*, p. 35.

30. Warshow, *Immediate Experience*, p. 190.

31. Ibid., p. 196.

32. Chadwick Hansen, *Witchcraft at Salem* (New York, 1969), p. 87.

33. Miller, "Journey to *The Crucible*" and "Brewed in *The Crucible*," in *Theater Essays*, pp. 30, 173.

34. Boyer and Nissenbaum, *Salem Possessed*, p. 215.

35. Lionel Trilling, *The Middle of the Journey* (New York, 1947), p. 145.

36. "John Proctor's Petition to the Ministers of Boston," in Levin, *What Happened in Salem?*, p. 99.

37. "Letter of Thomas Brattle," ibid., p. 189.

38. Ibid.

# 9 / Hazards of the Border Country: Some Contemporary Historical Novels

Those who make a separate category out of the historical novel, Marguerite Yourcenar has remarked, forget that all novels, by interpreting past actions and memories, consciously or unconsciously are "woven out of the same stuff as History itself."[1] Nothing could be further from the currently fashionable critical emphasis on myth, symbol, and self-conscious artifice, in which the artist's own maneuvers tend to become the substance of his work. Even the leading American Marxist critic betrays his own deference to the prevailing mood by reducing Georges Simenon's detective stories to a narcissistic pattern in which their "essential content" is said to be not referential, but a disguised portrait of "the writer in the act of creating the work, a kind of peculiar structural deflection of that impulse which, on its way towards the real and towards some genuine referent, strikes a mirror instead without knowing it."[2]

Great novelists before the age of self-conscious modernism, like George Eliot and Joseph Conrad, were confident, however, that they addressed historical problems in their own fictional way. In his preface to *Under Western Eyes*, "a sort of historical novel dealing with the past," Conrad asserts that "truth alone is the justification of any fiction which makes the least claim to the quality of art." Yet he also insists that he has given "free play" to his "creative instinct" and his feeling for "the dramatic possibilities of the subject."[3] Similarly, George Eliot called for novels constructed by the "veracious imagination," working out "the various steps by which a political or social change was reached, using all extant evidence and supplying deficiencies by careful analogical creation."[4] Today, structuralist critics tend to oppose the fact/fiction polarity by fictionalizing the historical as a form of rhetoric. But Conrad and Eliot chose the quite different path of historicizing the fictional. They felt they had a stake in the same sort of truth historians valued.

The experimental French novelist, Michel Butor, is characteristically modern in stressing the nonreferential nature of fiction: "It is only by what he tells us about his characters, and by this alone, that they can convince us, can live, even if they have actually existed in reality."[5] The only pertinent witnesses about them are the sentences in the text. At the same time Butor warns that attributing to real historical characters adventures they did not have will lead to contradiction of the novelist by documental reference, or even to charges of lying and slander. Since "such characters are unique, he cannot give them other names without falsifying the situation which they must, precisely, designate."[6] The logical inference from this statement of the case is that actual persons ought to be left to biographers and historians.

One can reply that if the text is the only witness for the reader, it is not for the novelist, whose referential knowledge enters into his thinking through of his material, whatever his subject. Nor does Butor's argument allow for Georg Lukács's category of the historical novel that respects the singularity of the actual case, even within a fictional frame, by focusing on the general milieu rather than on specific historical events, and keeping actual persons in minor roles, relating to unknown rather than familiar episodes in their careers.[7] There are other strategies to avoid contradictions between the literary and historical imaginations. Robert Penn Warren in *All the King's Men*, for example, treated a historical figure (Huey Long) analogically under another name, (Willie Stark) and viewed him through the eyes of a fictional person, who became the central character. Warren has often emphasized that he only worked with the myth of "Huey" and that what the fictional narrator "thought about the story was more important than the story itself." [8] *All the King's Men*, arising in part out of Warren's reading of William James, Machiavelli, and Shakespeare's historical plays, is primarily a philosophical novel about the idea of history—the great man's event-making role, the dialectical relation between past and present as they shape each other, and the need to connect facts and ideas. [9] The tragic form of Willie Stark's life is a literary paradigm, and if Willie is finally more conscious of it than Long was, such awareness of one's role is what Lukács calls "a necessary anachronism" in historical novels. Yet the pattern it describes substantially matches the trajectory of Long's career as a corrupted reformer turned dictator.

Ralph Ellison in *Invisible Man* found another way of dealing with history in fictional terms. By using a technique of symbolism and a generalizable anonymous hero Ellison condenses in one story the major phases in the history of the American black from slavery and Reconstruction through the exodus to the northern cities, the involvement of some black intellectuals with the Communist party, the proletariat's enthusiasm for Black Nationalism, and an urban riot analogous to the Harlem riot of 1943. *Invisible Man* is structured not only by evoking these major shifts in Afro-American history, but by Ellison's psychosocial theory about the cultural roots of Negro indentity in a country where formal egalitarian ideology provides the possibility of protesting the violation of it. His symbolic, even surreal, mode of telling his story heightens its pertinence to the historical question of how mythmaking stereotypes held by both the friends and enemies of Negroes have obscured the responsible recognition of their humanity.

These solutions, by creating aesthetic distance from their historical analogues and by expressing generalized concerns about historical process, minimize the risk of cross-pressuring the reader by provoking him, on the one hand, to wonder if particular facts are invented, distorted, or ignored, and, on the other, to ask why the writer did not turn to biography instead of fiction. Dealing mainly with historical persons in the actual course of events, as a novelist, can result in a hybrid offensive to both literary and historical standards, the literary imagination being hobbled by documentary limits or the historical imagination being frustrated by the lack of authentic evidence. All too often, undistinguished historical novelists have either grossly offended against high standards of historical accuracy or have smugly prided themselves on their careful research, while lacking any novelistic talent for breathing life into their wooden characters and plots. In such cases critical readers understandably prefer the pleasures of good history and good fiction, finding them in separate books on different shelves, while recognizing at the same time the literary merits of the historian's writing and the historical pertinence of the artist's imagined world. Moreover, while professional historical novelists, like the radical Howard Fast and the conservative Kenneth Roberts, have exercised talents for research and craftsmanship, none would appear on any list of major American writers.

Yet distinguished historians have defended historical novels, and distinguished novelists have written them, even though little critical theory exists to justify them. The most interesting cases are those in which sophisticated writers, who are not specialists in the historical novel as a genre, have turned their attention to explicitly historical subjects. Historians speaking on behalf of the historical novel have tended to favor those which "recreate a world of past thought and feeling, rather than those which interpret or illuminate a personality or group of characters," because (as another one put it) "the supreme thing" is to catch the age's "way of looking at the world" and "of accepting life." [10] Such stories are also less likely to make the reader nervous about specific issues of historicity. Yet novelists are often attracted to writing about influential personalities, for stories need protagonists and good imaginative writers are frequently more subtle about issues of motive and character than most historians are.

In practice, novelists may resolve this dilemma by choosing actual persons who are neglected, shadowy, or obscured under a cloud of obloquy. In doing so, novelists can contribute to historical controversy and clarification as well as speak to the condition of their age. William Styron, Gore Vidal, and E. L. Doctorow illustrate this strategy, and each in his own way exemplifies some of the virtues and hazards of telling stories in fictional form about historical persons and events. Whereas Warren and Ellison used collective myths about their subjects, these three tried to break through popular myths that have obscured actual historical persons, whose place in the history books had previously never been large or creditable. In all three novels the authors deal mainly with historical persons and events, rather than making them peripheral to a fictional plot.

Styron's *The Confessions of Nat Turner*, Vidal's *Burr*, and Doctorow's *The Book of Daniel* are "revisionist" stories; they persuade readers to reevaluate the conventional images of historical persons who were tried for sedition; and each novel has set up powerful resonances with current politics. It used to be said in the early days of "scientific" history in America that "history is past politics"; these revisionist novels suggest that the motto can be turned around to read "history is present politics." Neither *Burr* nor *The Confessions of Nat Turner* speak directly about present politics and are seemingly only historical in their concerns, yet they were widely perceived as politically relevant; while *The Book of Daniel*, by including "revisionist" critiques of the Cold War and bringing its own story down to the recent rebellions of the late 1960s, seems more obviously political in its pertinence, yet it is deeply historical in its treatment of a fictional surrogate for the Rosenberg spy case.

All three novels develop imaginary memoirs which have been constructed by elaborating on actual documents, and all three thus have to face the demanding problem of seeking to marry artistic imagination to historical consciousness, a modern marriage in which neither partner tyrannizes over the other. The overlapping realms of history and fiction constitute a dangerous but intriguing border country. Travelers tend to say on their return that they have paradoxically both respected and transcended the historical past. Only specific analysis can clarify this mystery.

At a forum organized by the historian C. Vann Woodward to

discuss William Styron's intensely controversial novel, *The Confessions of Nat Turner*, both Warren and Ellison came to the embattled author's defense. Styron aroused a storm of polemics because a white Southerner had dramatized from the inside a black rebel, a folk hero of American Negroes, in terms that were profoundly offensive to militant Black Nationalists, who had their own politicized image of him. The debate over the novel, which was acclaimed and denounced with fervor, not only exposed the political hazards of Styron's venture but highlighted some of the intellectual issues about the artist's creative freedom and his historical responsibilities, questions which have been lurking, unresolved, in all historically oriented fiction.

Styron's title was taken from an actual account by a white lawyer of the confession, trial, and execution of Nat Turner, who had become for some modern militant Black Nationalists a symbol of the case against racial integration or even "coexistence" and of the alleged "purgative effect of violence," when exercised by apocalyptic revolutionary nihilism, seeking "total destruction" of the existing system.[11] Ten black critics replied to Styron's novel by angrily charging it with reflecting southern racial stereotypes and reductively psychologizing the Turner rebellion. A historian's scrupulous compilation of all the pertinent documentary material on the revolt critically pointed out in detail some of the factual differences between the novel and the record.[12]

Styron's main offense in the eyes of many critics was that he had portrayed the leader of a black revolt as a psychologically troubled messianic figure whose inhibitions and yearnings make him vulnerable to sexual fantasies of having intercourse with a white adolescent girl, and his feelings critically weaken his capacity to carry out his armed rebellion because he lets another girl escape and warn others. In an interview Styron spoke of his psychologizing of Turner as pointing to traits of character that "must have been true in history" and must "historically" have "helped undermine the rebellion." (The intensity of the attack on him compelled him later to insist that the literary works he admired "exist outside of history, which gain their power from history, to be sure, which are fed by a passionate comprehension of what history does to people and to things, but which have to have other levels of understanding, and have to be judged by other levels of understanding." [13])

In an essay that predated his novel Styron saw Turner in dramatic terms as having Hamlet's "access of guilt" and "fatal irresolution," as well as a decent dislike of violence that contributed to the failure of his own leadership. [14] Curiously, this image of Turner is much like Harriet Beecher Stowe's image of her benign but ineffective planter, St. Clare, in *Uncle Tom's Cabin*. For blacks, however, especially for contemporary proponents of black power and Black Nationalism, Turner was an uncompromising freedom fighter, and a sexually integrated man with a black wife. This Turner suited the political needs of the militant separatists; but some white critics as well have also complained that Styron's image of Turner reflected "the stereotype of the feared and hated Negro in the mind of the white southern slave-owner class" by projecting a rebel "who loves his masters, regrets his education because it has made him discontented and therefore unhappy, despises his friends whom he thinks of a sub-human," and lusts to defile white women. [15]

Both Styron and his critics could appeal to parts of the evidence. The historical *Confessions*, compiled by a racist white lawyer who interviewed Turner, does not mention his wife, as a contemporary newspaper account does, but it reflects no trace of remorse or irresolution in him, while it does show him as a devotee of biblical apocalyptic thought, adapted to his vision of race war, with an intensity that once made him fall ill in his mind. [16] Styron's account of the rebellion exaggerates its failure necessarily by its literary focus on the doomed leader's consciousness because Turner could not have known of the effect his rebellion had in provoking some demands in the Virginia legislature for an end to slavery.

Styron insisted that he would have given Turner a wife if the lawyer's document had mentioned her and rightly pleaded that in providing Turner with a psychological history and rationale he had transcended the lawyer's image of a fiend engaged in a deranged, directionless rampage. [17] In his 1967 interview at Yale Styron had claimed historical truth for his psychological portrait of Turner's irresolution and desire for a white girl, a point he conceded he could not prove. But in a later discussion at a convention of historians in 1969 he took another tack. His basic defense was to cite Georg Lukács on the point that historical faithfulness to the general structure of a given period may require the novelist to deal as freely as he likes with any particular historical facts.[18] On this score it is entirely understandable that Warren and Ellison came to Styron's defense at a meeting of the Southern Historical Association where he was subjected to angry ad hominem abuse from the floor. But their defense of the artist had its own unresolved problems. C. Vann Woodward wryly summed up the artists' case as one that relegated historians to the "outside" of history and the obligation of facts, while leaving to novelists the "inner" undocumentable truths, which seemed to constitute a "superhistory," better than historians can write, of history's "inside" or, alternatively, the timeless "abiding problems" of man.[19] Warren conceded, however, that the novelist was tied to the "historically possible," and Ellison admitted that "Damn it, there is a *problem* about re-creating historical figures," and so he warned against any "move into the historian's arena, because you can only be slaughtered there," unless the novelist cannily disguised his historical figures in trying to express "the symbolic significance of what actually happened."[20] Styron himself tried to transcend the historical issues by asserting that all three writers had written books which somehow "do exist outside of history," while gaining their power from it.

Focusing on the discrepancies between the document and the novel in Turner's case has obscured the literary form and meaning of Styron's story. He rightly called his book "a meditation on history" because the form of the story is the hero's extensive meditation in jail on the impact of his adventures on his soul. The suspense in the narrative at this level is whether or not Turner will move beyond the despairing, guilty feeling that God has repudiated him. Book One ends with Nat brooding about the lawyer's accusation that biblical Christianity in this case has only produced a futile carnage of reprisal, killing more than a hundred blacks, and the results prove that God is "dead and gone." In Book Two, after suffering his worst misfortunes

as a slave, Nat hears the Lord's message: "I abide." In Book
Three he has his apocalyptic vision of race war and becomes a
Joshua to lead his people out of Egypt through a doomed revolt.
In the last book of the novel he has conquered his despair and
regained a sense of God's presence, remembering now Margaret
Whitehead's recitation of a passage from the Gospel of
John—"love is of God"—which had once only aroused his lust-
ful anger at her innocent, unconscious, sexual provocation.
Having been forced to kill her during the revolt to prove that he
was ruthless enough to lead his men, Nat in jail concludes that
he would do everything again—except for her murder, for she
has showed him in that remembered passage the presence of
God, who had seemed to have abandoned him. In an interview
Styron has spoken of Nat as coming to have "a guarded understanding of the quality of Christian redemption, whether he accepted it or not." [21] In this light the story is more of a religious
than a political novel, being consistent with the documentary
evidence of Nat's role as a preacher and his passionately literal
appropriation of biblical apocalyptic ideas.

At the political level the offense of the novel is its psychologizing story of Nat's thwarted, ambiguous sexuality, his auto-
erotic and homoerotic experiences, and, above all, his inhibited
yearnings for the adolescent white girl. Styron was politically
naive not to see how offensive his image of Turner would be to
militant Black Nationalists, whose contrived political posture
was that of intimidating, doubt-free, manly, unguilty, proud
self-sufficiency, and they repudiated Christianity as the mere
ideology of slavery, or at best the rationale of the integrationist
leader, Martin Luther King, whose nonviolent and nonhating
tactics seemed to them much too mild.

Even so, Styron had no obligation to create a Turner they
would have admired, one which is no more required by the
lawyer's document than Styron's Nat. While the lawyer's
Turner was not a Hamlet, a favorite metaphor for white
planters in the plantation novel, he was not a Malcolm X
either. Like Stowe, Styron dramatized a range of possibilities
within an oppressive system, and he was well-read in the current historical literature about slavery. [22] Though he exaggerated
black collaboration with owners in resisting the revolt, his pic-

ture of Will's owner as a cruel drunkard did not do justice to the fact that in reality six free Negroes were living on his place.[23] The melodramatic touches were not all on one side.

Styron looked at the revolt in a binocular way. For him "the year 1831 was, simultaneously, a long time ago and only yesterday."[24] Thus with one eye he saw the nineteenth-century messianic preacher; with the other he saw the psychological etiology of hate, so evident in the urban violence and separatist ideology of the 1960s. But his hero's sexual ambiguities have more to do with Styron's fellow novelist James Baldwin than with Nat Turner. Even so, as a Southerner, Styron generously took the risk of trying to imagine a real person behind the conventional image of a deranged, fanatical fiend. The effort reflected certain limits which his own regional conditioning had imposed on his imagination, and his Turner is certainly not the only possible Turner one might construct from the paucity of biographical evidence. But historians themselves have argued that the historical novelist finds his legitimate opportunities precisely where the records are thin, expecially in the area of motives; it is appropriate for the novelist to focus not on the public consequences of the agent's deeds, but rather upon their personal meaning for his own salvation.[25] In these respects Styron's novel fits classic requirements.

It is easy to see how a novelist's imagination in a Freudian age would be teased by the fact that the only person the documentary Turner killed was an adolescent white girl. As in Freud's own thought, however, Styron's psychologizing tends to work against his religious theme by treating God as a surrogate for the kind owner, whose inability to carry out his promise of freeing Nat provokes the slave to think of him as "a disgraced and downfallen prince." Just as the psychoanalyst Erik H. Erikson had earlier portrayed the oedipal conflicts in the "identity crisis" of Martin Luther, a revolutionary who later encouraged suppression of a peasant rebellion, so also did Styron seek to orient his story by narrating the "identity crisis" of a rebel in terms of merging religious and sexual feelings in a pattern of agonized ambivalence.

The debate over his book at the historians' conference led Styron to take the position that the writer could "show how it really was" by "dispensing with useless fact."[26] No intelligent historian could disagree with the principle that not all facts are born free and equal in importance, but the historical issue over his book was whether or not he had excluded salient facts and invented misleading fictions. Styron gave no specific arguments on this score when specificity was the point. Invidiously, he conceded that "an historian can tell you just what happened at Borodino, but only Tolstoy, often dispensing with facts, can tell you what it really was to be a soldier at Borodino." The novelist provides "an imaginative truth which transcends, in this case, what the historian can give you."[27] This distinction, however, degrades historical narrative into a mere description of external happenings, while turning the novelist into a superior historian, who has the unfair advantage of not needing any documentation. But the historian's Borodino is the battle as it figured in the plans of generals, in contrast to the novelist's battle as it figured in the experience of anonymous soldiers. Neither story is either more or less real than the conflict perceived at another level.

The novelist who only pretends to be talking about actual events, because he gives his fictions "a local habitation and a name," may justly say with Aristotle that his poetry is more general in its significance than history; he may also say the same thing when he indirectly and symbolically deals with actual events, as Warren did in *All the King's Men*. However, when he explicitly bases his story on a historical document, as Styron did, and aims to tell in his own way the same story in outline as the one set forth in the document, he cannot claim to be telling us "what really happened" without also meeting historical standards of authenticity. Under the pressure of polemics, Styron had it both ways, sometimes suggesting his novel told how it "really" was and also suggesting that it transcended history altogether.

If it did both, it was only in the sense that it dramatically portrayed the workings of an actual oppressive system in concrete terms, while at the same time portraying a leader whose consciousness was developed in imaginary terms, unified more by a religious theme than by a historically tenable hypothesis. A reader might be historically enlightened by

Styron's dramatization of the slave system and of Turner's messianic faith, but not by his psychologizing about Turner's motives, while he might also aesthetically feel an Aristotelian pity and terror at the tragic form of the protagonist's consciousness. Styron's Turner was loyal to a cause that exacted the tragic price of his murdering a person who had given him his only hint of both human love and the redemptive presence of God.

The novelist's use of history can raise difficult and subtle questions about the relationship between the historical conscience and creative freedom of the literary imagination, but they were for the most part distorted in an acrimonious atmosphere where, as Ellison put it, "everybody is saying: Damn it, tell it like *I* think it is."[28] If you were not a part of the (my) solution, as the saying went in those days, you were part of the (my) problem. Ironically, Styron's critics in stressing their version of the record failed to recognize a crucial paradox. Styron's obligation in using an actual document and a real person would be met by creating a possible Turner, not necessarily the actual one, even if the value of the portrait for historians would be increased by his Turner being a probable one. Nat Turner's development, psychology, and belief system are only partially inferrable from the document that records his major action. For that reason he can have novelists of his life, but not biographers.

*Burr* deals in such voluminous detail with the entire career of a historical person that it inevitably raises the question posed by Gore Vidal himself: "Why a historical novel and not a history?" Vidal answered by arguing that fiction enabled him to attribute motive—"something the conscientious historian or biographer ought never do."[29] But conscientious historians do engage in disputes about purposes and motives, because they are suggested in actions and documents which have to be interpreted. Certainly historians are not entitled to attribute motives without reliance on documentary evidence, but the history of scholarship about Aaron Burr is marked by disputes about his character and purposes.

Henry Adams, who had unearthed from European ar-
chives evidence of Burr's dealings with the British and Spanish,
treated him as a disloyal conspirator and "vulgar swindler." [30]
Two biographers in 1925 argued that only his dealings with the
French government in 1810 amounted to an attempt to return
Louisiana to France by force, though they excused him by suggesting he had become mentally unhinged. [31] In 1937 the historian Nathan Schachner in his biography absolved Burr of any
motive to disrupt the Union at any time and found his record in
public and private life to be "considerably cleaner than that of
most rival politicians." [32] Analyzing the Burr trial for treason,
Richard B. Morris concluded in 1953 that "it is still impossible
to define with precision Burr's ultimate objectives" because of
his "devious and serpentine character," which had "a well-
equipped store of alternative plans." [33] Vidal's response to this
disagreement among historians was to turn one of Burr's admiring young wards, Charles Burdett, rumored to be one of his
natural sons, into "Charlie Schuyler," an amanuensis for the
aging politician's memoirs. In them Burr could construe
everything (as he admits) in a light favorable to himself, rather
than to his political enemies, Hamilton and Jefferson.

Insofar as the traditional view of Burr as a disloyal in-
triguer has survived in the popular mind, Vidal's strategy effectively used the novel to demythologize our most notorious
villain. At the same time it titillated readers with the speculation that Hamilton's offense in provoking Burr to the duel that
killed his reputation, as it did his rival, lay in a plausible accusation that Burr was the lover of his own daughter, Theodosia.
To add to the gamey flavor, the narrator, who had been trying
to establish the rumor that Van Buren was Burr's natural son,
discovers himself also to be one. At this level the novel seems to
be aimed at an audience for whom history and gossip have
merged in those supposed revelations about the sexual indiscre-
tions of the famous that are the staple diet of tabloid newspapers. But Burr's private journal, written for his daughter,
about his tour in Europe is notable for its candid record of his
indiscriminate sexual hyperactivity, and the novel is largely an
invented memoir about Burr's public life, narrating and analyz-

ing the complex political issues of his career with an impressive mastery of American history. Only the suppositions about Burr's sexual life and the narrator's affair with a female prostitute, who is murdered by a male one, offer any appeal to readers who are more interested in spice than history.

The place where these two dimensions intersect is in a deliberate (but concealed) invention. The narrator refers to a (fictitious) letter in the (actual) *Memoirs of Aaron Burr*, whose (actual) editor appears in the novel as a character. This semi-spurious reference is supposed to link Burr with the place where Martin Van Buren was born.[34] Otherwise Vidal fairly alerts the reader by explaining that he does not entirely share Burr's view of Jefferson or Jackson, that while in three instances he moved people about, "otherwise the characters are in the right places, on the right dates, doing what they actually did," and that he used actual phrases of the speaker whenever possible in the made-up conversations. "Although the novel's viewpoint must be Burr's," Vidal maintained, "the story told is history and not invention."[35]

This claim is true in the sense that Burr's "memoirs" are based on responsible research, rather than on fictionalizing attempts to make him interesting. Indeed, Vidal's Burr coincides closely with Schachner's favorable picture of "a man of extraordinary talents, approaching genius, of a man of human mold and human failings, of one who remained to the end erect against the gods."[36] Like Styron's Nat Turner, Vidal's Burr tells his own story, elaborating on documents that exist, and *Burr* in this way enters the space created by the absence of an actual memoir, except for the record Burr kept of his European tour.

The risk in such an enterprise is that the subject also becomes a mouthpiece for the author's views, riddling the work with anachronism. George Eliot once complained that "the least readable of silly women's novels are the *modern-antique* species" which clothe their authors' "mental mediocrity" in "a masquerade of ancient names," putting their own "feeble sentimentality into the mouths of Roman vestals or Egyptian princesses, and attributing their rhetorical arguments to Jewish high-priests and Greek philosophers."[37] Vidal was in no danger of projecting sentimentality into the eighteenth-century characters whose worldliness he admired. But as an expatriate, caustic critic, and politically ambitious reformer with his own unconventional sexual tastes, he was vulnerable to using Burr to express his own debunking animus; by looking at American history through Burr's eyes the novel cuts Washington, Jefferson, and Hamilton down to a size much smaller than the clothes even sober skeptical historians have made for them. Washington is portrayed as an incompetent general, acquisitive landowner, and serpentine politician absorbed in protocol, wealth, and status; while Jefferson emerges as a canting hypocrite, bedding his wife's black half-sister and sacrificing his principles to score against his rivals. For the most part one can say these versions are justified as Burr's opinions, but when he speculates psychologically about "the way Hamilton always fell out with his surrogate fathers," it is the post-Freudian voice of Vidal we hear.[38] Both in youth and middle age he fancied himself as president, and he once compared himself and Norman Mailer to "born usurpers, like Bolingbroke."[39] When Charlie Schuyler says that he is fascinated by "dreams of domination that make it possible for the dreamer to subvert with the greatest of ease class, nation, honour" and prefers "the man like Burr who, failing to gain power in the conventional way, breaks up the game—or tries to—seizes the crown—or tries to—and in failing . . .," there is perhaps more than a hint of the author's own interest in Burr as a persona.[40] Reviewers often spoke of *Burr*'s timeliness in 1973 when the newspapers were filled with stories about "low men in high places." The avid readers of *Burr*, whose protagonist insists "that the early republic of ours was no place for a man who wanted to live in a good world,"[41] could have found in it an entertaining and knowledgeable way of nourishing their growing mood of cynicism about American history. Whereas the old-fashioned historical novel was often a vehicle for celebrating the past, the new historical novel became a vehicle for deflating it.

The publication of Vidal's next historical novel, *1876*, in the bicentennial year clearly exposed the polemical point. In his earlier novel *Washington, D.C.* Vidal had paid his disrespect to the New Deal and McCarthy eras; in the one that followed *Burr* he filled a gap in his debunking history by portraying the corruption centering around the disputed election of 1876. Its narrator, carried over from *Burr*, is given historical credibility by interpreting events much in the same way as did a real Jacksonian, Montgomery Blair, an editor and a member of Old Hickory's "kitchen cabinet," who saw in Tilden's defeat a triumph for "jobbery" in the name of "reconciliation" and who never could understand Tilden's composure in accepting the "fraud." [42] Though the novel tends to give the conference at the Wormley Hotel between Northern Republicans and Southern Democrats more significance than the historian C. Vann Woodward does—Woodward emphasizes the prior existence of the crucial agreements that were only ratified at the conference— *1876* is solidly grounded in historical evidence; and Vidal had a historian check the manuscript for inaccuracies and anachronisms before it was published.

Henry Adams in his novel *Democracy* used the character of the cynical European, Baron Jacobi, to pour scorn on the American belief that the United States was constitutionally immune to the disease of corruption. Vidal openly borrowed the same character to observe that "history is nothing but fiction." Vidal's narrator quotes him with the modification that such fictions are "of varying degrees of plausibility." [43] As demythologizer, however, Vidal himself has to consider his account of events, which the narrator describes as the "collapse into ruins" of "the pretensions of this ludicrous republic," to be essentially truthful in the same way that C. Vann Woodward's history of the sectional bargain is. But the novel's difference from history is a matter of perspective. Woodward's more detailed account is not scandalized by the compromise in the way that Vidal's narrator is. Where Charlie Schuyler finds in his bitter disillusionment grounds for exile, Woodward finds instead that the men of 1877, while of "smaller stature than the great Federalists," were not unlike them in being "more concerned with preserving the pragmatic and practical gains and ends of revolutions than the more idealistic aims." [44]

Vidal's unconventional excursions into the traditional area of the historical novel, as old in American literature as James Fenimore Cooper's *The Spy* (1821), satisfied the revisionist mood of a public's anguished response to an era of assassinations, racial violence, and self-defeating war. In this respect E. L. Doctorow's *The Book of Daniel*, published two years before *Burr*, was more clearly recognized at the time as a political novel inspired by the revolutionary sensibility of the 1960s. But the less-recognized virtue of Doctorow's novel is not its counterculture idiom, but its historical rendering of an American passage in the life of the Jewish-American Left. In these terms it is an impressive example of what George Eliot specified as the novelist's power of "the veracious imagination" and of "analogical creation" in showing how a political or social change has come about. All of the characters are fictional, but nearly all are analogues of actual persons. The story dramatizes a famous political trial, but it also interprets the elements of the Rosenberg spy case in light of the social history of Jewish tradition.

The form of Doctorow's novel is an invented memoir, (like much of *Burr*), being written before our eyes by a graduate student at Columbia University who is struggling with a thesis, and it ends with the student take-over of the library where he is working. Very gradually we learn from his disconnected and disturbed account of his family that Daniel Isaacson is the son of parents who were executed for supposedly being atomic spies for the Soviet Union. Danny tries to clear his parents' name by figuring out what really happened. Gradually he develops his alternative hypothesis that another couple actually committed espionage, while his father and the confessing friend who implicated him conspired to cover for the others. This sacrifice reflected not only loyalty to the Communist party, but a sentimental confusion of its Popular Front posture with a second-generation immigrant belief in American democracy.

The reader soon begins to identify this story with the historical situation of Julius and Ethel Rosenberg. Though Doctorow has changed the younger son into a sister, the events involving members of the family, from the Popular Front era, the Peekskill riot of 1949, and the trial of the Rosenbergs in 1951 to the march on the Pentagon in 1967 and the student uprising at Columbia University in 1968, are historical. A reader who knew nothing about the Rosenbergs could still respond to the drama of the novel's extraordinary story and to the author's impressive talent for engaging our feelings with his characters and their situation. But to separate the novel from its major historical referent greatly diminishes the achievement of the writer and the enlightenment a reader can derive from it.

The Rosenberg case was not a mere point of departure for the author, something to set his imagination going, independent of the historical course of events that led to the execution. On the contrary, the story overlaps actual events so closely that even the difference in the personal styles of the children's radicalism (which their later book, *We Are Your Sons*, makes very evident) is accurately reflected in the novel. In both the novel and reality the older child is more reflective, more the heir of the father's didactic political rationalism, and more critical of New Left violence, while the younger one is more anti-intellectual, more involved in the counterculture, and more hospitable to New Left confrontational activism. Thus in the novel Susan is involved with a Yippie anarchist "Digger," while Danny feels out of place in the march on the Pentagon. Similarly, in reality Michael was arrested for picketing, Robert for a sit-in; Michael scorned SDS trashing at Madison, while Robert joined SDS at the University of Michigan, had Weatherman friends, and joined a commune. "It was not an easy transition from Old Left to New Left," Michael told an interviewer; and Robert declared in a memoir: "I was more of a hippie. Also politics for him seemed to me to be an intellectual, letter-writing, party-building affair, for me a series of confrontations." [45]

The narrative presents Danny's hypothesis about "the other couple" as tentative because both the "confessing" friend and the FBI may have fantasized events, as Danny speculates. But the arrest of the Rosenbergs did alert another couple to flee, and they were eventually arrested in England in a house as overloaded with espionage equipment, as Rebecca West has put it, as the ark was with animals. [46] Furthermore, the novel's picture of the angry wife's belated discovery of her husband's quixotic act is consistent with the recent revelation from FBI files that J. Edgar Hoover, for whatever reason, did not want to tie Ethel Rosenberg into the case, and she was actually arrested a month later than her husband. [47] More significant from a his-

torical point of view, "the other couple" theory rests upon the
novelist's portrait of Danny's father as a man who sincerely
believed that the safeguards of the Bill of Rights would keep
him from the electric chair. Michael Rosenberg himself, conceding that his parents "probably were members of the American
Communist Party," quotes "death-house" letters showing that
Julius did continuously expect both the law and public opinion
to exonerate him and his wife. In their last ten days he still
hoped to "*shame* the august court" to review the case. [48]

The quixotic idealism of Danny's father finds another historical correlative in the remark of Mrs. Sobell at a fund-raising
rally for the defense that "Julie and Ethel could save their own
skins by talking, but they will never betray their friends." [49]
(When it was pointed out to her that this remark hardly
squared with the premise of their total innocence, she fainted.)
The novel's unusual premise about "what actually happened"
is an elaboration of the implication contained in Mrs. Sobell's
observation, which does not easily fit into the stories told by the
defense and the prosecution. In this sense the novel performs a
historical function by accounting for some of the evidence more
plausibly than official versions do.

The issue of the novel's pertinence to history, however, cannot be confined to the detective-story question of "who did it?"
because it is to an important extent a novel of manners in the
sense of reconstructing several political milieus from the
Popular Front of the late thirties through the cold war forties
and fifties to the confrontational politics of the late sixties. For
this reason it functions as a historical novel, whatever the truth
of Danny's hypothesis about "the other couple." As such, it
explains Paul Isaacson's behavior in terms of Doctorow's historically perceptive insight into the rhetoric of Popular Front
Communism with its characteristic blurring of radical and
patriotic sentiments. The historical point of the novel's argument transcends the sterile opposition between those who accept the terms "guilty" and "innocent," as if the cold war rhetoric of the government's charges and Communist propaganda
about "witch-hunts" were the real alternatives. Danny's theory
of the other couple is equally distant from the "Hearst
philosopher," who totally accepts the government's position,

and the "liberal bleeder," who cannot imagine that left-wing idealists could be guilty of anything. [50] Doctorow's reformulation of the issues not only prevents the novel from collapsing into sentimental melodrama; it also can prevent historical discourse from suffering the same fate.

The novel also explicitly challenges the view of the Rosenbergs that two literary critics, Leslie Fiedler and Robert Warshow, set forth in the 1950s. In their eyes, as Danny says, the Rosenbergs were "crass and hypocritical" in calling on their Jewish faith to sustain sympathy for themselves. The critics complained that they hid their commitments behind the Fifth Amendment and had no thoughts of feelings undictated by propaganda about their role: "But if they had not had the political commitment could they have thought and felt at all?" [51] The novel restores them, however, to their humanity by taking seriously the idea that "the perfectionist dream of heaven and earth" can be a substitute religion for those who otherwise have given up their Jewish heritage and by showing how this Jewish yearning entered into their internalizing of the Popular Front ideology of communism as "twentieth-century Americanism." [52]

*The Book of Daniel*, as its title intimates, also puts the Rosenberg case in a long-range historical perspective. The biblical resonances in the story, which include the Isaacson name, compel the reader to think about the case in relation to Bible stories and Jewish experience, to see the Communism of the parents as itself a modern though illusory form of an ancient and continuously thwarted Jewish impulse of "looking for paradise on earth." The story exhibits the changing forms of this passion in the delirious memories of the immigrant grandmother, the radical idealism of the father and mother, and the anguished efforts of the children, who no longer can believe either in Russia or America, to carry on the family tradition by their own troubled connections with New Left politics.

Doctorow is fully aware that the political ideas of the Isaacsons are naive and deluded about Stalinist Russia, but like a good historian, he reconstructs their point of view without anachronism and without losing sight of the advantages which historical hindsight has given him. He also incorporates in the narrative long sections from revisionist historians of the cold war, who help Danny to develop a radical perspective that rejects his father's confused hybrid belief in both Stalinist Russia and American constitutionalism. The novel could not have been written without an extensive pursuit of historical understanding gained from reading historians, but it also enriches historical understanding by its exercise of the novelist's imagination applied to actuality.

The story matches real events in such a knowledgeable and consistent way that it implicitly proposes a question about what would happen to our appreciation of it should it turn out that the Rosenbergs, unlike the Isaacsons, were actually guilty of espionage. The novel, no more than the government, proves its case, and it deliberately leaves Danny unable to confirm his suspicions about what happened; when he goes to see the confessing dentist many years later, he finds him senile, unable to answer crucial questions. The story does not depend upon assuming the truth of a hypothesis which actually remains only a plausible one. Similarly, the revisionist history of the cold war appears as part of Danny's consciousness, not of an "omniscient" author's perspective. The novel's analysis of the unfairness in trying the accused by using a conspiracy clause in the Espionage Act, rather than the treason clause of the Constitution, agrees with a historian's recent discussion, giving weight to the most serious doubts about some features of the legal process in the Rosenberg case, which only Supreme Court justices Felix Frankfurter and Hugo Black consistently voted to review. But the historian scrupulously acknowledges that so far the evidence does not yet allow us decisively to answer the question of whether or not the Rosenbergs did commit espionage.[53] Should it someday clear them of being spies, this result alone would not affect Doctorow's argument, for his Isaacsons are not spies. Since the case against them depended on testimony, rather than on physical evidence (unlike the Hiss case), it is doubtful that future research could confirm the government's case unequivocally; but if it did, the pertinence of the novel would be changed. From being the possible truth about the case the novel's hypothesis would become instead a mere opinion of Danny's, plausible but no longer possible.

Aristotle formulated the often-cited rule that "for poetic effect a convincing impossibility is preferable to that which is unconvincing though possible." [54] This rule presumably would artistically justify the novel, assuming the Rosenbergs turn out to be guilty in a way that the Isaacsons are not, if we compare it to a novel based instead on the premise of their guilt, but lacking an equivalent artistic power. This condition of comparison, however, is an important feature of Aristotle's rule. One could say that Heinar Kipphardt's version of the Oppenheimer case is also "impossible" in putting into Oppenheimer's mouth words that he could not then have said within his own perspective, and its deviation from accuracy certainly makes the play dramatically interesting, perhaps more so than it otherwise would be. But a deviation of this sort in a drama claiming the authenticity of documentary truth is wounding to our historical consciousness in an important matter of fact. Doctorow wrote his story when the case was still unresolved historically, and this ambiguity makes a crucial difference to our appreciation of the argument the narrative unfolds. It was once possibly true, even if it should later turn out to have incorporated a false hypothesis about the Rosenberg case. Danny is not Doctorow, moreover, and the novel's historical understanding of Jewish-American Communism as a political religion would still stand.

The power of *The Book of Daniel* now, however, has both aesthetic and historical force, each reinforcing the other. The narrative explanation of the father's acting out of his quixotic Popular Front Communism is a dramatic irony, a transcendence of a Manichean version of either his innocence or his guilt. Should we have to judge this interesting version of his character to be inapplicable to Julius Rosenberg, we should then have to try to read the story as if it were not analogous to an actual family. The novel would still tell the truth about the Isaacsons, as far as Danny could guess at it. But we would have lost some of our historical interest in the story, and it would no longer have the compound power it now has. Because we could never entirely "bracket" our awareness of a presumed analogical relation between the Isaacsons and the Rosenbergs, we could not read the novel either as merely an imaginary story.

The full force of Doctorow's fiction depends upon the existing historical uncertainty about the Rosenbergs, unless it should turn out that "the other couple" theory is true. Read as a mythical version of the case, the novel could not match the hold it has on us because it now is a possible version. The point is not that the novel assumes the truth of the "other couple" theory; it wisely leaves the question of its truth ambiguous. But if the theory should turn out to be, in Aristotelian terms, a "convincing impossibility," we would in this respect be wiser than Danny, rather than being enlightened by him as we now are. As a historian of the Isaacsons, Danny cannot be refuted or confirmed; as a novelist of the Rosenberg case, Doctorow in some respects can be. It is a risk inseparable from his achievement.

Recently, two historians, working with access to all the FBI files released so far on the Rosenbergs, have also challenged the myths of their total innocence or total guilt. While the historians cite Communist witnesses who believe Julius was involved in secret work for the Party, their evidence is not detailed enough to discredit Danny's particular version of his father's guilt as a loyal Communist, covering for others; and Doctorow's scene of the wife, at the trial, being shocked to discover what her husband had been up to is consistent with the historians' account. They cite evidence to show that FBI agents never did know whether Ethel had been cognizant of her husband's secret activities, even though the government cynically included her in the indictment in the hope of pressuring her husband into revealing details of a postwar espionage network. The historians also provide confirmation from two left-wing witnesses, speaking twenty-eight years apart, for establishing a connection between Julius Rosenberg and a couple that fled to Mexico and vanished after his arrest.[55] Doctorow's imagination not only anticipated the outlooks of the children in the memoir without ever knowing them; he also anticipated much of the historians' recent verdict without ever seeing any FBI files. The novel is as uncannily prophetic as a book with that title ought to be, providing eloquent testimony to the power that can reside in a novelist's historical imagination.

Notes

1. Marguerite Yourcenar, "Notebooks on *Memoirs of Hadrian*," *Anchor Review* 2 (1957):168.

2. Frederic Jameson, *The Prison-House of Language: A Critical Account of Structuralism and Russian Formalism* (Princeton, N.J., 1972), p. 205.

3. Joseph Conrad, *Under Western Eyes* (New York, 1951), pp. vii, x.

4. George Eliot, "Leaves from a Note-Book: Historic Imagination," in *Essays of George Eliot*, ed. Thomas Pinney (New York, 1963), pp. 446–47.

5. Michel Butor, "The Novel as Research," in *Inventory: Essays by Michel Butor*, ed. Richard Howard (New York, 1968), p. 27.

6. "Butor, Balzac and Reality," ibid., p. 106.

7. Georg Lukács, *The Historical Novel*, trans. Hannah and Stanley Mitchell (London, 1962), pp. 167–68.

8. Robert Penn Warren, "Louisiana Politics and *All the King's Men*," in *"All the King's Men": A Critical Handbook*, ed. Maurice Beebe and Leslie A. Field (Belmont, Calif., 1966), p. 27; Ralph Ellison and Eugene Walter, "An Interview with Warren," ibid., p. 65.

9. Cushing Strout, *"All the King's Men* and the Shadow of William James," *Southern Review* 6, no. 4 (October 1970):920–34; R. Gray, "The American Novelist and American History: A Revaluation of *All the King's Men*," *Journal of American Studies* 6 (December 1972):297–307.

10. Helen Cam, *Historical Novels* (London, 1961), p. 18; Herbert Butterfield, *The Historical Novel: An Essay* (Cambridge, 1924), p. 112.

11. Addison Gayle, "Nat Turner and the Black Nationalists," in *Nat Turner*, ed. Eric Foner (Englewood Cliffs, N.J., 1971), pp. 169–71.

12. John Henrik Clarke, ed., *William Styron's Nat Turner: Ten Black Writers Respond* (Boston, 1968); Henry Irving Tragle, *The Southampton Slave Revolt of 1831: A Compilation of Source Material* (Amherst, Mass., 1971).

13. William Styron, "Slavery in the First Person," *Yale Alumni Review* (November 1967), pp. 36, 37, 39; "The Uses of History in Fiction: A Discussion," *Southern Literary Journal* 1, no. 2 (Spring 1969):72.

14. William Styron, "This Unquiet Dust," in *Writers and Issues*, ed. Theodore Solotaroff (New York, 1969), p. 239. For the changing images of Turner see Seymour L. Gross and Eileen Bender, "History, Politics, and Literature: The Myth of Nat Turner," in *The Achievement of William Styron*, ed. Robert R. Morris and Irving Malin (Athens, Ga., 1975), pp. 168–207.

15. Joan Rockwell, *Fact in Fiction: The Use of Literature in the Systematic Study of Society* (London, 1974), p. 133.

16. Richmond *Whig*, 26 September 1831, in Foner, *Nat Turner*, p. 27; "The Confessions of Nat Turner," *Nat Turner*, p. 45.

17. William Styron, "The Uses of History in Fiction," p. 83.

18. Ibid., p. 67.

19. Ibid., pp. 67–68.

20. Ibid., p. 64.

21. Styron, "Slavery in the First Person," p. 39.

22. See John White, "The Novelist as Historian: William Styron and American Negro Slavery," *Journal of American Studies* 4, no. 2 (February 1971):233–45.

23. Tragle, *Southampton Slave Revolt*, p. 411.

24. Author's Note, William Styron, *The Confessions of Nat Turner* (New York, 1967).

25. See Cam, *Historical Novels*, p. 10; Butterfield, *The Historical Novel*, p. 24.

26. Styron, "The Uses of History in Fiction," p. 75.

27. Ibid., p. 76.

28. Ibid., p. 90.

29. Gore Vidal, *Burr: A Novel* (New York, 1973), Afterword.

30. Henry Adams, *The Formative Years*, ed. Herbert Agar (Boston, 1948), 1:427–28.

31. Samuel Aandell and Meade Minnigerode, *Aaron Burr* (New York, 1925), 2:265–69.

32. Nathan Schachner, *Aaron Burr: A Biography* (New York, 1937), p. 285.

33. Richard B. Morris, *Fair Trial* (New York, 1953), p. 121.

34. Vidal, *Burr*, p. 179.

35. Ibid., Afterword.

36. Schachner, *Aaron Burr*, p. 516.

37. George Eliot, "Silly Novels by Lady Novelists," in *Essays of George Eliot*, ed. Thomas Pinney (New York, 1963), p. 321.

38. Vidal, *Burr*, p. 287.

39. Gerald Clarke, "Petronius Americanus," *Atlantic Monthly* 229, no. 3 (March 1972):48, 50; Gore Vidal, *Rocking the Boat* (Boston, 1962), p. 175.

40. Vidal, *Burr* p. 43.

41. Ibid., p. 456.

42. Quoted in C. Vann Woodward, *Reunion and Reaction: The Compromise of 1877 and the End of Reconstruction* (Boston, 1951), p. 210.

43. Gore Vidal, *1876: A Novel* (New York, 1976), p. 208.

44. Woodward, *Reunion and Reaction*, p. 215.

45. Jonah Raskin, "Life after Death: The Sons of Julius and Ethel Rosenberg," *Ramparts* 12 (November 1973):49; Robert and Michael Meeropol, *We Are Your Sons: The Legacy of the Rosenbergs* (Boston, 1975), p. 306.

46. Rebecca West, *The New Meaning of Treason* (New York, 1964), p. 282.

47. Allen Weinstein, "The Hiss and Rosenberg Files," *New Republic*, 174 (14 February 1976), pp. 16–17, 20–21.

48. Robert and Michael Meeropol, *We Are Your Sons*, pp. 352, n.; 221.

49. Louis Nizer, *The Implosion Conspiracy* (Greenwich, Conn. 1973), p. 469.

50. E. L. Doctorow, *The Book of Daniel* (New York, 1971), p. 227.

51. Robert Warshow, "The 'Idealism' of Julius and Ethel Rosenberg," in *Immediate Experience*, p. 80; See also Leslie Fiedler, *An End to Innocence* (Boston, 1955), pp. 41–43.

52. Doctorow, *Book of Daniel*, p. 119.

53. Michael E. Parrish, "Cold War Justice: The Supreme Court and the Rosenbergs," *American Historical Review* 82, no. 4 (October 1977):805–42.

54. Aristotle, *The Poetics*, trans. W. Hamilton Fyfe (London, 1965), p. 111.

55. Sol Stern and Ronald Radosh, "The Hidden Rosenberg Case," *New Republic* 180, no. 25 (23 June 1979):13–25.

# 10/The Antihistorical Novel

The future of narrative, according to two contemporary critics, lies in "new combinations" of the novel with romance and history. Such combinations are themselves as old as Hawthorne's historical and symbolic tales about New England, or as recent as Robert Lowell's stage version of them, *The Old Glory*. The critics concede that their division between empirical "representation" of historical, psychological, or sociological truth, on the one hand, and symbolic "illustration" of "ethical and metaphysical truth" on the other, does not fit Hawthorne's straddle of both realms.[1] His stories can be called both psychological and historical romances. In "My Kinsman, Major Molineux," for example, Hawthorne tells an enigmatic and surreal narrative about a young man who leaves his family to seek patronage from an uncle, only to have independence thrust upon him by discovering that his relative is a Tory victim of a Revolutionary mob. The highly condensed symbolic details in the story point to psychological and historical correlations so that the tale becomes an analogical working over of "growing up" as a historical metaphor for Hawthorne's measurement of the moral and social costs entailed in making the Revolution. Set during the time of royal governance in the 1730s when there was popular resentment of authority, the tale foreshortens time to include a dreamlike anticipation of the 1770s when the boy would be as old as his victimized and honorable uncle. Hawthorne is proof that a nonliteral, highly symbolic method of narration can be applied to a serious historical theme without doing any injustice to our historical consciousness, but amplifying it instead.

But it is also possible not to straddle but to corrupt both sorts of truth, and current critical taste provides no defense against it. (This issue surfaced in the *New York Times Book Review* for January 27, 1980, in "Do Facts and Fiction Mix?" by Michiko Kakutani, who observed that six books on the *Times* best-seller list "obscure the distinctions between the old categories" of fiction and nonfiction.) Doctorow's *Ragtime* combines novel, romance, and history, but it does so in a parodic way that affiliates it more to "black humor" than to Hawthorne. Or is it possible to say that John Dos Passos's *U.S.A.* "furnishes a crucial model for the blending of fact and fiction and supplies a mine of historical particulars that enrich the panorama of Doctorow's created world"?[2] But in Dos Passos fictional and real characters are separately dramatized, not fused, and the fictional histories are related to the biographical sketches of actual persons only by analogy, the invented stories being lowercase versions of similar themes in the lives of the real uppercase figures. Thus the story of Mary French as an unhappy radical resonates with the biography of Veblen, whose work she reads, just as that of the inventor Charlie Anderson resonates with the biography of the Wright brothers, and the account of the actress Margo Dowling's fictional adventures with Isadora Duncan's and Rudolph Valentino's actual biographies, while the "Camera Eye" sections separately incorporate the author's own memories and express his feelings. The trilogy, as Arnold Goldman has observed, is unified thematically as a sequential chronicle of the hope and defeat of native American socialism, international revolution, and Veblenian technocracy, and it provides a remedy only in "the magical contagion of past examples" from the Plymouth Pilgrims to Walt Whitman, Sacco and Vanzetti, and Frank Lloyd Wright.[3] Dos Passos believed in putting his characters "in the snarl of the human currents of his time" for the sake of "an accurate permanent record of a phase of history."[4] Yet this ambition, for all the novelty of his techniques involving newspaper headlines, stream-of-consciousness soliloquies, and biographical vignettes, is classical enough to be shared by George Eliot and Joseph Conrad. *U.S.A.* bitterly satirizes American society, but it assumes that history is real and explicable.

Mark Twain's *A Connecticut Yankee in King Arthur's Court* is a more convincing example of a precursor to *Ragtime*. King Arthur and his round table may have been more legendary than real, while many of Doctorow's characters are historically real; but both novels use deliberate anachronism for comic effect and define history in terms of conspiracies and violent confrontations. Hank Morgan goes back into the sixth century to battle the forces of feudal injustice, just as Coalhouse Walker, a character drawn from the black militancy postures of the 1960s, surfaces in the ragtime era to have a violent showdown with the racists of early twentieth-century America. But Doctorow's anachronism, unlike Twain's, is not the open candid premise of the story; it lies beneath the surface, for Walker is presented as if he did live in the ragtime era.

In this respect *Ragtime* is more like John Barth's *The Sot-Weed Factor* (1960) a pseudodocumentary, parodic eighteenth-century history, whose title derives from a poem by an actual Marylander. Its characters, as a defender of "black humor" has noticed, are really "twentieth-century sensibilities responding to a modern world of 'blind Nature which has neither codes nor causes.'"[5] All three novels are pastiches that spoof the historical novel and cast doubt on the intelligibility of history as either a process or an interpreted record. Tony Tanner has pointed out how Barth's pseudohistorical novel deliberately blurs the line so that "we cannot be sure when we are in touch with facts, as opposed to fictionalized versions of facts." The result is a book suggesting "that the author does not believe in such a thing as history even while his narrative pretends to evoke it."[6] Instead of linking narrative to explanation, the stories of Twain and Barth imply that the world can neither be understood or managed. *Ragtime* swims in the stream where the fish are fishily skeptical of documents, history, truth, and meaning, but its "deconstruction" is politically colored.

While ostensibly at first a "period" story in the traditional sense of the historical novel, including such actual figures as Houdini, J. P. Morgan, Henry Ford, and Emma Goldman, *Ragtime* develops into a subversion of the conventional form by its deliberate affronts to the historical imagination. Unlike *U.S.A.*, it presents improbable imaginary events in the lives of actual people, drawn from history, mixes them up with fictional characters, and thrusts a racial confrontation of the late 1960s sort into the era before World War I, when it never could have happened. Speaking about his novel, Doctorow exposed his strategy by ironically calling his tale "a false document" in comparison with "a true document," like the Gulf of Tonkin Resolution or the Watergate tapes, duplicitous documents embedded in plots for manipulating the public.[7] His strategy calls into question, as one admirer of *Ragtime* has said, "our concept of factuality and, indeed, of history itself."[8] Doctorow himself is quoted as saying: "there's no more fiction or nonfiction now, there's only narrative." Whereas Truman Capote's *In Cold Blood* as a "nonfiction novel" stressed its factuality, *Ragtime*, as fictional history, expressed Doctorow's insistence that "facts are as much of an illusion as anything else."[9]

*Ragtime* presupposes the 1960s attack on neutrality, objectivity, and impartiality as being mere conservative ideology. In the late sixties political dissent tended to repudiate all "irrelevant" disciplines and to politicize the "relevant" ones. In historical thought Hayden White in 1969 had openly called for a "metahistory" on behalf of a political radicalism that could specify a "world-transforming" vision of a desirable future that would give "form to one's account of past and present."[10] This call for a return to speculative philosophy of history challenged the professional tradition of empiricism because White identified it with conservatism. Giving shape to the past according to one's hopes for the future opens the door, however, to an instrumental view of the past as a resource for propaganda rather than for history. Conservatives have no corner on "what actually happened" as an ideal of truth. Speaking about his study of three tenant families in the thirties, James Agee, for example, insisted that "the centrally exciting and important fact, from which ramify the thousand others which otherwise would have no clear and valid existence, is: that was the way it was." [11] Agee was passionately interested in finding a mode of telling "without either dissection into science, or digestion into art," a wish belied by his aspiration to musical form and his reverential poetic eloquence; but he rightly thought his interest in telling of the actual with fidelity to "the cruel radiance of what is" was quite consistent with his choice of one of the mottos for his book: "Workers of the world, unite and fight. You have nothing to lose but your chains, and a world to win." [12] Like George Orwell, who anticipated the new journalism's nonfiction novel, he would have been astonished to be told that his wish—to give happenings and appearances "as they were and as in my memory and regard they are"—was a politically conservative one. [13] Visions of a desirable future need all the guidance they can get from a realistic knowledge of the past and present, neither diluted nor distorted by current hopes and fears. Neither the erudite historian White nor the antihistorical and often anti-intellectual "activist" students appreciated the possibility of a nonconservative "realism" like Agee's.

Doctorow's blurring of the fact/fiction distinction reflects this political background in terms of his use of racial confrontation as the main focus of his plot. His tinkering with history is not just playful, as is Nicholas Meyer's in his overimitated and overpraised novel based on the amusing premise that Sherlock Holmes once visited Sigmund Freud for assistance. Nor is it just a salutary subversion of popular nostalgia for an earlier time. Like Mark Twain, Doctorow has political intentions, and the weight of his narrative is its suspenseful story about a black man's struggle for his dignity in a racist society. But whereas Twain undercut his reformer by exposing the elements of the Boss and of P. T. Barnum in him, Doctorow celebrates his fictional hero. The difficulty in reading *Ragtime* is that 1960s' preoccupations keep coming between us and the earlier era.

Given the weight of the racial issue in the novel we must be able to take it seriously. But this is impossible if we read *Ragtime* as a mosaic of a specific era. Even if we accept *Ragtime*'s jazzlike syncopation of its material in interconnecting fictional and real persons, just as the music itself links African and Western rhythms, this suspension of disbelief cannot countenance the disruption in our historical consciousness produced by the Coalhouse Walker story. Its unannounced anachronism makes incredible this tale of a ragtime pianist, who has no identifiable parentage or school records because "it is still not known how he acquired his vocabulary and his manner of speaking. Perhaps by an act of will." [14] The act of will, of course, is his creator's. He has put an uncompromising, defiant black man and his small band of supporters into the position of blowing up a fire station and occupying the Morgan Library; they threaten to destroy the library unless their terms are met. Walker succeeds in negotiating to have his Model T rebuilt by the vandalizing fire chief who had started the trouble; but the black leader in return forefeits his life to trigger-happy policemen. The hostage, a bomb-making, white supporter of the rebels, flees with the other blacks in the car and eventually joins the Mexican revolutionary, Zapata. All these details are in a contemporary idiom at odds with the era of ragtime.

Mark Twain also used anachronism in putting a nineteenth-century Hartford mechanic into sixth-century Camelot, which was also a disguised antebellum South; and he too ended his tale with a violent showdown, a confrontation between the Yankee's small band of supporters and the massed might of feudalism. Twain could not maintain control over the themes of his story, and his deep ambivalence about the idea of progress ultimately wrecked the novel. Hank Morgan as a showman, adman, commonsense mechanic, republican ideologist, ward boss, dictator, and, finally, nostalgic sentimentalist about a feudal past he has always ridiculed, contains too many contradictory meanings to be a coherent figure. But at least with Twain anachronism is always the point of the joke from the earliest exchange: "'Bridgeport?' said I. 'No, Camelot,' said he." But *Ragtime* begins with fidelity to the historical details in 1902. The only early and enigmatic warning of strange things to come is a little boy telling Harry Houdini to "warn the Duke," a fantastic anticipation of the assassination that triggered a world war and ended the era of ragtime. The magician only remembers the prophetic remark some 260 pages later when he is hanging upside down in a straitjacket over Times Square. Doctorow straight-facedly documents the memory from the magician's "private unpublished papers," a spurious reference in a "history" as topsy-turvy as Houdini's position.[15]

Playing such literary tricks on a magician is part of the fun, but Doctorow's cleverness ultimately is self-defeating, robbing the novel of any serious relation to the history it "deconstructs." Twain's book has the merit of subverting the idea of linear progress in an age that took it very seriously, but Doctorow's treatment of the issue of racism challenges no contemporary pieties. Instead his picture of the era presents stupid and callous capitalists, sexually inhibited WASPs, and victimized workers, immigrants, and blacks in terms that are not false, but too easily caricatured, being cut to suit contemporary radical rhetoric.

In this respect Doctorow's "updating" compares with Robert Lowell's in his dramatic version of Melville's *Benito Cereno* in *The Old Glory*. Lowell turns the American Captain Delano into a more aggressive, pecuniary, smug, and vindictive character, who ends the play by pumping six shots into the leader of the mutiny and shouting, "This is your future!"[16] In Melville's story, however, Delano's prejudices about blacks and Spaniards are also exposed, but we see how his temperamental optimism and complacency move him to urge forgetting the past, rather than avenging the mutineers. Lowell has made the muted perspective of the novella more obvious, crude, and melodramatic to fit a contemporary (1964) mood about American race relations.

Doctorow's unusually simple, declarative style of narration seems never to comment, making its point only through ironic juxtapositions. But sometimes the objective tone turns editorial. The anarchist Emma Goldman teaches Evelyn Nesbit, the chorus girl who had once been Stanford White's mistress, that her sexual corruption is a consequence of capitalism and that Negroes and immigrants really do exist, in spite of majority prejudice. "And though the newspapers called the shooting the Crime of the Century," Doctorow remarks, "Goldman knew it was only 1906 and there were ninety-four years to go."[17] When she is asked if the black rebel is a follower of hers, she replies: "The oppressor is wealth, my friends. Wealth is the oppressor. Coalhouse Walker did not need Red Emma to learn that. He needed only to suffer." [18] She has the requisite political consciousness, but Houdini, Doctorow laments, "never developed what we think of as a political consciousness" because he could not "reason from his own hurt feelings" or see "the great map of revolution laid out by his life," as a Jew whose entertainments charmed everyone but the upper classes, who made him uncomfortable. [19] The author also tips his political hand when he comments on the path that will lead Tateh, the Jewish immigrant artist of socialist opinions, to become one of the early founders of the movie business and to conceive the "Our Gang" comedies: "Thus did the artist point his life along the lines of flow of American energy." It is this entrepreneurial energy, as explained in the same paragraph, that leads the evil genius of Ford to invent mass production as a system for making the men who built the products "be themselves interchangeable parts." [20]

Twain's hero speaks proudly in his own dehumanizing way about his reformist "man factories," but in *A Connecticut Yankee* it is the hero who is hoist by his own petard in being trapped by the stench of the corpses he has created by his own ingenious devices for war. In *Ragtime*, however, it is not Younger Brother, the alienated terrorist, whose ingenuity in making explosive devices is exploited by Father as war-contractor, but Father (in Freudian style) who is torpedoed on the *Lusitania* with its cargo of "grenades, depth charges, and puttied nitro" invented by Younger Brother. The terrorist himself dies in a skirmish with government troops in the same place where "Zapata himself was to be gunned down in ambush." [21] The Yankee's destructiveness recoils on himself; Younger Brother is done in by oppressive government forces. Doctorow does satirize him by having him put on blackface with burnt cork "to suggest his good faith" to the rebels by "appealing to their sense of irony," [22] but like his accusations against Father for being an oppressor, his guerrilla raids on oil fields and federal garrisons for Zapata's peasant army are presented with no comment whatever. Father is finally ridiculed as an "establishment" figure; Younger Brother's "alienation" is at first comically presented, but in the end he is taken straight.

Sexuality in *The Book of Daniel* is always justified by its relation to character, whether in Danny's disturbed, morbid eroticism with his wife or in the healthy passion of the Isaacson parents. But in *Ragtime* a gamey scene of lesbian and voyeuristic sexuality, involving corrupted Evelyn Nesbit, emancipated Emma Goldman, and frustrated Younger Brother is played for farce. Its only point lies in its political overtones which seem to be pitched to glibly "liberated" readers of the *Village Voice*. When Doctorow invents a ludicrously solemn belief in reincarnation to deck out Morgan's passionate interest in Egypt and juxtaposes it to Houdini's desperate burial stunts after the death of his mother, nothing is served except the author's cleverness, a half-truth about Morgan matched to a plausible psychoanalytic interpretation of the mother-dependent Houdini.[23] Doctorow's manipulations of the past create an ambiguity about his judgment that the era of ragtime ended "as if history were no more than a tune on a player piano."[24] The remark implies that real history is no frivolous tune, but his book's rearrangement of history subverts the implication, for the ragtime era is as frivolously manipulated in *Ragtime* as if it were only a tune. Appropriately, his book was promoted in the media like a popular song, whatever his own intentions may have been.

The real irony in *Ragtime* is a concealed one about the novel's most exciting story. As an openly duplicitous history, *Ragtime* also has its own secret. Its major plot about the embattled black man and his wife is actually a refurbishing in detail and in contemporary dress of a story about a horse dealer locked in struggle with an oppressive aristocracy, as told by Heinrich von Kleist, an early nineteenth-century German dramatist, in *Michael Kohlhaas* (1810).[25] Doctorow's pun (Coalhouse) on the name is the only clue to his Americanization of the German protagonist and the change of the pair of horses to a Model T. This hidden literary theft is part of the novel's trickiness and its freewheeling play with anachronisms. The drama of the book derives from Kleist's retelling of a medieval chronicle. *Ragtime*, in this sense, reverses the Connecticut Yankee's time travel from modern to medieval. To make anachronistic history out of literature, itself made out of chronicle in this case, is a complex way of making Doctorow's point that "there is only narrative now." This cleverness is akin to John Barth's where everything tends to resolve itself into linguistic sport. But linguistic omnipotence is an atmosphere in which history cannot flourish.

One critic paradoxically praises Doctorow for "calling into question our concept of factuality and, indeed, of history itself," while also "enhancing the historical self-consciousness of his readers."[26] But these aims point in different directions. The critic's best defense is her argument that Doctorow's outrageous anachronism simply underlines the continuation into our own time of a racism that survives as a legacy from the ragtime era. In this light Doctorow sees the groundwork for the sixties being laid in the paternalism of Father and Mother and the conservatism of Booker T. Washington, who appears in the story to try to persuade the rebel to abandon his violent tactics and nearly swoons when Walker declares that he might be serving his race by insisting on respect for his manhood.

It is useful to compare *Ragtime* on this score with Hawthorne's "My Kinsman, Major Molineux." He also disrupts chronology by having young Robin encounter a political mob evocative of the Boston Tea Party, an event some forty years after the time in which the story is set. By this foreshadowing Hawthorne makes a point about the future that Robin will one day confront and about the long-run implications of the popular resentment of authority already active in the boy's present climate of public opinion. While Hawthorne sympathizes with the tarred-and-feathered honorable Tory, rather than with the mob, and Doctorow with the rebels, rather than with their opponents, the crucial difference is not political, but artistic. Hawthorne's story is a fable of types and his anachronistic mob scene has the texture of a vivid nightmare. Doctorow's types, including the "monumental negritude" of Walker, are mingled with actual persons, who tend to be tendentiously caricatured (as Washington is) in order to cohere with the others. There are no visible seams in Hawthorne's fictional world; Doctorow's is crudely patched.

*Ragtime* has flashes of the remarkable historical imagination that lights up *The Book of Daniel* when, for example, it pays attention to immigrant dimensions in the life of Houdini and the Hollywood career of Tateh. But one cannot read *Ragtime* consistently either as playful fantasy or serious history. It is too historical for farce, too light-hearted for the rage of black humor, and too caricatured for history. Doctorow's motto for the novel is Scott Joplin's warning: "Do not play this piece fast." Taking it slow reveals its cleverness, but the trouble is that there is nothing else to be learned, because it lacks an integrating historical point of view. Doctorow, like Houdini, performed to a wide audience by escaping from the usual restraints. Houdini, as *Ragtime* points out, made a show of appearing to struggle in making his straitjacket escape, because otherwise people would not believe he was legitimate. *Ragtime* appears to struggle with the complexities of history, but it is only a clever trick. Modern art rightly celebrates artistic freedom, yet its victories are cheapened when there is no resistance from the pressure of a responsibility to historical consciousness. To make historical characters do whatever suits one's fancy makes for amusing entertainment or for political manipulation, but the veracious imagination is corrupted.

The nineteenth-century "realist" novel is not prescriptive. Speculative imaginary worlds, like *Brave New World* or *1984*, achieve the power and insight we expect from serious novels. But Huxley and Orwell worked within the limits of a definite logic of extrapolation; they achieved their force by their respect for those limits. We are at a loss in reading *Ragtime* to know by what logic Doctorow's speculative history is created. He may seem to be a magician in his capacity to blur the actual with the illusory, but his dictum that "facts are as much of an illusion as anything else"[27] contrasts with Houdini's knowledge that some "facts" only appear to be such because other facts are real. His skill (like Doctorow's) depended upon matter-of-fact knowledge of the difference between the illusion spectators saw and what actually happened. To confuse others about that distinction by blurring it for political reasons, as some recent presidents have done, is widely recognized as being corrupting. The artist dealing with matters of history is not exempt, however, from the temptation or the corruption.

Samuel Johnson's philosopher in *Rasselas* reflects that the Great Pyramid in Egypt seems to have been erected only in compliance with "*that hunger of imagination which preys incessantly upon life.*"[28] Similarly, novelistic cleverness can be a preying upon history when the novelist thinks of it as "nothing but words. Accidental accretions for the most part, leaving most of the story out." The words are supposedly those of Richard Nixon, a character in Robert Coover's *The Public Burning* (1978), a hyperbolic parody of the Rosenberg case. "We have not yet begun to explore the true power of the Word, I thought," this Nixon announces. "What if we broke all the rules, played games with the evidence, manipulated language itself, made History a partisan ally?"[29] Coover himself writes from this premise, and his Nixon flirts with Doctorow's hypothesis about the Rosenbergs' martyrdom on behalf of the spying activities of their friends, becomes infatuated with Ethel, and tries to save her. This farrago of fact and fiction ends with the couple trying to copulate in her cell as she writes I AM A SCAMP on Nixon's rump with lipstick, while in Times Square, where the execution is to take place, the justices of the Supreme Court skid about on elephant droppings. Nixon enters with dropped pants and calls upon the crowd to follow suit, and in an obscene Epilogue the Uncle Sam of folklore brutally sodomizes Nixon, who then confesses his love for this "incorrigible huckster." Ironically, *Ragtime* prepared readers for this scatalogical frivolity, which preyed upon the history of a case that Doctorow had fictionalized with such moving imaginative veracity.

As the best artists have shown, there are many and subtle ways to respect both the documentable and the imaginative without sacrificing either to the other. The artist has no monopoly on imagination, the historian no monopoly on the past. The writer of either history or fiction has to be discriminating, synthesizing, and evocative. Neither one can afford to ignore the other, especially the other in himself. Doctorow's *The Book of Daniel* performed an act of both the literary and the historical imagination without literalism or anachronism. *Ragtime* disappoints the expectations it arouses of a comparable achievement. It took the easier way out of the problem of reconciliation by giving the hungry lion of the imagination a fresh lamb of humble fact every day to devour as he wished. When that happens, the veracious imagination becomes voracious.

## Notes

1. Robert Scholes and Robert Kellog, *The Nature of Narrative* (New York, 1971), pp. 88–90.

2. Barbara Foley, "From *U.S.A.* to *Ragtime*: Notes on the Forms of Historical Consciousness in Modern Fiction," *American Literature* 50, no. 1 (March 1978):89.

3. Arnold Goldman, "Dos Passos and His *U.S.A.*," *New Literary History* 1, no. 3 (Spring 1970):481.

4. Quoted in Melvin Landsberg, *John Dos Passos's Path to "U.S.A.": A Political Biography 1912–1936* (Boulder, Colo., 1972), p. 220.

5. Max F. Schultz, *Black Humor Fiction of the Sixties: A Pluralistic Definition of Man and His World* (Athens, Ohio, 1973), p. 87.

6. Tony Tanner, *City of Words: American Fiction 1950–1970* (New York, 1971), pp. 242, 245.

7. Quoted in Foley, "From *U.S.A.* to *Ragtime*," p. 99. (Interview, *New York Times*, 11 July 1975.)

8. Foley, "From *U.S.A.* to *Ragtime*," p. 97.

9. Quoted in Foley, "From *U.S.A.* to *Ragtime*," pp. 102, 104. Foley confuses Doctorow's "creative" fictionalizing of history with R. G. Collingwood's theory of the historical imagination in *The Idea of History*. But he explicitly says that the historian's "business is not to invent anything, it is to discover something." *The Idea of History* (Oxford, 1946), p. 251. For Collingwood historical truth is a matter of coherence with evidence, not of creation.

10. Hayden V. White, "The Politics of Contemporary Philosophy of History," *Clio* 3, no. 1 (1973):44.

11. James Agee and Walker Evans, *Let Us Now Praise Famous Men* (New York, 1966), p. 217. Orig. pub. 1941.

12. Ibid., p. 11.

13. Ibid., p. 218.

14. E. L. Doctorow, *Ragtime* (New York, 1974), p. 153.

15. Ibid., pp. 9, 267.

16. Robert Lowell, "Benito Cereno," *The Old Glory* (New York, 1965), p. 194. But Lowell's revisionism fleshes out Hawthorne's *Endecott and the Red Cross*, rather than simplifying it.

17. *Ragtime*, p. 5.

18. Ibid., p. 233.

19. Ibid., p. 29.

20. Ibid., pp. 111, 113.

21. Ibid., p. 259.

22. Ibid., p. 205.

23. Eric T. Carlson, a psychiatrist, agrees that Houdini's attachment to his mother was excessive even for a Victorian. See "Psychoanalysis, Biography, and Houdini," *Bulletin of the New York Academy of Medicine*, second series, 54, no. 6 (June 1978):594.

24. *Ragtime.*, p. 270.

25. Foley, "From *U.S.A.* to *Ragtime*," p. 94.

26. Ibid., pp. 96–97.

27. Quoted in Foley, "From *U.S.A.* to *Ragtime*," p. 104.

28. My colleague M. H. Abrams called my attention to this striking metaphor, which W. Jackson Bate analyzes in *Samuel Johnson* (New York, 1977), pp. 298–300. For a witty critique of vanguard literary theorists who defend "double-dealing" with texts see Abrams, "How to Do Things with Texts," *Partisan Review* 46, no. 4 (1979):566–88.

29. Robert Coover, *The Public Burning* (New York, 1979), p. 168.

# PART 4
# Psychological Biography

I emphasize that for psychoanalysis, one *tells*
a history; one does not *have* a history.
It is a history of something, however;
a fabrication won't do. In this history
the past and the present mutually define
one another in a complex manner. . . . The
inner world of experience is a kind
of telling, not a kind of place.
    —Roy Schafer, *Language and Insight*

# 11 / William James and the Twice-Born Sick Soul

I became a doctor through being compelled
to deviate from my original purpose; and
the triumph of my life lies in my having,
after a long and roundabout journey,
found my way back to my earliest path.
—Sigmund Freud

Historical determinism was much in fashion in 1880 when William James published his essay on "Great Men and Their Environment." He had to attack the superstition, derived from Herbert Spencer, that great men were mere resultants of that "aggregate of conditions" out of which both they and their society had arisen. Spencer's method, as James pointed out, was like that of "one who would invoke the zodiac to account for the fall of the sparrow."[1] To offer the whole past as an explanation of something specific in the present was no better than explaining every event by saying "God is great." James acknowledged that society, in Darwinian terms, could preserve

or reject the great man, but it did not make him before he re-
made it. Physiological forces, with which social conditions had
no discernible connection, genetically produced the hero. Even
at the level of intellectual history, the same Darwinian point
applied: society confirmed or refuted the spontaneous variations of ideas produced in great thinkers by the "functional
activity of the excessively instable human brain."[2]

Certainly the movement of pragmatism cannot be explained apart from William James who became, as Ralph
Barton Perry has said, "the Ambassador of American Thought
to Western Europe." It is consistent with James's theory of the
great man to note that social circumstances played their part in
favoring the development of pragmatism into a force which influenced American philosophy, psychology, religion, political
theory, education, and historiography. Voluntaristic, democratic, tough-minded, and optimistic, pragmatism had qualities
well suited to American culture at a time when science had
great prestige and humanistic values needed new underpinnings
because of the erosion of older theological supports. But it was
James's own wide-ranging intellectual curiosity, his familiarity
with Europe and its languages, and above all his fervent conviction that pragmatism was "something quite like the protestant
reformation" and destined for "definitive triumph" that made
him "the revivifying force in European thought in the decade
and a half preceding the outbreak of the First World War."[3] Intellectually gregarious, gifted with a talent for popular lectur-
ing, passionately attached to American life by affection and
critical commitment rather than by habitat, he was (like
Franklin and Jefferson) a cosmopolitan American who could
speak to the world in a voice that resonated with a specific
identity.

Yet James's own struggle in forming a personal identity
and finding his proper vocation was acute. His growth to greatness was precarious and painful, vulnerable to chronic debility,
depression, and distress. James's theory of the great man has
one conspicuous weakness: it does not cover himself. There is
more to the great man than favorable social conditions, the
spontaneous variations of genetics, or what James called the
"seething caldron of ideas" in the "highest order of minds." He

believed that the "genesis [of ideas] is sudden and, as it were, spontaneous,"[4] but the history of his own development is a refutation of any such sudden spontaneity. Spontaneity was in his case a hard-won achievement of a personality threatened by imminent disorganization. What James needed to round out his theory of the great man was an ordered way of talking about the inner history of the great man's relation to himself and to the significant others in his family.

In this sense, the great man is made, in part, by that intimate society, filled with resounding echoes of the world in the significant speech, gesture, and silence of parents and siblings, which he in turn remakes by his appearance in it. If he is truly great, he conspires with circumstance to turn his private conflicts into public issues with relevance for others. He learns to speak not only to his family and his society but, in principle, to all men. Paradoxically, he might even learn to speak to all men just because on certain matters he cannot speak openly to his family. The sign of that inability would be a kind of sickness, a bafflement of development, referring to the unspeakable. For such individuals, as Erik H. Erikson has taught us in *Young Man Luther*, the identity crisis of early manhood may be a period in which endangered youths, "although suffering and deviating dangerously through what appears to be a prolonged adolescence, eventually come to contribute an original bit to an emerging style of life: the very danger which they have sensed has forced them to mobilize capacities to see and say, to dream and plan, to design and construct, in new ways."[5] Erikson suggests that "born leaders seem to fear only more consciously what in some form everybody fears in the depths of his inner life; and they convincingly claim to have an answer."[6] The conscious fear that James grappled with was the apprehension that scientific determinism, what he called "medical materialism," would leave no meaningful space for the human will. That fear was closely connected with his fears as a member of the James family. I propose to analyze that linkage in narrative form, trying to do justice to the relevant claims of psychoanalysis, history, and philosophy.

The historian is justified in asking the James family to sit for a portrait of upper-class Victorian life. The bearded, revered, religious father, the domestically devoted mother, the effusive language of family endearment, the endless trips to Europe for convalescence—all these familiar features we recognize with the usual smile. The intellectual issues of James's life—the conflict between science and religion, the revolt against rationalism, and the moral cult of "the strenuous life"—are part of the texture of that period, which writers like Walter E. Houghton have brought to vivid life.[7] James's own depressed invalidism also had many counterparts in the lives of other eminent Victorians, like Mill, Darwin, and Jane Addams. A pre-Freudian, James was inevitably a mystery to himself, but he welcomed the work of Freud and his pupils on the ground that it might shed light on "the twilight region that surrounds the clearly lighted centre of experience." He looked forward to biographical studies that would show "the various ways of unlocking the reserves of power" exemplified in individual lives.[8] Let us begin, therefore, with a striking peculiarity of James's career—the long deferment of a youthful philosophical ambition, which he did not fully commit himself to as a vocation until he was nearly sixty.

William James first decided to become a painter. As a boy he had shown a spontaneous interest in drawing, and with his first real youthful friend shared a hope of becoming an artist. Unfortunately, in 1859 his father whisked young William off to Europe, away from his friend and from William Morris Hunt's studio at Newport. The father explained to a friend:

> Newport did not give the boys what they required exactly, and we didn't relish their separation from us. Willy especially felt, we thought, a little too much attraction to painting—as I suppose from the contiguity to Mr. Hunt; let us break that up, we said, at all events. I hoped that his career would be a scientific one . . . and to give up this hope without a struggle, and allow him to tumble down into a mere painter, was impossible.[9]

In the end, the elder James relented because his son pleaded, very respectfully and humbly, that his life "would be embittered" if he were not allowed to try painting. The father need not have worried; the son himself echoed his father's judgment by declaring before entering Hunt's studio: "There is nothing on earth more deplorable than a bad artist." For a conscientious boy who much admired his father, this venture in vocation must have engendered a bad conscience. Within the year he had abandoned art school, though he kept up his drawing for several years. In 1872, he was to confess that he "regretted extremely" letting it die out.[10] Meanwhile, the Civil War was a call to action, and in 1861 both William and Henry sought to enlist in the Union Army. Once again their father had other plans: "I have had a firm grasp upon the coat tails of my Willy and Harry, who both vituperate me beyond measure because I won't let them go."[11] Both boys soon developed illnesses that incapacitated them for service anyway, and it was the younger brothers, Wilkinson and Robertson, the forgotten Jameses, who with father's blessing joined the army.

In 1861, William dutifully gave his father a plan of his future life: to study chemistry, anatomy, and medicine as preparation for spending several years with Louis Agassiz in natural history. The plan was shaped to his father's hopes for him. That fall William entered the Lawrence Scientific School in Cambridge as a student of chemistry. "Relentless Chemistry claims its hapless victim," he wryly wrote to a friend. As his teacher later recalled, nervous illness began to interfere with his work at this point.[12] In 1863 he entered medical school where Jeffries Wyman taught, a man for whom James had "a filial feeling," perhaps because Wyman was also an excellent draftsman. The next year, under the spell of the "godlike" charm of Louis Agassiz, William went to Brazil as part of an exploring and collecting expedition. There he caught varioloid, a mild form of smallpox, and spent over two despondent weeks in the hospital, resting his eyes and rethinking his future. His experience convinced him that he hated collecting and was "cut out for a speculative rather than an active life." Having recovered the use of his eyes and having lost his respect for Agassiz's pretensions to omniscience, he joyfully returned home with a new resolution: "When I get home I'm going to study philosophy all my days."[13]

Privately James read philosophy voraciously, but publicly he resumed his medical studies and undertook a brief internship at the Massachusetts General Hospital. His comments on the medical profession, except surgery, were always contemptuous, convicting it of "much humbug." Nevertheless, his disenchantment with Agassiz and natural history forced him to consider medicine as a possible career unless he were to abandon the scientific bent of his education. In retrospect, the Brazil expedition gave him a "feeling of loneliness and intellectual and moral deadness." In the fall and winter of 1866 he complained of digestive disorders, eye troubles, acute depression, and weakness of the back. His symptoms are characteristic of hypochrondriasis, and in psychosomatic illness unconscious imitation often plays a part in the selection of discomforts. He revived those symptoms which he had felt in Brazil, and he now also spoke, in revealing language, of a "delightful disease" in the back "which has so long made Harry so interesting." [14] Henry had developed this symptom from a trivial accident incurred while he was trying to put out a fire in 1861. When his father was thirteen, he had, under similar circumstances, sustained an injury that led to a leg amputation and two years in bed. William's back and eye trouble provided him with an excuse for not practicing medicine. Shortly before taking his exams for the medical degree in 1869, he wrote his brother: "I am perfectly contented that the power which gave me these faculties should recall them partially or totally when and in what order it sees fit. I don't think I should give a single damn now if I were struck blind." [15] In the winter of 1867, he felt himself on the "continual verge of suicide" and sometime during these years he was paralyzed in panic fear by the image of a greenish, withdrawn epileptic idiot whom he had seen in an asylum. *"That shape am I*, I felt, potentially," he confessed, and for months he dreaded being alone in the dark. [16]

What did this paralyzing recollection mean? As a medical student he might easily have read the well-known work by the English doctor William Acton, *The Functions and Disorders of the Reproductive Organs*. Steven Marcus has pointed out in *The Other Victorians* that Acton's book is a classic statement of Victorian attitudes toward sex; indeed, one of Acton's themes is the moral need to break willfully the habit of introspection in order to ward off the temptation of masturbation, luridly imagined as a threat to sanity. Acton points up his moral by a description of inmates of an insane asylum: "The pale complexion, the emaciated form, the slouching gait, the clammy palm, the glassy or leaden eye, and the averted gaze, indicate the lunatic victim to this vice." [A decade after my essay was published a colleague discovered a more exact image of James's patient in an illustration of a French work on mental illness (1838), representing an *onaniste*. This French source may explain James's pseudoattribution of his panic fear (in *The Varieties of Religious Experience*) to an anonymous Frenchman. See Sander L. Gilman, "Seeing the Insane: Mackenzie, Kleist, William James," *Modern Language Notes* 93 (1978):882. Cf. Acton in Marcus, *The Other Victorians* (New York, 1966), p. 20.] This image resembles James's memory of the epileptic patient, and in the late 1860s he was unsuccessfully courting Fanny Dixwell, whom his friend Oliver Wendell Holmes, Jr., married in 1872. James was thirty-six when he married, and no doubt sexual frustration had plagued him, but his vocational problem persisted after 1878. That hideous figure, we may speculate, objectified not only the self-punishing guilt in his own symptoms, but also his fear of being trapped in a medical career which seemed to be his only option after his disillusionment with natural history. Neither Wyman nor Agassiz had shaken his belief that his father was, as James had written in Brazil, "the *wisest* of all men" he had ever known.[17] And his father was a metaphysician—not a physician.

James defined his dilemma to a despondent friend: "I am about as little fitted by nature to be a worker in science of any sort as anyone can be, and yet . . . my only ideal of life is a scientific life."[18] His whole program, outlined to his father in 1861, had collapsed along with his health and spirits. In submitting his prospectus, he had prophesied wryly that the last stage would be "death, death, death with inflation and plethora of knowledge."[19] That jest had come symbolically true, as if he had unconsciously feared the worst in the pursuit of his scientific career. In 1867 he sailed for Europe, which served him as a psychic moratorium from commitment. Subjecting himself to the tortures of the baths and galvanic remedies, he felt ashamed not to be earning money like his brothers. He found solace in the theater, art galleries, music, novels, and glimpses of pretty frauleins, while he read philosophy and dutifully attended university lectures on physiology. After passing his medical exams for the degree in 1869, he wrote a sketch of his philosophical gropings which put his own pain at the center of things: "Three quantities to determine. (1) how much pain I'll stand; (2) how much other's pain I'll inflict (by existing); (3) how much other's pain I'll 'accept,' without ceasing to take pleasure in their existence." [20] To a friend he confessed: "I am poisoned with Utilitarian venom, and sometimes when I despair of ever doing anything, say: 'Why not step out into the green darkness?'" [21] Similarly greenish in hue was his image of the idiotic, epileptic patient, huddled in the corner of his cell. To stick to his chosen path would be, in short, a kind of suicide. He could not find himself in medicine nor the acting self in medical materialism's picture of the world.

By 1872 James had discovered a desperately needed sense of initiative in the French philosopher Charles Renouvier's arguments for free will. He also passed up an opportunity "to strike at Harvard College" for a subprofessorship of philosophy, accepting instead an appointment there to teach physiology. "Philosophy I will nevertheless regard as my vocation and never let slip a chance to do a stroke at it," he confided to his diary. [22] Reluctant to accept a reappointment in physiology because he had such "arrears of lost time" in "the line of mental science," he nevertheless acquiesced on psychological grounds: "Philosophy as a *business* is not normal for most men, and not for me." Philosophic doubt was too unnerving because he was not yet prepared to make that much of a bid for autonomy: "My strongest moral and intellectual craving," he confessed, "is for some stable reality to lean upon." [23] In 1874, thirteen years after the onset of his psychosomatic troubles, his mother complained: "Whenever he speaks of himself he says he is no better. This I cannot believe to be the true state of the case, but his temperament is a morbidly hopeless one, and with this he has to contend all the time, as well as with his physical disability." [24]

In the year of his marriage in 1878 he signed a contract to write the *Principles of Psychology*. He spent twelve years on the book, delivering it at last like a man relieved of a kidney stone. "Seriously," he wrote an admiring reader, "your determination to read that fatal book is the one flaw in an otherwise noble nature. I wish that I had never written it." [25] As Perry notes, "he never afterwards produced any considerable article or book on the standard problems of psychology." [26] Not until the late 1890s, however, did he cut himself free of the laboratory work which he had always disliked; he advised a fellow sufferer to study philosophy with a good conscience because the best thing a man can work at "is usually the thing he does most spontaneously." Not until 1899 could he write:

> I have surrendered all psychological teaching to Munsterberg and his assistant and the thought of psycho-physical experimentation and altogether of brass-instrument and algebraic formula psychology fills me with horror. All my future activity will probably be metaphysical—that is, if I have any future activity, which I sometimes doubt. The Gifford Lectures . . . are a fine opportunity were I only able to meet it. [27]

At the age of fifty-seven James was at last prepared, with some trepidation, to give his full attention to those philosophical issues which had defined his ambition at the age of twenty-three. Suffering from a valvular lesion of the heart, he then spent six years trying to resign from Harvard. Four years after his resignation he died, convinced that his philosophy was "too much like an arch built only on one side." [28] Nearly all his major philosophical work, as Perry points out, began when he thought his professional career was finished.

The basic clue to understanding James's search for a vocation is provided by Erikson's remark in *Young Man Luther* that it is usually a parent, who has "selected this one child, because of an inner affinity paired with an insurmountable outer distance, as the particular child who must *justify the parent*," that by an "all-pervasive presence and brutal decisiveness of judgment" precipitates the child into "a fatal struggle for his own identity." [29] If in contemporary America that parent would usually be the mother, in Victorian America it would have been

the father. It is significant that James's vivid memory of the
shape in the asylum closely resembles a similar experience his
father suffered in 1844 when he felt "an insane and abject terror" before "some damned shape squatting invisible" to him
within his room "and raying out from his fetid personality influences fatal to life." [30] Henry James, senior, had written
Emerson one or two years earlier to seek help:

> What shall I do? Shall I get me a little nook in the country
> and communicate with my *living* kind, not my talking
> kind—by life only—a word, may be, of *that* communica-
> tion, a fit word, once a year? Or shall I follow some com-
> moner method, learn science and bring myself first into
> men's respect, that thus I may the better speak to them? I
> confess this last theory seems rank with earthliness—to
> belong to days forever past. [31]

Son of a rich Calvinist merchant, William's father had been cut
off without a legacy because of his worldly tastes and heretical
opinions. He had temporarily fled college to work as a
proofreader, made an abortive attempt to please his father by
studying law, and revolted against the Presbyterian orthodoxy
of Princeton Theological Seminary to become an original, if obscure and eccentric, theologian. Having broken his father's will,
he was able by his inheritance to devote himself entirely to his
writings and to his remarkable family, whom he shuttled
constantly about in America and Europe. In 1846 he was rescued from the "endless task of conciliating a stony-hearted
Deity"—*his* father's Calvinist God—by a conversion to Swedenborg, as William would be rescued from propitiating the deterministic god of medical materialism by conversion to the
philosophy of Renouvier and the idea of free will.

"The children were constantly with their parents and with
each other," as William's son later described his father's childhood, "and they continued all their lives to be united by much
stronger attachments than usually exist between members of
one family." [32] The elder James refused to send his sons to
college out of contempt for a gentleman's conventional education. Depositing them briefly with a succession of instructors,

he involved his sons mainly with his own spirited intellectual and moral reactions to the world. In his eldest son he must have seen an opportunity to realize his own forsaken alternative of trying to "learn science" and bring himself "into men's respect." A visionary advocate of freedom and spontaneous love, he was also a fierce polemicist. In the family circle as with strangers, the elder James spoke his mind with trenchant, witty, and brusque decisiveness. "What a passion your father has in writing and talking his religion!" exclaimed Oliver Wendell Holmes, Jr., a tough-minded skeptic. "Almost he persuadeth me to be a Swedenborgian."[33] For William, his father was a vivid, perpetual presence. After his father's death in 1882, the forty-year-old son made a significant confession:

> It is singular how I'm learning every day now how the thought of his comment on my experience has hitherto formed an integral part of my daily consciousness, without my having realized it at all. I interrupt myself incessantly now in the old habit of imagining what he will say when I tell him this or that thing I have seen or heard.[34]

His father was still an inner court of tribunal for him long after that is normally the case.

In this family it was easy for William to revolve his feelings and thoughts about his father because his mother had a soft spot for Henry, who was known in the family as "the Angel." Father himself, after his wife's death in 1881, felt that he had "fallen heir to all dear mother's fondness" for Henry, who had "cost us the least trouble, and given us always the most delight."[35] William, the oldest brother, had reason to be envious of Henry, who first achieved literary fame and financial independence. William's "hypochondriacal condition"—as his family called it—involved a set of highly charged elements: his career choice, his attraction to philosophy, but fear of embracing it; his dislike of practical scientific work, whether as collector, medical student, or laboratory psychologist; and his need to become financially independent. His father was closely linked to all these issues, and because Henry was obviously the mother's favorite, it was especially important for William to feel that he was in good standing with his father.

The sickness in this family gives deeper meaning to Perry's innocent remark about the James household that "the region of family life was not empty, but was charged with palpable and active forces." There is a strong hint of suppressed hostility in Alice James's confession that in her hysteria she sometimes felt "a violent inclination" to throw herself out of the window or "knock . . . off the head of the benignant Pater, as he sat, with his silver locks, writing at the table." The same point could be made of the benign father's remark to Emerson that he "wished sometimes the lightning would strike his wife and children out of existence, and he should suffer no more from loving them."[36] As the head of a religion with only one member, the father's life had something of the smell of futility about it, and his son felt uneasy about the prophet's role. "Certainly there is something disheartening in the position of an esoteric philosopher," he wrote in a letter he did not want shown to his father.[37] Although he followed his father's wish for a scientific career, the son could not but be aware that his father believed that science was ultimately inferior to metaphysics and religion. During his depressed years in Europe, he received from his father a nineteen-page letter of ontological speculation which boasted: "I am sure I have something better to tell you than you will be able to learn from all Germany—at least all scientific Germany. So urge me hard to your own profit."[38] Ambivalently attracted and repelled by both science and philosophy—an ambivalence connected with his feelings about his father's wishes, attitudes, and example—the son found his path hard to see clearly. He could not follow both his father's example and his advice—yet he tried to do both. The "sicker" he became, the more guilt he felt for prolonging his financial dependence. In his worst years, he made himself a pathetic parody of his father—a crippled philosopher without a job. "The crisis in such a young man's life," as Erikson has noted, "may be reached exactly when he half-realizes that he is fatally overcommitted to what he is not."[39] James made that discovery in medical school.

These emotional issues were linked to intellectual conflicts, for young men need ideological convictions to support their growing identity. During his period of invalidism, William wrote his brother Henry that their father was "a religious genius," but unfortunately his "absence of *intellectual* sympathies of any sort" made it hard to respond to "the positive side of him." [40] William James found himself in late adolescence "tending strongly to an empiristic view of life." Unlike his father, he was willing to believe that "God is dead or at least irrelevant, ditto everything pertaining to the 'Beyond,'" but the consequences left him full of doubt. The problem was "to get at something absolute without going out of your own skin!" [41] During his depression years, he was "going slowly" through his father's books; though he was impressed with their "definite residuum" of "great and original ideas," he could not find in them an explanation of his own torments. "For what purpose we are thus tormented I know not," he wrote his suffering brother in 1869. "I don't see that Father's philosophy explains it any more than anyone else's." He could not bring himself into so much sympathy "with the total process of the universe as heartily to assent to the evil that seems inherent in its details." He refused to "blink the evil out of sight, and gloss it over. It's as real as the good, and if it is denied, good must be denied too. It must be accepted and hated, and resisted while there's breath in our bodies." Like his father's peculiar blend of Swedenborg and Calvin, scientific determinism seemed to make these evils inevitable too—on physiological grounds. In April 1870 he finished reading Renouvier's essay on freedom and made his first act of positive belief: "My first act of free will shall be to believe in free will." [42]

James found a solution to the problem of determinism by sustaining a thought *"because I choose to* when I might have other thoughts." If he could not yet choose his vocation, he could validate choice in principle, and that freedom was enough to defend the moral power to fight evil. Erikson has relevantly observed that an aggravated identity crisis tends to generate a state of mind in which actual commitment is minimized, while an inner feeling of retaining the power of decision is maximized; at such a time, a person attempts to rebuild the shaky identifications of childhood, as if he wanted to be born again. [43] The general problem of determinism for William gained personal force from its association with his medical-scientific training and his need to find autonomy as a person. This issue was also intimately related to his involvement with his father. In his diary for 1868 the son noted: "My old trouble and the root of antinomianism in general seems to be a dissatisfaction with anything less than grace." He acknowledged that his antinomian tendency was partly derived from the example of his father, who always made "moralism the target of his hottest attack, and pitted religion and it against each other as enemies of whom one must die utterly, if the other is to live in genuine form." [44] The elder James routinely condemned moralists as prigs who believed that their good works entitled them to salvation. His "amiable ferocity was," as Perry well puts it, "an exercise in contempt for selfhood, on his own part and in behalf of others." [45] This contempt was an unrecognized threat to a conscientious boy struggling to find his own sense of self and to be responsive to his father's attitudes. The elder James believed that men fell from grace individually, but could be saved collectively in a redeemed socialized society. His son, however, needed an individual salvation not only through faith, but also in works. To translate this theological idiom, he needed to believe that there was point and purpose to some particular work of his own with social meaning. He would finally save himself through his writing, finding courage in Carlyle's gospel of work, forgetting complaint and rapture alike in "the vision of certain works to be done . . . for the leaving of them undone is perdition." [46] To his father's antinomianism, he would oppose an Arminian emphasis on work, a moral equivalent for "the strenuous life" idealized in his period by Roosevelt, Holmes, and the naturalistic novelists London, Norris, and Dreiser.

The connection between the intellectual and emotional development of William James can be followed in the growth of his work and the betterment of his health, as he successfully but slowly came to terms with his father's teachings and example. Four days before his father died in 1882, the son wrote him from Europe: "All my intellectual life I derive from you. . . . What my debt to you is goes beyond all my power of estimating—so early, so penetrating and so constant has been the influence." And he concluded this great and touching letter with a final benediction: "Good-night, my sacred old Father! If I don't see you again—Farewell! a blessed farewell!"[47] At the age of forty, the son would also very slowly bid farewell to his scientific career and gradually move from psychology toward those deep interests he shared with his father in religion and metaphysics. As he abandoned his image of himself as a scientist, he learned to yield to his spontaneous interest in philosophy, which had been born in his crisis of health and career in Brazil. He would increasingly see himself as well enough in body and strong enough in ego to become a philosopher by vocation, assimilating and rejecting aspects of his father's personality in a new configuration.

The father died a year after the mother. James was now the eldest in the family. He was alone in Europe, seeking respite from the burdens of his own family and having trouble getting his book under way. He was also in correspondence with Renouvier, whose philosophy had "saved" him in 1870. In the French philosopher, James found much-needed intellectual sympathy and encouragement for his own philosophical talents. "Your thinking," the Frenchman told him, "springs from a source that is original and profound, and bears the stamp of what you yourself feel—of something that comes, indeed, from your very self." The American was, he felt, much too modest about his philosophical efforts. "It seems to me when I read you," he wrote him, "that you are called to found an *American philosophy*."[48] The power of Renouvier's productive energies in his old age would later prompt James in his last years to form the intention of writing "a somewhat systematic book on philosophy—my humble view of the world—pluralistic, ty- chistic, empiricist, pragmatic, and ultra-gothic, *i.e.*, non-classic in form."[49] By then, Renouvier himself would seem "too classic in the general rationalism of his procedure," and James would be too near the end of his life. In 1883, however, he was under- going a new sense of health and direction. Suffering from eye trouble, he had written but six pages of the *Psychology*. Two weeks after hearing of his father's death, he wrote his brother Henry that he felt "a different man" and was resolved to return home to his wife and children, amazed that a "change of weather could effect such a revolution."

In the winter following his father's death James wrote "The Dilemma of Determinism"—a blow for freedom against both scientific and religious monistic views of the world and the first of the characteristically Jamesian essays on the open universe which he had struggled to glimpse out of the pain of his own constricted conflicts. That same year, in filial tribute, he edited his father's *Literary Remains*, as he had promised, and in the following year he noted a definite improvement in his eyesight: "It has continued gradually, so that practically I can use them all I will. It saves my life. *Why* it should come now when, bully them as I would, it wouldn't come in in the past few years, is one of the secrets of the nervous system which the last trump . . . may reveal." [50] James now found in Josiah Royce a worthy beloved opponent, provoking James's "highest flight of ambitious ideality," as he affectionately told him, to become his conqueror and "go down into history as such . . . rolled in one another's arms and silent (or rather loquacious still) in one last death-grapple of an embrace." [51] It was as if he had transferred some of his emotions about his father to the monistic religious idealist he had brought to Harvard in the year of his father's death.

The accounts, however, were not yet settled with his scientific career. Not until the late 1890s had he worked himself free of laboratory work. Philosophy was still a source of morbid feelings. In 1895, he confessed to a fellow philosopher:

> I am a victim of neurasthenia, and of the sense of hollowness and unreality that goes with it. And philosophic literature *will* often seem to me the hollowest thing. . . .
> —When it will end with me I do not know. I wish I could give it all up. But perhaps it is a grand climacteric and will pass away. At present I am philosophizing as little as possible in order to do it the better next year, if I can do it at all. [52]

That summer he delivered his famous lecture on "The Will to Believe"—the justification of believing, under certain circumstances, beyond the evidence, the argument of a man who, as Perry notably remarked, had always "suffered from incredulity." At the turn of the century a heart lesion forced him to postpone the Gifford Lectures, finally published in 1902 as *The Varieties of Religious Experience*. This book was his grand effort to incorporate "Father's cry" that "religion is real," a cry the son had earlier resolved someday to voice.[53] Now he did so on his own terms. He, like his father, was a "twice-born sick soul," the type he placed at the center of religious insight, and like his father, James was now convinced that religion was closer than physical science to ultimate reality: "Assuredly the real world is of a different temperament—more intricately built than physical science allows." Religion, because of its concern for the private destiny of the individual, grasped the personal nature of reality, which science lost hold of in its search for symbolic generalizations. Like the psychiatrist, the artist, and the existentialist philosopher, James felt that the self was the locus of fundamental reality: "The axis of reality runs solely through the egotistic places—they are strung upon it like so many beads."[54] Yet James remained honestly agnostic, making no personal "over-beliefs" in God or immortality and steadfastly refusing to give any cosmic apology for evil. While his sympathies went out to the "sick souls," who had a more profound sense of existence than the "healthy-minded," he was also drawn to the healthy-minded pluralists who resolutely gave no quarter in their struggle with evil. This divided sympathy reflected his personal history. He had been a sick soul who became healthy minded through intellectual resistance to scientific and theological monism. While he always felt that his episode of panic fear had a religious bearing because he had afterward clung in desperation to scriptural texts, it was rather through his own "twice-born" pluralism that he made an original contribution to the varieties of religious experience.

Having settled his intellectual accounts with his father, he was now prepared to devote himself to philosophy, writing freely "without feeling in the least degree fatigued." But he had only a few years left. "I live in apprehension lest the Avenger should cut me off," he wrote in 1906, "before I get my message out. It is an aesthetic tragedy to have a bridge begun and stopped in the middle of an arch."[55] James died with his "somewhat systematic" book unfinished. He had been able to assure Royce in 1877 that "a young man might rightfully devote himself to philosophy if he chose," an assurance James found so very difficult to achieve for himself.[56] From a psychoanalytic point of view, the resolution of critical emotional issues in infancy "will determine whether an individual is apt to be dominated by a sense of autonomy, or by a sense of shame and doubt," and the way in which adults meet the child's shame and doubt "determines much of a man's future ability to combine an unimpaired will with ready self-discipline, rebellion with responsibility." Significantly, the father's crisis happened when the son was two years old, struggling to form his first sense of will. His later development illustrates the psychoanalytic point that "the neurotic ego has, by definition, fallen prey to overidentification and to faulty identifications with disturbed parents."[57] The historian must add that while the elder Henry James had made the son's struggle for identity particularly difficult he had also made the resolution of that struggle particularly fruitful. His influence largely determined the kinds of problems that would be central for his son's intellectual development. That influence delayed the son's maturity, but it also enriched it by giving him that double focus on science and religion and that note of authenticity in dealing with the issues of freedom and determinism which stamped his work as vividly original. The father must also have engendered the son's charming tolerance of cranks and vigorous scorn for prigs of all kinds. William James had selectively assimilated and rejected what his father meant to him in a struggle of fifty years' duration.

The creative man, as Erikson has observed, has to face the risks of neurotic suffering:

> Once the issue is joined, his task proves to be at the same time intimately related to his most personal conflicts, to his superior selective perception, and to the stubbornness of his one-way will: he must court sickness, failure, or insanity, in order to test the alternative whether the established world will crush him, or whether he will disestablish a sector of this world's outworn fundaments and make a place for a new one.[58]

James would have understood this point better than most philosophers. "In any minute of moral action where the path is difficult," he wrote George Santayana, "I believe a man has deeper dealings with life than he could have in libraries of philosophizing." [59] His own life was a painful, eloquent witness to this truth.

Most people, faced with such a parent as James had, learn how to evade or compromise in order finally to get their way. William's own son, "Billy," tried medical school for a melancholy year and then happily took up painting—the reverse of his father's sequence. Others make nothing distinctively great out of similar troubles. William's Swiss friend Théodore Flournoy was also depressed by his laboratory work in psychology, but could never marshal the strength to follow James's advice to give it up for philosophy. Sometimes, as Erikson has remarked, an individual feels "called upon" instead to "try to solve for all what he could not solve for himself alone." [60] By whom and by what he is called, the psychoanalyst adds, are mysteries which only theologians and bad psychologists dare to explain. James himself believed that individuality is founded in "the recesses of feeling, the darker, blinder strata of character." [61] In *The Varieties of Religious Experience*, he modified his earlier theory of the great man and offered a radical explanation for the mystery of his appearance: "Thus, when a superior intellect and a psychopathic temperament coalesce . . . in the same individual, we have the best possible condition for the kind of effective genius that gets into the biographical dictionaries." [62] Such men are possessed by their ideas, he added, and inflict them, for better or worse, upon their contemporaries. It is part of the ethical meaning of James's greatness that in this case the suffering was his, the enlightenment ours.

Looking backward, it seems an extraordinarily symbolic moment in time when James met Freud at Clark University in 1909. A decade earlier James had praised Freud's work on "the buried life of human beings"—that "unuttered inner at-. mosphere" in which the nervous patient "dwells alone with the secrets of its prison-house," full of "old regrets, ambitions checked by shames and aspirations obstructed by timidities," breeding "a general self-mistrust." [63] James spoke from experience, but unlike Freud, he was never able to systematize his troubles into a revolutionary new theory of the mind. Rather, his genius was for sketching a world in which truth was profoundly human and, like action itself, a genuine addition to a reality still in the making. "Admit plurality, and time may be its form," he wrote in "The Dilemma of Determinism," a remark which points toward a profoundly historical view of the world. Pluralism characterized his life as well as his thought. Perhaps the incompleteness of his philosophy is a mark of his failure to achieve that masterful and compelling power which the greatest thinkers have, exerting their force on followers and critics alike for generations to come, as Freud certainly did. But in an age when all systems are undergoing revision, and many have collapsed beyond repair, there is still something fertile in James's critique of "the block universe" and the synoptic vision which would claim to encompass it.

Psychology itself now reflects a more existential and historically oriented mode of analysis, of which Erikson's work is a primary example. Surely the author of *The Varieties of Religious Experience: A Study in Human Nature* would have found *Young Man Luther* a deeply congenial book. It is aesthetically satisfying that the kind of study which Erikson's book illustrated and spurred two decades ago should be luminously relevant to explaining William James's troubled history. James would not have been surprised, for he knew that the discovery of the "subliminal self"—as he called it—was the door through which entered the experiences that have had emphatic influence in shaping religious history, including (we must add) his own.

For James, however, the subconscious was not always the same concept that it was for Freud. Sometimes James spoke in Freudian terms of "whole systems of underground life, in the shape of memories of a painful sort which lead a parasitic existence, buried outside the primary fields of consciousness, and making irruptions thereinto with hallucinations, pains, convulsions, paralyses of feeling and of motion, and the whole procession of symptoms of hysteric disease of body and of mind." [64] He could also say that "on our hypothesis it is primarily the higher faculties of our own hidden mind which are controlling," a position reminiscent of the transcendentalists.[65] This dual emphasis partly reflected his distinction between the *"farther side"* and the *"hither side"* of the subconscious self; he focused on the nearer side in order to examine religious experience. Certainly he had something of the healer in him—a residue of his medical training, as well as something of the Swedenborgian mystic, like his father. Unfortunately, James's interest in the cults of "mind-cure" and Christian Science made him vulnerable to being classified as a facile "positive thinker." We too often forget that in his mature work, the *Pragmatism* of 1907, he cried out with a tragic sense that John Dewey never had:

> Is the last word sweet? Is all "yes, yes" in the universe? Doesn't the fact of "no" stand at the very core of life? Doesn't the very "seriousness" that we attribute to life mean that ineluctable noes and losses form a part of it, that there are genuine sacrifices somewhere, and that something permanently drastic and bitter always remains at the bottom of its cup?[66]

And he associated this theme with his willingness to treat pluralism as a serious hypothesis.

James presented pragmatism as a reasonable synthesis of the two temperaments he called "the tough-minded" and "the tender-minded," but he personally believed that "the prodigal-son attitude . . . is not the right and final attitude towards the whole of life."[67] In the end, he remained a sympathetic agnostic, flirting with the idea of a finite God who needed men. In his more "tough-minded" moments, as Donald Meyer has acutely noted in *The Positive Thinkers*, James was (in retrospect) an important figure in the history of the movement which—from Anna Freud, through Heinz Hartmann, Ernst Kris, and David Rapaport, to Erik Erikson—has developed an existentially oriented ego psychology.[68] For all of them, the life of the self is portrayed not as a bland voyage on a smooth sea, but as a rugged willingness to encounter conflict and evil and so to transform oneself. A thinker sometimes comes into perspective as a leader only after those who come later can identify him as a forerunner of their own leadership. William James was such a man, and those who can revise our conception of ourselves are surely, at last, as influential as any leaders that history knows.

(1968)

## Notes

1. William James, *Selected Papers on Philosophy* (New York, Everyman Edition), p. 180.
2. Ibid., p. 181.
3. James to Henry James, 4 May 1907, in *Letters of William James*, ed. Henry James, 2d ed., 2 vols. (Boston, 1926), 2:279; H. Stuart Hughes, *Consciousness and Society: The Reorientation of European Social Thought 1890–1930* (New York, 1958), p. 397.
4. William James, "Great Men and Their Environment," in James, *Selected Papers*, p. 192.
5. Erik H. Erikson, *Young Man Luther: A Study in Psychoanalysis and History* (New York, 1958), pp. 14–15. Erikson's concept of the identity crisis has proved to be of great value in understanding James.
6. Ibid., p. 110.
7. Walter E. Houghton, *The Victorian Frame of Mind 1830–1870* (New Haven, Conn., 1957), especially pp. 58–109.
8. Ralph Barton Perry, ed., *The Thought and Character of William James* (Boston, 1935), 2:122. Perry explains James's troubles only by reference to "morbid traits," as if they had no history.
9. Ibid., 1:192.
10. James to Charles Ritter, 31 July 1860, ibid., 1:193; James to Henry James, Jr., 10 October 1872, ibid., 1:330.
11. Quoted in Leon Edel, *Henry James: The Untried Years, 1843–1870* (Philadelphia, 1953), pp. 174–75.
12. James to Katherine Temple, September 1861. *Letters of William James*, 1:40; ibid., p. 32.
13. Perry, *William James*, 1:220. James to his family, 3–10 May 1865, ibid., p. 219.
14. James to Tom Ward, 24 May 1868. James Papers, Houghton Library, Harvard University; 12 September 1867, Perry, *William James*, 1:244.
15. James to Henry James, Jr., 12 June 1869, Perry, *William James*, 1:300.
16. James to Tom Ward, January 1868, *Letters of William James*, 1:129; Perry, *William James*, 2:675.
17. Perry, *William James*, 1:142.
18. James to Tom Ward, 9 October 1868, ibid., p. 287.
19. James to his father, November 1861, ibid., p. 211.

20. Ibid., p. 302.

21. James to Tom Ward, 9 October (1868), ibid., p. 287.

22. Diary, 10 February 1873, ibid., p. 335.

23. James to Henry James, Jr., 10 October 1872; ibid., p. 341; Diary, 10 April 1873, p. 343.

24. Ibid., 2:673.

25. James to Mrs. Whitman, 15 October 1890, *Letters of William James*, 1:304.

26. Perry, *William James*, 2:125.

27. James to Theodore Flournoy, 19 September 1892, *Letters of William James*, 1:325; James to Carl Stumpf, 10 September 1899, Perry, *William James*, 2:195.

28. William James, *Some Problems in Philosophy: A Beginning of an Introduction* (New York, 1911), p. viii. Also see chapter 3.

29. Erikson, *Young Man Luther*, p. 65.

30. Quoted by Austin Warren, *The Elder Henry James* (New York, 1934), pp. 56–57; Perry, *William James*, 1:21.

31. James to Emerson (1842?), Perry, *William James*, 1:43.

32. *Letters of William James*, 1:19.

33. O. W. Holmes, Jr., to James, 15 December 1867, Perry, *William James*, 1:507.

34. Ibid., p. 142.

35. James to Henry James, Jr., 9 May (1882?), ibid., p. 112.

36. Ibid., p. 171; F. O. Matthiessen, *The James Family* (New York, 1961), p. 276; Perry, *Wiliam James*, 1:3.

37. James to O. W. Holmes, Jr., 15 May 1868, Perry, *William James*, 1:517.

38. Henry James, Sr., to James, 27 September 1867, ibid., 2:711.

39. Erikson, *Young Man Luther*, p. 43.

40. Perry, *William James*, 1:151.

41. James to O. W. Holmes, Jr., 18 May 1868, ibid., pp. 516–17; James to Tom Ward, 9 October 1868, ibid., p. 287.

42. James to Henry James, Jr., 2 October 1869, ibid., pp. 306–8; 7 May 1870, *Letters of William James*, 1:158; Diary, 1 February 1870, and 30 April 1870, Perry, *William James*, pp. 322–23.

43. Erik H. Erikson, "The Problem of Ego Identity," *Psychological Issues*, 1 (1959):123–24, 129.

44. Diary, 21 April 1868, James Papers, Houghton Library, Harvard University; Perry, *William James*, 1:164, quoted from introduction, *The Literary Remains of the Late Henry James*.

45. Perry, *William James*, 1:133.

46. William James, "The Dilemma of Determinism," in *Essays on Faith and Morals*, ed. Ralph Barton Perry (New York, 1947), p. 174.

47. James to Henry James, Sr., 14 December 1882, *Letters of William James*, 1:218–20.

48. Renouvier to James, 28 May and 5 September 1882, Perry, *William James*, 1:678–79.

49. Ibid., p. 710.

50. James to Henry James, Jr., 23 January 1883, ibid., p. 389; April 1885, *Letters of William James*, 1:242–43. He did complain again about his eyes in 1887, but not severely, and presbyopic spectacles seem to have solved the problem. *Letters of William James*, 1:262. In his pictures he does not wear spectacles.

51. James to Josiah Royce, 26 September 1900, Perry, *William James*, 1:817.

52. James to G. W. Howison, 17 July 1895, ibid., 2:207–8.

53. Ibid., 1:165.

54. William James, *The Varieties of Religious Experience: A Study in Human Nature* (New York, 1928), pp. 519, 499.

55. James to Théodore Flournoy, 8 February 1905, Robert C. LeClair, ed., *The Letters of William James and Théodore Flournoy* (Madison, 1966), p. 163; to Henry James, Jr., 10 September 1906, *Letters of William James*, 2:259.

56. Perry, *William James*, 1:779.

57. Erikson, *Young Man Luther*, p. 255; Erikson, "Identity and the Life Cycle," *Psychological Issues* 1 (1959), p. 90.

58. Erikson, *Young Man Luther*, p. 46.

59. James to George Santayana, 2 January 1888, Perry, *William James*, 1:403.

60. Erickson, *Young Man Luther*, p. 67.

61. James, *Varieties of Religious Experience*, pp. 501–2.

62. Ibid., pp. 23–24.

63. William James, *Talks to Teachers of Psychology* (New York, 1916), p. 203.

64. James, *Varieties of Religious Experience*, pp. 234–35.

65. Ibid., p. 513,

66. William James, *Pragmatism: A New Name for Some Old Way of Thinking* [1907] (New York, 1919), p. 295.

67. Ibid., p. 296.

68. Donald Meyer, *The Positive Thinkers* (New York, 1965), p. 284.

# 12 / Ego Psychology and the Historian

From the standpoint of methodological puritanism historians have always lived in sin, loosely cohabiting with a variety of mistresses from theology to sociology. Historians have drawn on other fields for metaphors, data, categories, and explanations, yet whatever they have borrowed they necessarily have made over in their fashion to suit their own terms and purposes. With proper pride they have refused the role of being mere field hands for other explainers, self-appointed overseers on the plantation of knowledge. This point is often puzzling to social scientists, who are sometimes tempted to complain that historians have no specific subject or method and that therefore their manners should be more humble. For their part, historians are likely to be particularly on guard against presumed friends who offer them methodological help in the form of disguised contempt for the historian's alleged dependence on a primitive common sense. Properly understood, his common sense is at its best a recognition of the nature of documentary reasoning and of the particular kind of focus that historical questions bring to bear on evidence. At its worst such common sense is only another name for ignorance and fear of the unfamiliar, an unearned and inflated professional pride that masks an anxious fear for a threatened status in an academic world in which other subjects currently have more prestige. It is not always clear whether the best or the worst motives are operative because they may be deeply entangled.

The present condition of the historian's ordinary attitude toward psychoanalysis is an important case of this problematic mixture of motives; it needs careful discrimination for the sake of highlighting the genuine methodological issues at stake. I shall plunge into this thicket as an intellectual historian with an interest in both philosophy and psychoanalysis and a recent experience of collaboration with a psychiatrist.

During its formative years in Europe psychoanalysis was often most attractive to humanistic scholars, rather than doctors, and Freud himself was strongly opposed to having it treated as a medical specialty. While "depth psychology" has notoriously permeated American culture, it has had surprisingly little impact on the historical profession. Unfortunately, when psychoanalysts, professional or amateur, have turned to history, they have often bolstered the historian's easy conscience about his indifference to their method by confirming his worst fears that it is incurably polemical, farfetched, and crudely oblivious to the rational, cognitive, and moral capacities of men.[1] A dogmatic assumption that man's fate is a monotonous repetition of early childhood conflicts not only offends the historian's sensitivity to change and development, but it also misdirects his attention to stages of life for which he can seldom find documentary evidence. Furthermore, such data themselves seem to depend upon first being seen through controversial psychoanalytic categories before they can even be identified as "fact" for confirming the hypotheses offered to explain them. It is no surprise, given this conception of psychoanalysis, that historians commonly conclude that in this area professional ignorance is bliss.

Yet, whatever the status of Freud's views on dream interpretation, libidinal energy, and the oedipus complex, many of his terms for "defense mechanisms" have proved to be useful in historical interpretation, while at the same time the development of modern ego psychology in a style more existentialist than scientific has made psychoanalytic thinking much more congenial to historical inquiry. At the level of historical analysis of group attitudes, it is increasingly clear that in discussing such familiar topics as messianic zeal, ethnic prejudice, ideological suspicion, or persistent images of other countries and peoples, historians have profited from using (sometimes implicitly) the concepts of *displacement, projection, compensation, repression, and ambivalence.*[2] The processes to which Freud gave these names are capable of being lifted from his clinical and theoretical contexts for them because they point to the fact that groups employ various strategies to protect a threatened sense of identity, to objectify fears and hopes, or to compensate for unsatisfied needs. Their verification does not depend upon the validity of the connections that Freud made between these defenses and his specific sexual theories, nor does it depend upon any dubious analogies between the psychosexual etiology of an individual and the social history of a group. If there are any causal connections between child-rearing practices and group characteristics, they "explain" too much to be of any particular use in accounting for specific social events. A given social character is compatible with a very wide range of ideals and actions.

The historical relevance of psychoanalytic theory would appear to be strongest in the biographical case when individual character formation is at issue. Historians commonly acknowledge the importance of biographies by writing and reading them voluminously. In some circumstances individual character may be important even for understanding the course of events, whenever a person has an opportunity to influence the outcome by tenacity or by vacillation, flexibility or rigidity, timidity or courage, shrewdness or obtuseness, magnanimity or spitefulness. Because public and universal issues come to a focus of clarification in individual minds, the historian cannot read individual persons out of his story, and those who once protested against a drum-and-trumpet historiography that was too fond of kings and generals transformed it not by eliminating individuals from their accounts, but by replacing the familiar figures with businessmen, inventors, scientists, philosophers, and artists.[3] Even "institutional historians" speak of individuals when they treat of innovation or describe "representative men." To abstract entirely from individual persons would be to transcend history itself. Even so, historians may rightly say that though they pay attention to individuals and sometimes speak of character, they do not necessarily need to rely on Freudian theories.

For some purposes of historical analysis we want to know a man's self-conscious ideas, opinions, and values; for others we want to know his conscious feelings, often demonstrated in his actions; for still others we want to know his deep-rooted biases. In none of them are we *compelled* to appeal to psychoanalytic categories. We may find it more appropriate to talk about the explanatory relevance of social class, regional loyalty, national customs, religious traditions, occupational traits, or ethnic dispositions—all produced by historical experience. The historian may be forced by his evidence, however, to consider problems and raise questions that he cannot treat intelligently without benefit of the psychoanalyst's experience. The historical subject may have experienced bouts of depression, suicidal inclinations, inorganic illness, inability to work, intense phobias, bizarre visions, inappropriate affects, or paradoxical behavior—all signs of deep internal conflict. Such material has invited psychoanalytic probing of figures like Luther, Darwin, Mill, Schopenhauer, Goethe, Johnson, Boswell, Swedenborg, William James, Henry James, and Freud himself. With these men psychic disturbance is intimately connected with the development of their work and ideas, as Charles Renouvier saw clearly when he said of William James: "Your thinking springs from a source that is original and profound, and bears the stamp of what you yourself feel—of something that comes, indeed, from your very self."[4] For many creative men, whose willingness to probe reality may lead them to be open to deeper conflicts than most people dare to let themselves in for, the depths of their lives call out for an analysis that common sense cannot make. Such people only make more evident and intense the conflicts which in ordinary psychic growth are more blandly resolved.

For understanding such historically influential and significant figures the development of ego psychology has been particularly relevant. Erik H. Erikson has sketched a schedule of stages in the life cycle in which a balance between opposing psychic tendencies is struck and reintegrated at successive levels, with new strengths and new vulnerabilities, qualified by the earlier resolutions. Its most familiar and useful concept has been that of the "identity crisis" of late adolescence and early adulthood, because it is that period in which the historian's subject is self-conscious and mature enough to produce literary evidence and because it is then that he faces most directly the identity-defining choices of vocations and mates which are critical for his future development. In that crisis the subject's conflicts reanimate earlier tensions of his psychic growth, as he seeks to renew or redefine identifications made in childhood.[5] Erikson's scheme also provides a central clue: if the crisis is deeply disturbing, beyond the usual intensities of adolescence, it is commonly because a parent "out of an inner affinity and an insurmountable outer distance has selected this child as the particular child who must *justify the parent*" and who by an "all-pervasive presence and brutal decisiveness of judgment" precipitates the child into "a fatal struggle for his own identity."[6]

To work out the implications of this framework for a particular case is not a question of fixing labels but of thinking one's way into the specific situation of such a person, so far as the evidence can support it, in order to see how in detail his thoughts, feelings, and actions can be understood as a process over time of an unconscious effort—*in conjunction with conscious aims*—to assimilate and reject in a new configuration aspects of identity which the significant others in his family (or their surrogates) represent for him. In this light "symptoms" are not disease entities, like foreign bodies, but dramatic expressions of the ego's difficulties in finding its way to autonomy, and their interpretation calls for incorporation of psychoanalytic thinking into the historian's mind by way of his ability to see psychic disorder, distress, and disability as a language which, because of repression, cannot be put into words. That repression may, in fact, as Freud found, be a widespread cultural trait. For this work the investigator has to be as attentive to the symbolic meaning of language and experience as literary critics are, and no amount of information about "rules" will substitute for that empathetic effort which taxes the historian's own capacity to be aware of his own feelings and conflicts. For this reason the historian is well advised to do such work in close collaboration with a psychoanalytically trained person, who can teach the historian as he is taught by him, so that they can bring together the kind of insights which their particular training has engendered.

This kind of collaboration is in principle possible because Eriksonian psychoanalytic thinking is closer to individuating humanistic thinking than to scientific "covering law" thinking. It provides the historian with a task, and he can fit himself for it only by acquiring a balanced awareness of social and intellectual factors, as well as of the psychic strengths and weaknesses of a growing young person. This work demands a heightened sensitivity to the intersections of the development of family-centered difficulties with social and cultural history, for they interact and resonate with each other. Such analysis can be convincingly presented, in large part, only in the form of a story, not in the abstraction of a kernel of generalization from a mere husk of detail. (Perhaps for this reason, it is avant-garde dramatists who have recently been fascinated by such figures as Luther, Oppenheimer, Marat, Sade, Thomas à Becket, St. Thomas More, and Tom Paine.)

The Eriksonian framework has the advantage for the historian of indicating specific things to look for: idological turmoil, a psychic "moratorium" or postponement, an overcommitment to a wrong choice, a harking back in the identity crisis to the shame and doubt of an earlier stage of emotional development, a perfectionist conscience that inhibits helpful apprenticeships, and the expression of overidentification with troublesome parental figures. Tracing the course of this crisis, the historian stays alert to the way in which private and public matters intermingle, each imbuing itself to some extent with the nature of the other. Just as young people are formed in part by elements at work in the wider world beyond their family circle, so also do parents themselves incorporate cultural forces in their behavior and values. These complications demand binocular vision.

Procedural principles may emerge more clearly in the light of a brief sketch of the course of inquiry that issued in my own psychohistorical essay on William James.[7] I undertook the research on James's identity crisis in close collaboration with a historically interested friend and psychiatrist, Dr. Howard Feinstein. We set ourselves the problem of understanding the genesis and resolution of James's troubles in the hope that they would illuminate his vocational and intellectual career, perhaps helping to explain the paradox of his long deferment of an early ambition to be a philosopher by compromises made with other vocations—natural history, medicine, and laboratory psychology. His classic biography pointed out that he did most of his professional work in philosophy after he thought his academic career was finished, and it gave attention to his "morbid traits" without accounting for their genesis.[8] We found that the biographer had considerably foreshortened the actual period of James's nervous difficulties and in some cases elided from his letters material having a direct bearing on those troubles. Having established a more accurate chronology, we were able to discriminate some typical psychosomatic symptoms. One of these had originally been organic (disease-connected) and had disappeared only to be revived later in a context of anxiety over career choice, the same sort of setting in which the disease-connected symptom had first appeared. Our research—seen in abstraction from its buzzing, disputatious, and groping actuality—was then directed by a series of questions, each triggered by the finding of documentable answers to the preceding ones:

In what context (vocational, familial, sexual) did the symptoms reach a crisis? In what context did they tend to disappear? What covert protest or excuse did they serve? Why was a covert language needed? What enduring, recurring intrapersonal conflict of wishes could be documented? How were these wishes related to identifications with persons revered as models? Were the identifications unusually ardent and enduring? What were the specific difficulties of identifying with such a person? What "messages" did the older person give to the younger? Were they consistent or conflicting? If conflicting, how did they relate to the ambivalence of the younger person toward certain career goals? Were there signs of conflict, interpersonal and intrapersonal, in the older person himself? When did his crisis occur in relation to his growth and that of his child's? Why, in this family, should this particular relationship be so important to both? How did the younger react to the older's death? How did ideological concerns relate to identity-formation struggles? What congruence and resonance could be found between intellectual texts and their contexts of emotional conflict? What adaptive functions did the "troubles" serve, what ego strengths were also developed, not merely complicated, by the troubled relationship? What intellectual sustenance did it provide? How did the historical milieu, throughout, frame the range of the person's choices, color the imagery of his symptoms, and influence his feelings about sex, work, family, and ideals?

Documentable answers to these queries can be presented in narrative form only by constant exercise of a binocular vision of both emotional and intellectual problems, familial and cultural issues. Just as the Eriksonian description of the identity crisis had helped us to orient our investigation, so also did our research tend to confirm the explanatory pertinence of four of Erikson's points: (1) the neurotic ego has "fallen prey to overidentification and to faulty identifications with disturbed parents";[9] (2) a parent of dominating presence who selects a child to justify himself precipitates in the child a struggle for his identity; (3) the crisis is often reached when the young person "half-realizes that he is fatally overcommitted to what he is not";[10] (4) the resolution of early childhood isssues, when shame and doubt are in tension with feelings of autonomy, will "determine much of a man's future ability to combine an unimpaired will with ready self-discipline, rebellion with responsibility."[11] It is important to emphasize, however, that we did not begin with these propositions; they became relevant through our inquiry. It is necessary, furthermore, to show the *specific* difficulties in *this* child's involvement with *his* parent, to see why *this* father had *these* hopes for his child, and to show that the crisis of the symptoms *did* coincide with the troubled discovery of an overcommitment. Furthermore, the fourth proposition (in this case) is only a possible inference, consistent with psychoanalytic theory, from the fact that the father's disrupting hallucination coincided with the developmental stage of infant will in his son; it cannot be supported by direct evidence of the child's troubled feelings. What can be shown, however, is that James's paradoxical postponement of a youthful philosophical ambition is intelligible in the light of his conflicted efforts to assimilate and reject aspects of his father's personality in a new configuration. It is equally clear that the development of the son's philosophy was deeply implicated in his identity crisis and his profound engagement with his father's example, advice, and theories. Analysis of this genesis illuminates the meaning of James's voluntarism, pluralism, and meliorism, though it does not, of course, encompass it. No *historical* questioning can ever properly lead to answers that would make irrelevant the need to confront James as a philosopher with *philosophical* questions.

These connections are of configural congruence and resonance, not of causality. They settle nothing about the truth or error of James's philosophy. They do help us, however, to appreciate the chronology of his works and the meaning and urgency of many of his ideas. They illuminate, for example, his divided sympathy for "healthy-minded" pluralists and the monistic insights of the "sick soul" because he himself had been a sick soul who became healthy in the course of formulating his pluralistic philosophy, a goal toward which he moved more confidently and steadily after his father's death. Since James characteristically emphasized the existential context of thought, the investigation of his own struggles for autonomy is peculiarly appropriate. Finally, just as Freud's own troubles provided the basis for his psychoanalytic theory and practice, so also did James's psychological difficulties powerfully suggest to him the importance for psychological theory and religious experience of what he called "the subliminal self."

This combination of psychoanalytical and intellectual history can also stimulate other potentially significant questions: Are there significant patterns in the identity crisis of Victorian intellectuals which may tell us something about the Victorian upper-class family? Do the differences in the imagery (supernaturalistic versus naturalistic) of the pathogenic visions experienced by both father and son locate a cultural transition point between the treatment of psychic troubles as "sins" and as "neuroses"?[12] Why did James, who was acquainted with Freud's work and the man himself, come to significantly different psychological conclusions? Does James's extraordinary popular influence have anything to do with the troubles he experienced? Could one find in his followers some echo of his own difficulties? Is American optimism, so often associated with James, perhaps more often affiliated by "reaction formation" to experiences of despair and suffering? They led James himself, in his classic *Pragmatism*, to say of experience that "something permanently drastic and bitter always remains at the bottom of its cup," surely one of the most neglected passages in all the commentary on American philosophy.[13] Our work provoked, without answering, such historical questions.

Our interior view of the lives of the James family also deepened our appreciation of how cultural issues, connected with religion, had powerful repercussions on the formation of personalities. We understood better how the grandfather's rigid Calvinism posed problems for William's father, who rebelled against his parent, and how the residual Calvinism in the elder Henry James undermined William's need for self-respect and for belief in the efficacy of moral striving. In this way we felt that our research had contributed something not only to biography but also to intellectual and to social history, however special a case the James family may seem to be. The historical value of such unusually articulate and conflict-ridden people is the power they have of bringing issues of general significance to a more vivid, intense, and clarifying focus. We not only see into them; they enable us to see into some of the profound issues of their time. As leaders, they consciously grapple with problems that others only obscurely feel.

Freud pointed out in a brilliant passage that "in one way the neuroses show a striking and far-reaching correspondence with the great social productions of art, religion, and philosophy, while again they seem like distortions of them. We may say that hysteria is a caricature of an artistic creation, a compulsion neurosis a caricature of a religion, and a paranoiac delusion a caricature of a philosophical system."[14] This affinity of psychic "illness" with self-conscious mind is the fundamental reason why those who are accustomed, in Collingwood's phrase, to "reenact" the actions of others in the course of constructing historical narratives can, by extension, learn to envisage for themselves the deeper motives at work in the growth of a personality.[15] Such historians will not find themselves able to proceed by pasting labels; they will be forced instead to undertake the plunge into the depths of trying through the evidence to envisage at every significant stage of the person's career how the conflicting feelings at work in him are entangled with his rational thinking, as he strives to become a person in his own right. If we ask how unconscious feelings can be grasped, the answer is that language itself, as well as action, is full of hints for observers ready to be attentive to them. When, for example, James wryly observes that "relentless Chemistry has claimed its hapless victim," or predicts that his following his father's wishes for his son's scientific career will eventuate in "death, death, death with plethora of knowledge," the historian who does not know that such jests can tell deeper truths is listening with an insufficiently sensitized antenna. Only acquaintance with the psychoanalyst's habit of learning to listen for such overtones and undertones can remedy his defect. No doubt the historian will not always have evidence in such abundance as introspective and articulate people like James have produced, but it is wise not to foreclose the possibilities that open up when historians begin to look for evidence that they commonly have not sought. Historical evidence is not a previously known entity, like a continent; when it emerges, it comes in response to questions which need it. A generation of historians trained to listen with a "third ear" will, in their fallibility, hear some things that are mere gossip—particularly if they treat theories canonically rather than pragmatically—but there is a good chance that with tact, subtlety, industry, and experience they may also hear belowstairs some news that sheds a good deal of light on what is going on above.

Hegel said that if no man is a hero to his valet, that is only a comment on the limitations of his valet. The same might be said of psychohistorical investigators, who should be committed not to depreciating ideals and aspirations but to connecting them with the deeper springs of action in order the better to respect what Freud called "the intensively tilled soil from which our virtues proudly emerge." [16] The later Freud, however, believed that "the events of human history, the interactions between human nature, cultural development and the precipitates of primeval experiences (the most prominent example of which is religion) are no more than a reflection of the dynamic conflicts between the ego, the id and the super-ego, which psychoanalysis studies in the individual—are the very same processes repeated upon a wider stage." [17] Historians, however, cannot accept this dogmatic and reductionist conclusion. The advantage for them of the identity-crisis concept is that it is more descriptive than explanatory. The concept itself does not explain why some young men know how to evade or defy difficult parents, or why others should make their troubles the source of a creative encounter with general issues. My own use of it did not entail any position on Freud's theory of libidinal energy in its oral, anal, and genital stages, nor any presupposition that the oedipal complex "explains" neurosis. My paper claims only to show in detail that in this case a disturbed father did seek justification in his eldest son and that the disturbed son did to his cost and to his benefit "overidentify" with him. Fully describing *how* that relationship worked out answers questions about James's career and the development of his ideas that otherwise remain puzzling. The identity-crisis concept, because it focuses on problems that to some extent do emerge into self-consciousness, does not objectify the subject in a naturalistic way nor depend upon reference to submerged material that only clinical interaction with a patient could bring to consciousness. These are advantages to historians, for whom no theory is canonical.

Whether such exposition proves its case is not a matter of external recourse to the alleged universality of a general theory; it is instead a matter of establishing a coherent dynamic pattern, without loose ends or patchwork suppositions, of documented actions, thoughts, and feelings in specific social contexts. Only detailed examination of the historian's account can test its truth; it cannot be assessed by examining the general truth of a few propositions extracted from it. He who thinks that this standard is not rigorous enough, let him try to meet it first. The historian as psychohistorical biographer must make his way on the power he can demonstrate to make more coherent the sequence and form of a man's life. For some, psychoanalysis is a theory of history. At the other extreme are those historians who relegate psychoanalytic thinking to the clinician's office. This essay will have served its purpose if it has convincingly staked out a middle ground which historians should be willing to explore. A complacent skepticism can instead indulge itself by pointing a scornful finger at the obvious abuses in some recent psychohistorical work. It will always be easier to do so than to undertake the arduous efforts that collaboration requires. But in failing to make them, historians will only perpetuate the second-rate work that they rightly deplore.

From the point of view of intellectual history the kind of study that I have described enables the historian to carry out Ortega's theory of an idea as "the reaction of a man upon a definite situation of his life . . . *an action* taken by a man in view of a definite situation and for a definite purpose." [18] Of abstractions as such there is no history. If we pursue the effort to see how ideas function in individual lives, we shall have to talk in some cases about the relevance of inner conflicts to their formulation, even though it is *not* possible to ascertain the consistency or profundity of thinking by psychological investigation. From the point of view of the artistry of historiography the presentation of such research will demand a difficult balance between generalizing analysis and individuating narration, between paying attention to conscious aims and recognized problems, on the one hand, and to unconscious strategies and unrecognized difficulties, on the other. From the perspective of the philosopher of history, this kind of historical writing will complicate and enrich our sense of the range of meaning which "understanding" and "explaining" may have. To some extent psychohistorical study seeks to understand the agent in his own stated terms in order the better to understand him in the light of the unacknowledged purposes which his "symptoms" express. To some extent, as well, such study is oriented by generalizations about the life cycle, derived from psychology, which draw the historian's attention to the probable interpersonal setting which influences identity formation or its failure.

The identity-crisis concept is primarily a phenomenological description of identity diffusion rather than a causal theory. Even its precipitating cause is intelligible as the logic of a situation—a familiar form of historical explanation—in which "illness" is understandable as a covert protest against obedience and as an excuse for disobedience to parental wishes that have too much prestige to be openly challenged without incurring excessive guilt. Erikson himself in *Young Man Luther*, despite his emphasis on the adaptive, not merely the defensive, functions of the ego and on the neglected place of work in illness and recovery, goes beyond this logic to use libido theory and the oedipus complex in tracking down the ultimate sources of Luther's troubles. The difficulty is, however, that the historian cannot carry his analysis into infantile sexual areas without leaning far more heavily than he has a right to do on clinical theory without clinical evidence or experience. The utility for him of the identity-crisis concept is its work orientation and its refusal to subordinate the later stages of life to those of childhood in a deterministic way. The vicissitudes of libidinal energy constitute a Freudian quest that leads too far back into a "prehistoric" context for which the evidence itself is usually generated by the clinical encounter.[19] Freud himself insisted that the clinical phenomena of "resistance" and "transference" are the essential facts for psychoanalysis, which is fundamentally an explanation of them.

Psychohistorical biography will have to come to terms with the logic of history, but so will the philosophy of history have to accommodate itself to successful empirical studies. They require revision, for example, of R. G. Collingwood's opinion that biography is intrinsically antihistorical:

> Its limits are biological events, the birth and death of a human organism: its framework is thus a framework not of thought but of natural process. Through this framework—the bodily life of the man, with his childhood, maturity and senescence, his diseases and all the accidents of animal existence—the tides of thought, his own and

others', flow crosswise, regardless of its structure, like sea-
water through a stranded wreck. Many human emotions
are bound up with the spectacle of such bodily life in its
vicissitudes, and biography, as a form of literature, feeds
these emotions and may give them wholesome food; but
this is not history.[20]

The point is clear enough if the historian does, in fact, take
birth and death as the meaningful limits of his problem, but he
does not in practice accept such accidental boundaries. What
the biographer really talks about is the development of a self,
and a part of that story is the emergence of the person into the
role of a historical agent. Birth and death *might* be significant
in particular cases because of their meaning to the agent
himself, or they might merely be matters of information. Similarly, the ills that flesh is heir to are often merely natural
(nonhistorical) events, as Collingwood says, but "mental illness" is not external, nor in many cases is medical disease when
it has meaning for its victim.

It is true that the psychohistorical biographer will often
have to discuss intrafamily problems, but the voices of the
family, as well as its critical silences, are full of resounding
echoes of the outside world and times past. Collingwood's dismissal of biography depends on a misunderstanding of the
biographer's interest and on an artificial separation of the individual from the historical process. He himself protested against
positivism on the ground that "individuality, instead of appearing in history only now and then in the shape of the accidentall
or contingent, is just that out of which history is made. . . ."
The positivistic conception of individuality, he argued, makes
the inner and the outer "mutually exclusive," like the individuality of a stone. But human individuality, he believed,
"consists not of separateness from environment but of the
power to absorb environment into itself."[21] No psychohistorical
biographer need quarrel with these assertions, which contradict
Collingwood's own strictures against biography.

Collingwood's theory of historical knowledge, however,
must be revised to include a place for the historian's effort to
understand emotional difficulties which the agent could, in

principle, bring to self-consciousness, but which in fact he does not. James, for example, explicitly recognized, after his father's death, his own deep engagement with him: "It is singular how I'm learning every day now how the thought of his comment on my experience has hitherto formed an integral part of my daily consciousness, *without my having realized it at all.*" [22] In Collingwood's terms the statement is certainly self-conscious; yet it confesses to the prior significance of an unconscious attitude, whose full implications James never did comprehend. On Collingwood's principles only the self-conscious statement should enter into an historical account, yet the statement itself points toward the relevance of an unconscious attitude. This example is a good crux for Collingwood's theory: should the historian ignore a fundamental insight, provided by the historical subject himself, in order to be consistent with a philosophical theory, or should the theory be revised to take account of what any intelligent historian must surely do with such a confession— make the most of it? Can there be any legitimate doubt about which alternative to follow, with all due respect to Collingwood's impressive insights and arguments? The power of the identity-crisis concept, as illustrated in James's biography, is its ability to fill the historical gap between Freud's naturalistic determinism and Collingwood's voluntaristic idealism, to mediate between the view that men do not know the psychosexual process that has made them what they are and the view that a historical process is one in which the mind knows itself to be living.

Historians working in this area will have to hammer out procedural rules under the pressure of decisions made in research, but a few guidelines are clear from the best work already done. Just as in clinical practice not every problem nor every person is explored at the same level, so also the historian needs justification for seeking understanding at the level of "depth psychology." Evidence points toward internal conflict when antagonistic wishes generate paradoxes that invite analysis, when surprising, inappropriate affects provide cues, or when there is discordance between a man's image of himself and his idealized image of what he ought to be. "In biography," as Erikson has said, "the validity of any relevant theme can only lie in its crucial recurrence in a man's development, and in its relevance to the balance sheet of his victories and defeats."[23] In such work, he adds, the law of parsimony needs to be adjusted to the material; only a certain "extravagance" in first searching for possible relevances can open up the material and lead to a later, more considered condensation of it. It is at this point that the clinician's experience and the historian's parsimony are likely to collide. What, for example, did James's paralyzing memory of an idiotic, epileptic patient mean? He had seen him in an asylum and felt panic fear at the possibility that it might be himself. The image connects most directly with his own distaste for medical school, his sense of entrapment in a wrong choice of career, but it may also be related to self-punishing guilt feelings, perhaps, given his extended bachelorhood and chastity, to masturbation-guilt, as clinical practice suggests. Here the historian can find his own ground in the fact that Victorian sexual theory did, in William Acton's well-known work, specifically describe asylum inmates *in similar terms* as the inevitable products of the practice of masturbation. The point gives a possible (but not farfetched) additional meaning to an "overdetermined" symbol. In this way accommodation is reached between the likely surmises of the clinician and the historian's sense of the milieu. Since work, rather than sex, continued to be a problem for James, however, it is proper to give this erotic point a subordinate place in the biographical account.

The historian's fallacy is likely to be evident in a desire to trace "symptoms" to textbook diseases, rather than to specific life circumstances in a historical milieu about which these symptoms speak in a covert way, translatable into ordinary language. It is the mistake of seeing the psychoanalyst as an exotic, alien specialist, called in only to provide labels in an emergency upsetting to common sense. But it is a psychoanalyst himself who has warned against seeing men "of creative intensity and of an increasing historical commitment" as "cases" to be measured in terms of some hypothetical but inappropriate norm of "inner repose."[24] The historian is also deceived if he thinks of psychoanalytic interpretation as the attempt to establish causal links in a deterministic series, as early formulations of Freudian ideas unfortunately suggested. In its modern form it is instead "more concerned with emotional relevance and affective equivalence than with locating events in their literal sequences. . . . Memories, as such, do not determine the living present, but the emotional context of the present determines which events will be recalled. . . . It is necessary, however, to recognize the events which *endure* longer, not just those which occurred a very long time ago. The enduring events are discovered and rediscovered in many recurrent moments of existential time. They survive by evoking fresh relevance and fresh reality sense for the organic meaning of the present." [25]

Psychohistorical investigation will deservedly fail to win respect if it is used to discredit opponents, belittle achievements, or circumvent rational arguments where they are appropriate. Its benefits can be realized only if historians and clinicians are willing to learn from each other at the price of disturbing unexamined professional habits. It is of course begging the question to interpret objections to psychohistorical work as only signs of emotional resistance. Logical criticisms have to be met on their own ground. But it is often deep reluctance, rather than logic, which is most striking in some critics of such investigation. The reluctance is understandable. To seek interpersonal and intrapersonal conflict in historical materials, which demand emphathetic efforts of the imagination, must make the historian aware of the place of such conflicts in all experience, including his own. It is a commonplace that the investigator's inquiry may disturb what he examines—at least he must inevitably reconstruct it rather than reproduce it. It is more unsettling, however, to realize that what he examines and the way in which he examines it may disturb the investigator himself. One can only hope that some historians will be willing to run the risk for the sake of the adventure, the excitement of genuinely adding to our comprehension of the historical past. Psychology without historical insight dehumanizes the individual into a "case"; history without psychological insight drowns the individual in a sea of social forces or elevates him to mythical heights.[26] Only binocular vision can keep him in a focus that does justice to his social role and his uniqueness, to the troubles of his common humanity and the glories of his uncommon achievements.

The skeptic may suspect that the psychosocial stages of development spelled out in Erikson's schedule of the life cycle are applicable only to particular cultures in a given period of time. It may be that the extension of adolescence characteristic of modern times and Western society is a favoring condition for the identity crisis. It may be too that Christianity has a special relation to the generation of the identity crisis, whether in its converts or its heretics, much like the "twice-born" gospel of "the sick soul" that William James found at the core of his study of the varieties of religious experience. It may also be the case, as Robert Jay Lifton has provocatively suggested, that identity diffusion, rather than being a more or less pathological confusion, is becoming instead a new historical style of self-process, the signature of a "protean man" evident in youth movements and in many art forms.[27] For such people in a time of instability the old symbols that mark important transitions in the life cycle have no authenticity and for them only temporary precarious identities are possible. Historians must always seek the limits of universal statements about human nature, including those of their own common sense. But such limits do not excuse neglect. The concept of the identity crisis has already infiltrated popular speech, but it has not yet been assimilated by historians as a working tool rather than as a fashionable phrase. [Historians have applied Erikson's categories to Jonathan Edwards, Benjamin Franklin, Alexander Hamilton, Andrew Jackson, Margaret Fuller, Ralph Waldo Emerson, and Henry David Thoreau. The results are very uneven. For a cogent analogy with Luther see Joel Porte, *Representative Man: Ralph Waldo Emerson in His Time* (New York, 1979), pp. 289–99.] That difference is the measure of our neglected opportunities. Perhaps we are beginning to appreciate them just as the old inner struggles traditionally associated with ideological shifts are losing their severity in a protean world. If so, then it is another illustration of the rule that for the historian the owl of Minerva flies only when the shades of dusk have fallen.

## A Note on the Terms *Identity* and *Identification*

For Erikson identity is largely unconscious or, at best, preconscious. It has both positive and negative features, the latter being elements of what the child has been warned not to become. The positive elements, far from being static, are always in conflict "with that past which is to be lived down and by that potential future which is to be prevented." Despite his own warning to social scientists that the term cannot be reduced to "social roles, personal traits, or conscious self-images" and that it should not be indiscriminately used to "fit whatever they are investigating," he himself has applied the identity concept to groups, particularly Negroes in America. But this extension detaches the idea from the connections it has with the life cycle and the family situation. See Erikson, "The Concept of Identity in Race Relations: Notes and Queries," *Daedalus* 95 (1966): 146, 151, 155. I think that the ordinary use of identity in talking about groups quite properly points to *conscious* self-definition, direction, and cohesiveness. A strict psychoanalytic application of identity to groups is methodologically obscure and dubious.

The term *identification* is also a vexed concept in the literature of psychological theory, particularly with respect to the process, or mechanism, of psychological forces that generate emulative tendencies in any individual. The historian need not enter this controversy. It is sufficient for him to observe specific emulating or internalizing of a given model's actions, standards, or expectations and to see if it is appropriate (in terms of psychic balance) at a given stage in the life cycle. Identification in childhood is part of normal development; at a later stage its intensity points to a barrier against identity formation. For the various meanings and difficulties of the term *identification* see Urie Bronfenbrenner, "Freudian Theories of Identification and Their Derivatives," *Child Development* 31 (1960): 15–40.

(1968)

## Notes

1. Two recent examples, both polemical and reductionist, are Sigmund Freud and William C. Bullitt, *Thomas Woodrow Wilson: A Psychological Study* (Boston, 1967); and Meyer A. Zeligs, *Friendship and Fratricide: An Analysis of Whittaker Chambers and Alger Hiss* (New York, 1967). For an excellent critical review of the Wilson book by a psychoanalyst see Erik H. Erikson, *The International Journal of Psycho-Analysis* 48 (1967), pt. 3, pp. 462–68. Zeligs reduces all of Chambers's acts to infantile fantasies and treats Hiss's at face value. While professing his refusal to judge matters of fact, Zeligs presupposes that Chambers is lying and that Hiss is telling the truth, thus flagrantly begging the historical question.

2. For historical use of *repression* and *anxiety* see Michael Walzer, "Puritanism as a Revolutionary Ideology," *History and Theory* 3 (1963): 59–90; for *projection* see David Brion Davis, "Some Themes of Counter-Subversion: An Analysis of Anti-Masonic, Anti-Catholic, and Anti-Mormon Literature," *Mississippi Valley Historical Review* 47 (1960): 205–224; and for *ambivalence* see Cushing Strout, *The American Image of the Old World* (New York, 1963). For a bold (but in my opinion debatable) use of the *oedipal* "family romance" idea see Alan C. Beckman, "Hidden Themes in the Frontier Thesis: An Application of Psychoanalysis to Historiography," *Comparative Studies in Society and History* 8 (1966): 361–82.

3. See Sidney Hook, *The Hero in History: A Study in Limitation and Possibility* (New York, 1943), p. 9. See also Fred I. Greenstein, "The Impact of Personality on Politics: An Attempt to Clear Away Underbrush," *American Political Science Review* 61 (1967): 629–41.

4. Ralph Barton Perry, ed., *The Thought and Character of William James* (Boston, 1935), 1:678.

5. Erik H. Erikson, "The Problem of Ego Identity," *Psychological Issues* 1 (1959).

6. Erik H. Erikson, *Young Man Luther: A Study in Psychoanalysis and History* (New York, 1958), p. 65.

7. See chapter 11.

8. Perry, William James, 1:430; 2:670–681. Gay Wilson Allen in the most recent biography of James tends to explain his troubles on the ground of a conflict between his sexual longings and his idealization of women, a conventional point about Victorians that fails to come to terms with the vocational problem of James's life. See Allen, *William James: A Biography* (New York, 1967), p. 149. Dr. Edward Hitschmann, a devout Freudian, misses the point even more widely, observing very inaccurately that William's "kind father" did "not influence the choice of profession of his sons." See Hitschmann, *Great Men: Psychoanalytic Studies* (New York, 1956), p. 233.

9. Erik H. Erikson, "Identity and the Life Cycle," *Psychological Issues* 1 (1959): 90.

10. Erikson, *Young Man Luther*, p. 43.

11. Ibid., p. 255.

12. I am indebted to Erikson for this suggestion.

13. William James, *Pragmatism: A New Name for Some Old Ways of Thinking* [1907] (New York, 1919), p. 295.

14. Sigmund Freud, *Totem and Taboo*, in *The Basic Writings of Sigmund Freud*, ed. and trans. A. A. Brill (New York, 1938), pp. 863–64.

15. As Louis O. Mink points out, the interpretation of neurotic behavior as being unconsciously purposive conforms implicitly to Collingwood's account of historical knowledge with some modifications that do not challenge his main thesis. See Mink, "Collingwood's Dialectic of History," *History and Theory* 7 (1968): 16.

16. Freud, *The Interpretation of Dreams*, in Brill, *Basic Writings*, p. 548. Surprisingly, however, Freud was willing to admit that "for all practical purposes in judging human character, a man's actions and conscious expressions of thought are in most cases sufficient." Historians commonly take the same position.

17. Sigmund Freud, *Autobiography*, trans. James Strachey (New York, 1935), p. 149.

18. José Ortega y Gasset, *Concord and Liberty*, trans. Helene Weyl (New York, 1946), p. 99.

19. The clinical encounter *produces* evidence from the patient's relation to the therapist and from the therapist's own emotional responses to the patient, as Erikson points out in *Insight and Responsibility: Lectures on the Ethical Implications of Psychoanalytic Insight* (New York, 1964), pp. 72–73. Otherwise "the evidence is not 'all in'," as Erikson says. The historian's situation with respect to his subject is very different, a point insufficiently recognized by psychoanalysts who practice history, particularly if they discuss presumed crises of infancy.

20. R. G. Collingwood, *The Idea of History* (Oxford, 1946), p. 304.

21. Ibid., pp. 150, 162.

22. Perry, *William James*, 1:142. (My italics.)

23. Erikson, *Young Man Luther*, p. 50.

24. Ibid., p. 34.

25. Avery D. Weisman, *The Existential Core of Psychoanalysis: Reality Sense and Responsibility* (Boston, 1965), pp. 93–94.

26. As David Brion Davis suggests, "by showing how cultural tensions and contradictions may be internalized, struggled with, and resolved within actual individuals," biography offers the most "promising key to the synthesis of culture and history." See Davis, "Some Recent Directions in American Cultural History," *American Historical Review* 73 (February 1968): 705.

27. Robert Jay Lifton, "Protean Man," *Partisan Review* 35 (Winter 1968): 1–27.

# 13 / Personality and Cultural History in the Novel

In a critical review of contemporary directions in the study of American cultural history, David Davis has pointed out that the American Studies movement has characteristically produced works that "expose a contradiction or cluster of tensions embedded within the culture itself as the result of an interplay between past choices and commitments and new ideas or situations." Many of these literary studies have been alert to the way in which symbols and myths have concealed or accommodated conflicts in belief and value: the myths of the West or of the American Adam; the pastoral ideal of the middle landscape between primitive nature and urban civilization; the image of Europe as the Old World; and the contrary types of Cavalier and Yankee as stand-ins for the American character. But Davis properly notes that "one must guard against relegating all conflict to the world of symbol and myth," and he adds that it is still necessary to find some means of seeing how cultural patterns find "internalization and adaptation within individual personalities." Pointing to Erik Erikson's *Young Man Luther*, he suggests that biography, "by showing how cultural tensions and contradictions may be internalized, struggled with, and resolved within actual individuals," offers "the most promising key to the synthesis of culture and history."[1]

It is no longer unusual to hear scholars refer to identity crises, any more than it is for students to speak of having them. I have done it myself at length in a study of William James, using the psychohistorical concepts of Erikson,[2] but I know there are those who would say that such analyses express what they describe—identity diffusion. They ask, "Who is the fellow anyway, a psychoanalyst or a historian?" What I shall propose may provoke a further accusatory query: "Who is he anyway, a literary historian or a social psychologist?" The only proper reply is that to see some things clearly you must have binocular vision, especially in matters of the historical and cultural meaning of personality.

Strictly speaking, the identity-crisis concept is a semi-clinical description of the emotional turmoil characteristic of late adolescence and early adulthood facing decisive choices of mate and vocation. Erikson has expanded its usefulness by his own sensitivity to the historical elements that enter into such dramas, particularly in the lives of creative men whose development is marked by intense and disruptive difficulties in the very measure that the problems which they generate and suffer have a wide relevance to the major intellectual, cultural, or political problems of their time. Erikson's revision of Freud has its own framework, a schedule of opposing emotional tendencies for each of his eight stages of the life cycle. It mediates between the deterministic view that men do not know the psychosexual process that has made them what they are and the voluntaristic view that a historical process is one in which the mind knows itself to be living, because in practice it finds in the search for vocation and the experience of work a neglected clue to the meaning of psychic conflict. Erikson's theoretical concept of identity, nevertheless, makes it largely unconscious, or preconscious at most, in any case not to be confused with "social roles, personal traits, or conscious self-images."[3] His limiting definition is meant to be a useful warning against loosely using the concept of identity to apply to whatever we happen to be investigating.

Certainly the clinical context of Erikson's concept is necessary when the presence of inorganic disabilities, inappropriate feelings, or paradoxical behavior is striking enough (as with Martin Luther or William James) to compel the analyst to become a part-time alienist in order to make sense of the bizarre data. But there are few people now at work in our academic life who can confidently follow the path that he has charted by virtue of his unusual training and experience in clinical and anthropological study, and the number of cases where extensive appropriate evidence is available for depth analysis, though greater than we thought before we began to look for it, is still small enough to act as a deterrent for most scholars against straying from more traditional scholarly routes.

Yet many of Freud's terms—repression, ambivalence, projection, compensation, and displacement—have been exploited out of their original context in his specific theory of the individual's psychosexual etiology because contemporary historians need a vocabulary to explore a broad range of more or less conscious strategies for dealing with powerful feelings generated by the conflicts of group life, conflicts not reducible to "the family romance" that both Freud and Erikson have emphasized. Similarly, Erikson's concern for identity-formation tends to appear nowadays in sociological formulations of historical problems that are usually much more matters of the conscious assertion of group ideologies, interests, and images than they are of unconscious feelings and assumptions, for example, the movement for "black power," for various anti-imperial nationalisms, or for woman's liberation. For the purpose of bringing together culture and history in the analysis of individual or group conflicts there will be a range of formulations between the terms appropriate to Freud's vocabulary and the terms of "habits, opinions, usages, and beliefs" that have been characteristic of sociology ever since Tocqueville used them in *Democracy in America*.[4]

It would seem to be a major problem, however, that we do not have a vocabulary of analysis as specific as Freud's, Erikson's, or Tocqueville's for the difficult, shifting middle ground between ego psychology and sociology. I would like to suggest that we can be compensated to some degree for the missing vocabulary by the narrative method of certain novelists whose imagined characters, drawn indirectly from experience, dramatize in their lives the sort of intellectual, cultural, and psychological interplay that has attracted Erikson's attention. The novel tends to focus on the growth of personality through conflict and crisis, and if the novelist has a strong sense of time and place, combined with perception into the individual motivations of his characters, those changes will resonate with the historical and cultural issues that enter into them. I want to illustrate this proposition with two neglected novels, *Esther* and *The Rise of David Levinsky*, one closer to the psychoanalytic end of the spectrum, the other closer to the sociological, though both incorporate shades of meaning at the complementary opposite pole.

Over a decade ago Edward N. Saveth found an ambivalence toward women in Henry Adam's work that led him to lament the historical decline of the Virgin as force, while dooming his fictional heroines to be without husbands or children. Saveth speculates that Adams's expectation of a coming cataclysm is masochistically linked to his guilt for quarreling with the "dynamo" as an embodiment of the male principle, like the fantasy of killing the father. Adams's doomed heroines are seen as revenge-fantasies against the mother, aggressive dreams harbored by "meek children and impotent men."[5] In this Freudian interpretation the novels are reduced to projections of Adams's inner tensions, and the origin of these is merely deduced from psychoanalytic theory, rather than being historically traced to a specific biographical context.

Saveth's treatment of Adams needs to be revised in the light of a post-Freudian psychology that can do justice to the historical situation to which Adams addressed himself in his reflections on women. Whatever his own conflicts, he was, as a novelist, seeking to comprehend those of his characters, drawn from his experience of the women he knew well, and the cultural limits of their problems found an echo in his own personal sense of the limitations of contemporary masculine attitudes.

Adams's own psychohistory must remain elusive because he destroyed his private diaries and many of his letters after the suicide of his wife in 1885. There is one unnoticed clue, however, in his autobiography: "the fourth [child], being of less account, was in a way given to his mother, who named him Henry Brooks, after a favorite brother just lost."[6] According to Henry's brother, Charles Francis, their mother delighted in the dark side of anticipation, in "the forecast of evil."[7] This trait became a notorious one of her fourth child, reflecting his own incorporation of an aspect of his mother's personality. His mother probably had on her side a special feeling for the child she had named for her recently lost brother, and Adams's fascination with women was probably in part rooted in his response to this relation. More important for the historian (if not for the biographer) is the point that Adams's empathy with his heroines, his cult of the Virgin, and his role as an avuncular mentor to his flock of "nieces" can be seen as ways of expressing certain aspects of himself traditionally designated in his culture as more "feminine" than "masculine," qualities of sympathy, artistic feeling, and flirtatious wit, not favored by men in the hard, power-oriented capitalist world of his age.

Despite his success as an editor, scholar, and teacher, his autobiography monotonously laments his "failure" from the point of view of a person who sees himself as a passive spectator rather than as a participant "playing the game" of life. This sense of his own displacement from that world of aggressive power, which "sensitive and timid natures" could not regard "without a shudder," gave him an unusual and penetrating sympathy with women. By analogy he could understand with particular keenness the plight of women who for whatever reason did not find their destiny adequately summed up in the image of meekness or of frivolity. In a lecture in Boston, given in 1876 on "The Primitive Rights of Women," Adams used Lewis Henry Morgan's findings about American Indians to show that primitive peoples did not treat women as property, and he blamed the Church for having "stimulated or permitted" woman's degradation, which is later softened by idealizing the image of woman as "the meek and patient, the silent and tender sufferer, the pale reflection of the Mater Dolorosa."[8]

Adams's *Esther* exploits his own personal knowledge of such American figures as his cousin Phillips Brooks, pastor of

Boston's Trinity Church; John La Farge, who painted its murals and decorated St. Thomas Church in New York; Clarence King, the geologist and explorer of the West; Elizabeth Cameron, wife of a senator; and Adams's own wife.[9] But the novel's value is not that of a roman à clef; it hovers instead about the competing values of religion, science, and art as they bear on an intellectual woman's search for herself.

The heroine of *Esther* has artistic interests, does charity work, and is not conventionally religious. She complains of her "feminine want of motive in life" (p. 273), confessing that she wished that she earned her living. Two weeks after her father dies, Esther submits to a minister's passionate insistence that they be engaged. It is clear that she finds her geologist cousin's scientific naturalism and devotion to abstract truth far more congenial than the minister's sensuous and passionate supernaturalism, but she loves him and not her cousin. Her mother is dead and, as her father says, she has been "brought up among men, and is not used to harness,'" and "'a woman who rebels is lost'" (p. 231). Hearing the minister preach of love, she feels that the privacy of her own love has been violated by his public expression of passion. He is persuasive, but she "could no more allow him to come into her life and take charge of her thoughts than to go down into her kitchen and take charge of her cook" (p. 306). Her aunt, trying to break up what she knows is a bad match, appeals to Esther's feminine pride by pointing out that a woman cannot afford to be "'thrown over by a man, not even if he is a clergyman.'" Esther should therefore make it clear to him that she is jealous of the church, which she can never accept as a minister's wife should. In the climax she is determined to turn their relationship into a mere friendship, "even if it cost her a lover as well as a husband" (p. 364). But the minister confesses that he wants her soul for his church and demands that she share his faith, which she cannot feel. "'It is not my fault if you and your profession are one,'" Esther protests; "'and of all things on earth, to be half-married must be the worst torture'" (p. 366). Threatened by "the thunders of the church" that are "already rolling over her head," she confesses that to her he always has seemed to be an archaic "priest in a Pagan temple" (p. 368). The minister then loses his case forever by appealing to her to accept the hope of resurrection and immortality on the ground that "the natural instincts" of her sex should lead her to want to meet once more the relatives she loves. This appeal to her weakness revolts her: "I ask for spiritual life and you send me back to my flesh and blood as though I were a tigress you were sending back to her cubs" (p. 370). She has succeeded in driving the minister away, and she knows that "the romance of her life was ended" (p. 371). In this light Esther's integrity prevents her from succumbing to the great pressure put upon her by both the scientist and the minister to "have" a faith that she does not have.

Adam's conception of his heroine gives her the dignity of her principled rejection of her suitor as well as the pathos of her troubled identity. but a careful reading shows that there is another level to her story. It is parallel, incidentally, in this respect to Adams's other novel, *Democracy*, in which the cultivated heroine eventually rejects a powerful amoral senator and is unable to respond emotionally to a powerless but honorable statesman because of her loyalty to her first husband and child, whose deaths have left her with the fire of her emotional and sexual life "burned out."

There is a powerful undercurrent to Esther's conflicts that connects her story with the biographical fact that the death of the father of Adams's wife sent her into a depression that ended in suicide. That Adams saw the connection, as his biographer Ernest Samuels observes, is evident from his own suppression of the novel after the tragedy had happened. Esther's father scorns clergymen and jokes about his hatred for Esther's potential suitors whom in fantasy he has hated all his life and twice a year "treacherously stabbed . . . in the back" (p. 229). Esther's inability to accept the minister has another dimension suggested by the intensity of her outburst: "'I despise and loathe myself, and yet you thrust self at me from every corner of the church as though I loved and admired it!'" (p. 369). The church, she complains, cries "'flesh-flesh-flesh' at every corner." When Catherine Brooke at Niagara Falls compares the fall to a pretty, self-conscious woman like herself, Esther "vehemently" protests that the roaring cataract is really "a man," too powerful to be a woman (p. 352). Adams's comment on the minister has a psychological resonance: "To have Niagara for a rival is no joke" (p. 349). In one sense the fall is for Esther a "huge church," thundering its naturalistic gospel before her eyes, suggesting the traditional attributes of God, "eternity, infinity, and omnipotence," reducing her fret about her love affair to an "impertinence." In another, unconscious sense, her image of it may express a wish to be a man. In a strange passage she "feverishly" proposes to "elope together" with Catherine on a "wedding journey" (p. 332) as a flight from the problems of their suitors. Her language is appropriate to a fantasy-role as a man. These intense reactions on her part, in their range of possible meanings, compel the attentive reader to look for a deeper trouble in her feelings than any rational disagreement with the minister can account for. Her self-revulsion and horror of the flesh suggest a deep-seated difficulty in accepting her own body, her sexual identity. Her aunt, who understands Esther, the minister, and the geologist better than anyone else in the story, believes that "if Esther is sensible she will never marry" (p. 231).

These psychological considerations should lead us back to historical ones. Something in the culture of these women has predisposed them to unhappy histories. Esther's friend, Catherine Brooke, rebukes the dominating, erratic painter who loves her: "'Men are always making themselves into ideals and expecting women to follow them'" (p. 359). Esther is conventionally expected to accept the preacher's faith if she is to marry him. The best option in the judgment of Esther's tart-tongued aunt is for women to fall in love with clever men and then "marry dull, steady men in Wall Street, without any manners, and with hands in their pockets," using the rest of their lives for the business of "educating their husbands" (p. 351). But, at bottom, in her view the situation is much worse than that. She tells Esther's father, who is worried that Esther will make a mistake in her marriage: "'Marriage makes no real difference in their lot. All the contented women are fools, and all the discontented ones want to be men. Women are a blunder in the creation, and must take the consequences'" (p. 231). Woman's identity could hardly be more problematical than her aunt's bleak jest would have it. At the end of the story the heroine and her female companion flee to Europe to escape the pressures put upon them by rejected men.

Popular writers, Adams wryly observes in *Democracy*, "have decided that any woman will, under the right conditions, marry any man at any time, provided her 'higher nature' is properly appealed to" (p. 158). Both heroines, Madeline and Esther, come to the verge of illustrating Adams's aphorism that "the capacity of women to make unsuitable marriages must be considered as the corner-stone of our society" (p. 159). Their interest for him is that ultimately they do not. But such women, who challenge the ordinary rules, are themselves scarred and troubled by earlier family life. Their curiosity and conviction are isolated from their sexuality, and they can see themselves as active agents only in their agonized refusals. They purchase their self-respect at the price of alienating their suitors. In so presenting them, Adams dramatized the effects on female character of a cultural definition of women as beings assumed to be irrelevant to politics and to rational thought. The depth of the educated American woman's trouble in this era was that she herself, to a painful extent, internalized the definition that cramped her. Their own previous roles have not fitted them for new beginnings. Esther's identification with her anticlerical father has confused her own sexual identity. If the men demand too much of the heroines of both novels because of their interest in power—political or spiritual—the women are more attracted to them than to the available suitors who do not threaten their individuality. To some extent their suffering is self-inflicted.

In his autobiography, published twenty-three years after *Esther*, Adams's view of women shifts in two ways. He expands his vision downward in the social scale of women to include "telephone and telegraph-girls, shop-clerks, factory hands, running into millions of millions, and, as classes, unknown to themselves as to historians."[10] But he sees this new "free" woman as "sexless" and bound, like the man, to "marry machinery."[11] He also looks far backward to the time when woman was a historical force by virtue of her power of sex, expressed in her role as beauty and as mother, as Venus and as Virgin. Traces of this power of woman remain in France, but in

America, he laments, "an American Virgin would never dare command; an American Venus would never dare exist." Both symbols represent energy, and woman in this sense is "animated dynamo," or the power of reproduction—"the greatest and most mysterious of all energies; all she needed was to be fecund." The Middle Ages charmed him because the combination of Venus and Virgin, evident at the Louvre and at Chartres, had exercised "vastly more attraction over the human mind than all the steam-engines and dynamos ever dreamed of; and yet this energy was unknown to the American mind."[12] This mythmaking was a lament for the historical passivity of women in an age of the machine, and a criticism of merely "masculine" images of power and energy. If he had the good sense to see that "the Marguerite of the future could alone decide whether she were better off than the Marguerite of the past," he was afraid that she would substitute for submission to the man or the church, submission to the machine.[13] He is at his best on women in the autobiography, however, when he speaks without mythologizing:

> The study of history is useful to the historian by teaching him his ignorance of women; and the mass of this ignorance crushes one who is familiar enough with what are called historical sources to realize how few women have ever been known. The woman who is known only through a man is known wrong. . . . The American woman of the nineteenth century will live only as the man saw her; probably she will be less known than the woman of the eighteenth . . . and all this is pure loss to history, for the American woman of the nineteenth century was much better company than the American man; she was probably much better company than her grandmothers.[14]

If some women were not able to be happy in the passive roles that their culture had invented for them, neither was Adams, as a reformer, a historian, and a poet, content to be judged by the dominant standards of economic and political power. Every reader of the autobiography knows that Adams was ambivalent about what William James called "the bitch-goddess SUCCESS" if only because the author so monotonously insisted on his own "failure." A self-styled "pilgrim of power," Adams knew that he did not have the power that his illustrious ancestors had wielded, but he "saw no office that he wanted." [15] He could therefore sympathetically understand his heroine's ambivalence about submitting to masculine power or defying it:

> "I want to submit!" cried Esther piteously, rising in her turn and speaking in accents of real distress and passion. "Why can't some of you make me? For a few minutes at a time I think it done, and then I suddenly find myself more defiant than ever" [319].

Looking backward in his autobiography through a poetic haze of nostalgia, Adams could celebrate the time when the Virgin had the power over men to make them want to build the Chartres cathedral. But that celebration was flawed by its reduction of woman's humanity to a symbol of maternity, transcending sex, his own version of the characteristic misogyny of his class and culture. Elegant, witty, and penetrating, his novel tells another story, however, and proves the force of D. H. Lawrence's advice to trust the artist's tale and not his opinions.

As a novelist, Adams was more sympathetic to Esther than Freud was to Dora, one of his most famous cases. What Freud missed in her, as Erikson has pointed out, was a "vital identity fragment" of "the woman intellectual which had been encouraged by her father's delight in her precocious intelligence, but discouraged by her brother's superior example as favored by the times." [16] Freud's blindness to certain aspects of the Dora case, as Philip Rieff has suggested, reflected a common type of nineteenth-century misogyny that depreciated the intellectual aspects of woman's personality: "the child-bearing female represents the natural heritage of humanity, while the male carries on in spite of her enticements the burden of government and rational thought." [17] If Adams tended to approach the same view in his myth of the Virgin, he could transcend it as a novelist, finding sympathy for a woman's agnosticism and rebellion against male domination, even if, like Freud with Dora, he suspected that all was not well with Esther's sexual identity, as it was not with his own wife's relation to her father. For himself he valued *Esther* more than his nine-volume history. Though it has remained largely neglected by American scholars, it is one of the few American novels, after *The Scarlet Letter*, whose heroine has a similar name, that sympathetically portrays an intellectual woman outside the church.

With *The Rise of David Levinsky* we must shift our focus toward the sociological without losing sight of the individual personality of its hero, who undergoes the representative experience of an immigrant encountering what Tocqueville saw as "a virtuous materialism" that might in the future "not corrupt, but enervate the soul and noiselessly unbend its springs of action," unfitting men for public responsibility.[18] Abraham Cahan's novel, published in 1917, is set in the same time period, the 1880s, as *Esther*, but it deals with the other end of the social scale.[19] It brings us into intimate knowledge of the inner meaning of the cultural strain implied in the movement of a Russian Jew to America, and it modulates our understanding of that process in a way that dramatization can achieve better than any sociological generalization. At the same time it links certain ideological currents with the social pattern of economic upward mobility and clarifies the function of Jewish religion in the life of immigrants. Just as Adams's novel circles over the intellectual issue of the conflict of science and faith to probe at a less rationalistic level, so also Cahan's story in all its "thick" social detail goes much deeper than the conventional literature of economic success ever did.

The usual history of a religious group that breaks in a reformist spirit from its institutional tradition is characterized by sociologists as the development of a "sect" in tension with its surrounding society in contrast to a "church" that accepts it. But America had already blurred this distinction in the history of the Puritans who became the established church in New England. The American Reform Jews illustrated another variation by splitting off from the tradition of Orthodoxy in order to have *less* tension with the larger society. But the Jews, like both Protestants and Catholics in the American world of the late nineteenth century, experienced a common process of accommodation to the secular, rationalistic, and middle-class ethos of a modernizing industrial and urban society with democratic traditions. In this sense Jewish history was not an anomaly, and it produced its own version of this process in *The Rise of David Levinsky*. Cahan himself represented the new immigration of Jews from eastern Europe, a great influx that was markedly different from the earlier German middle-class emigrants. Its grimmer circumstances of ghetto life had made for a more tenacious traditional piety, a stronger sense of peoplehood among different nationalities, or a more radical passion for secular social justice. The small group of American Jews who had in 1885 formed the Jewish Theological Seminary Association in New York as a protest against the sacrifice of tradition by the reform movement would find its opportunity for influence in the flood of the new immigration. Cahan himself was a Russian Jew with a passion for Russian literary culture and for socialism. Emigrating to America in 1882 as a political exile, he mastered both English and Yiddish, edited the *Jewish Daily Forward* in the language of its readers, and worked as an organizer in Jewish labor unions. By the turn of the century his literary work had earned the praise of William Dean Howells, and *The Rise of David Levinsky* was, in one sense, a Russian-Yiddish study in "realism" to match the American's *The Rise of Silas Lapham*.

Howells's Yankee hero finally forsakes the material advantages which complicity with sharp practices could have brought him and abandons Beacon Street for his native Vermont. More faithful to representative social actuality of its period, Cahan's novel portrays the slow economic rise in the garment industry of the lower East Side of a Jewish immigrant from Russia. Levinsky begins as a rabbinical student in the Russian ghetto, steeped in the Talmud, but distracted by guilty sexual desires. Stricken by his mother's death, he is rescued from sinking into desperate poverty by an educated and prosperous Russian girl who is close to Gentile culture. Subsidizing his exodus, she resolves to achieve her vision of him as an educated man. On American shores the process of his adaptation to the economic and social conditions of his new world completes his alienation from Orthodoxy. Levinsky begins to see Americanization as the "tangible form of becoming a man of culture," because he regards even the most learned and refined Europeans as "greenhorns." Yet at the same time he retains an ambivalent feeling that American education is a "cheap machine-made product." All the outward earmarks of his conventional earlier identity as a rabbinical student, his earlocks and beard, disappear in his struggle for economic advancement and for sexual satisfaction in the teeming world of the East Side. The hope of going to City College, occasional lectures on ethical culture, the Darwinism of Herbert Spencer's *Sociology*, and the dream of a close family life come to take the place of his training in rabbinical studies. Evading union regulations, thereby winning the support of big manufacturers, and copying his rivals' designs, Levinsky becomes increasingly prosperous, able to donate to the Antomir Synagogue, which is a sentimental link for him to the world of his mother, who had been killed by anti-Semites. If he studies poetry it is as a strategy to get to the poet's daughter. But he is as out of place in her Hebrew-speaking milieu of advanced literature, socialism, and Zionism, as he is among pious traditionalists. Both ends of the eastern European spectrum of Jewish life are equally distant from his new life.

Levinsky fashions for himself a new identity as a highly successful leader in the women's ready-made cloak and suit business, but his doggedly honest account of his rise is also a recurrent lament for his lost ambition, his disappointments in love, his aching, nostalgically distorted feeling that the talmudic student that he was in Russia has more in common with his "inner identity" than the self that he has made in America. His autobiography is the only way he can express his wistful vision of himself as a person "born for a life of intellectual interest." But his own story also shows that even as a schoolboy he had a vengeful dream of becoming rich and influential so as to punish his tormentors and that after his mother's death he had lost his interest in the Talmud and was looking for "some violent change, for piquant sensations." It is in this mood that the image of America seized his imagination. His divorced Russian-speaking patron had made it clear to him that she found his piety and his Jewish look equally ridiculous. She prophetically expects America to make "another man" of him. Shaved and outfitted in his first American clothes, Levinsky mentally parades his "modern" makeup before his patroness. In America his reading of the Talmud at the Antomir Synagogue is only a stay against homesickness and a refuge from the strains of his struggles as a pushcart operator. Levinsky feels that his rigid native religion cannot be bent to the spirit of his new surroundings without breaking. But what makes the most critical difference in his development is the shame reflected in his decision to shave: he cannot bear to be called a "green one." His teacher in a public evening school, an American-born Reform Jew of German descent, devoted to the English Bible, Dickens's novels, and the Democratic party, is his instructor in accommodation to the New World, a midwife to the immigrant's representative experience of a second birth.

Cahan himself, though equally alienated from Orthodoxy, had a quite different development in the New World, preserving his ties to Russian literature, to socialism, and to the Yiddish culture of the East Side Jews. The artfulness of his novel is not so much its authentic documentation in detail of a closely observed world but rather its cumulative exposure of the psychology of a Jew whose successful adaptation to American life of the late nineteenth century leaves him with a residual melancholy sense that his past and his present "do not comport well." David Levinsky is not destroyed but successfully made over in a businessman's role that only fitfully troubles him in retrospect. His wistful feelings are derived from the ideals that his mother and his patron have fostered in his youthful imagination. Despite his adaptation, however, Levinsky knows that he cannot marry a Gentile to whom he is attracted, and he is still enough of a Jew to know that he is not really an educated man, that he has not served the cause of social justice, and that his connection with a fashionable synagogue is quite external. Levinsky earns our sympathy for his plain prosaic honesty in accounting for his success. If he has missed much in achieving it, he knows, as his creator does, that it has been a representative experience in a country testifying to the power of worldliness.

That power has been able to exert its force over him so thoroughly because a process of change had already begun in him before he crossed the sea. In Levinsky's life Cahan dramatized the portentous fact that Judaism in America, like Catholicism, would be intimately connected with the problem of ethnic identity, thus complicating the problem of religious belief in America to the benefit of sociologists, if not of believers. Tocqueville had observed a peculiar mingling in America of patriotism and religion. If he had returned at the turn of the century, he would have had to add a chapter on immigration. Even in 1835 he had briefly noted with his usual keenness that economic success in American often forces the European emigrant "to unlearn the lessons of his early education."[20] Cahan's novel refines that observation by making it clear that for many of those who find the motive and the means to emigrate, the unlearning has already begun before the crossing.[21]

These novels, as I have read them, are not so much "a mirror set up in the roadway" as they are small lasers with a focused beam that is very penetrating. They demonstrate the power of the novelist's imagination to link into a narrative unity those elements of psychology, history, and sociology that have also challenged the talents of scholars who seek to make the kind of integration that modern psychobiography demands but rarely achieves. What they provide is an invaluable resource for advancing our understanding of the complex transactions between the self and its culture in a historical moment. But only if we bring to them a curiosity and a knowledge informed by these concerns will they answer in kind to our questions.

There are other kinds of novels—and in the American case, at least, they may often be the best ones—that explore wider meanings through symbols removed from the ordinary settings of their own time into, for example, the Puritan past, the legendary wilderness, or the whaler's ocean. These too can be shown to bear indirectly upon the specific culture to which they were directed, just as some novels which pretend to a "realistic" foreground actually transform it in symbolic terms that engage writer and reader with powerful myths. Critics have been much attracted to these efforts, but usually at a level where their interest in historical and cultural problems finds expression in ways that are as speculative and provocative as they are often ungrounded in precision of historical knowledge or respect for the limits of literary evidence.[22] My plea has been for the neglected value of stories which through imaginative art openly explore a middle range of identity problems that occur when an individual's emotional life, representative, in part, of a group, class, or movement, entangles itself in cultural patterns that are subject to the deeper tides of historical change. These novels are not "historical" in the sense of recreating specific events that we already know about from historians, a superfluous and dubious enterprise, nor do they seek the cachet of the old or the exotic. They are "historical" in a more modern sense because they deliberately show us how personality and culture interact in a particular style of life to pose issues in the life cycle of developing individuals whose imaginary existence still has a local habitation and a name in actuality. If that paradox is somehow a mystery, it is a familiar magic of one of the powers of art that is congenial to a modern kind of cultural history. If this be treason to fact or to fiction as traditionally understood, let us make the most of it.

(1970)

## Notes

1. David Brion Davis, "Some Recent Directions in American Cultural History," *American Historical Review* 73 (February 1968):700, 704, 705.

2. See chapter 11.

3. I have discussed the methodological advantages and limits of psychobiography in chapter 12. For Erikson's warning about the overextension of the identity concept see his "The Concept of Identity in Race Relations: Notes and Queries," *Daedalus*, 95 (1966):146, 151, 155.

4. Alexis de Tocqueville, *Democracy in America*, ed. Phillips Bradley (New York, 1945), 2:322. I have discussed Tocqueville's method in "Tocqueville's Duality: Describing America and Thinking of Europe," *American Quarterly* 21 (Spring 1969):87–99.

5. Edward N. Saveth, "The Heroines of Henry Adams," *American Quarterly* 9 (Fall 1956):231–42.

6. Henry Adams, *The Education of Henry Adams*, (New York, 1931) p. 23.

7. Quoted in Ernest Samuels, *The Young Henry Adams* (Cambridge, Mass., 1948), p. 93.

8. Ibid., p. 264.

9. *"Democracy" and "Esther": Two Novels by Henry Adams*, introduction by Ernest Samuels (Garden City, N.Y., 1961), pp. xvi–xviii.

10. Adams, *Education*, p. 445.

11. Ibid., p. 447.

12. Ibid., pp. 384–85.

13. Ibid., pp. 447.

14. Ibid., p. 353.

15. Adams asks "why had no President ever cared to employ him?" and suggests that it would require "a volume of intricate explanation." Yet he concludes that "from his own point of view, in the long run, he was likely to be a more useful citizen without office." The missing "volume" is eloquent by its absence. Similarly, in estimating his success he says that he and John Hay could look out their window "with the sense of having all that any one had; all that the world had to offer; all that they wanted in life. . . ." But he concludes, "this was not consideration, still less power in any of its concrete forms, and applied as well or better to a comic actor." Ibid., pp. 322–23; 326–27.

16. Erik H. Erikson, *Insight and Responsibility: Lectures on the Ethical Implication of Psychoanalytic Insight* (New York, 1964), p. 172.

17. Philip Rieff, *Freud: The Mind of the Moralist*, rev. ed. (Garden City, N.Y., 1961), p. 201.

18. Tocqueville, *Democracy in America*, 2:128, 133.

19. I have used the Harper Torchbook edition (New York, 1960) which has a valuable introduction by John Higham.

20. Tocqueville, *Democracy in America*, 2:298.

21. My reading of Cahan's novel agrees with the analysis of David Singer, "David Levinsky's Fall: A Note on the Liebman Thesis," *American Quarterly* 19 (Winter 1967):696–706. He points out that Charles Liebman's recent work confirms Cahan's story by emphasizing the prior secularization of Orthodoxy before its emigration to America.

22. One of the best examples of a historical and cultural reading of American literary classics is Leo Marx, *The Machine in the Garden: Technology and the Pastoral Ideal in America* (New York, 1964). But Marx also illustrates the tenuousness of his method of reading a writer like Hawthorne when he tortures "Ethan Brand" to find in it Hawthorne's sense of the "the doom awaiting the self-contained village culture." Yet Marx confesses that "taken by itself, the fable reveals no link between Brand's fate and Hawthorne's attitude toward industrialization" (pp. 267, 277). The best modern example of a novel that uses the method of symbolism to focus on historical and cultural forces as they enter into the development of an individual's identity problem is Ralph Ellison's *Invisible Man* (1952), which is both a condensed social history of the American Negro and a psychobiography of a "rabble-rouser" becoming a writer, using techniques that range from the quasi-documentary to the surrealistic.

# 14 / Psyche, Clio,
# and the Artist

In mythology Psyche is a rather equivocal figure. Apollo tells her that for all her beauty she is grimly destined to marry a terrible winged serpent; instead, in the end, she happily marries Cupid and becomes immortal. The prospects for psychoanalytic thought also seem to point in two directions. Either it is seen as subversive of true historical and literary understanding, or it is championed by a few as the ultimate oracle for all interpretation of history and art. Witness *The Journal of Psychohistory*, committed to reducing all history to the psychic story of the effects of child-rearing practices; while many historians and literary critics disdainfully ignore psychology for the more impersonal truths of quantitative or structural analysis.

It is difficult to insist on both the uses and the abuses of psychological interpretation without alienating those who have already chosen sides. But I think a restoration of humanistic critical and historical understanding requires both a sharper and a more irenic assessment of the issues. When Erik H. Erikson twenty years ago introduced the term "psycho-history" in *Young Man Luther*, the quotation marks and the hyphen stood for his own modest sense of the provisional nature of the enterprise. Even in 1973, when both the qualifying markers had disappeared from common usage, he looked forward to the day when history would "simply be history again, but now a history aware of the fact that it has always indulged in a covert and circuitous traffic with psychology which can now be direct, overt, and aware," just as "psychoanalysis will have become conscious of its own historical determinants, and *case history* and *life history* will no longer be manners of speaking."[1] I honor him, above all, for this ideal, which informs my remarks on psychological interpretation even when they sometimes criticize him.

Literature, history, and psychoanalysis belong to a common family, perhaps even to a somewhat incestuous one. The historian Hayden White has pointed out how histories may be organized by the literary categories of comedy, romance, irony, or tragedy; and the clinician Roy Schafer has translated Freud's scientific language of force, energy, and apparatus into "a historical, experiential, intentionalistic model."[2] In all three disciplines, moreover, the favored mode of explaining is telling a story. For all three the original data are interpretations, whether they are documents, texts, or dreams. Their facts are not like pebbles on a beach; they are acts of mind. A crucial difference among them, however, is that neither historian nor critic can benefit from the evidence-creating "feedback" produced by the clinical encounter in "transference," "resistance," and "free association," nor can their interpretations be tested by therapeutic results; on the other hand, scholars usually have a wealth of documentary evidence denied to the clinician.

Freud's genius, like some of his follies, lay in reading between the lines. The same may be said of historians, biographers, and critics, but they have a prior, greater obligation first to read the lines as scrupulously as possible. The humanistic scholar has to try to understand historical persons as they see themselves before he can see them in terms which may account for the mistakes they may have made about themselves. Even Freud thought that people sometimes said what they meant: "people make no mistake where *they are all there*, as the saying goes."[3] His examples—speaking to the king, making a declaration of love, or defending one's honor before a jury—reflect his preference for the seemingly casual as the locus of betrayal, rather than our most committed acts. No doubt, these sometimes might refute him, but his point stands that our acts do not always betray our inner conflicts. For that reason I think it is a wise procedural rule to recognize that even when the covert speaks its message louder than the overt, we still need much overt evidence to interpret it. Let me use an example from my own research. William James in his old age recorded a dream as supposed evidence for a mystical experience. "It seemed thus to belong to three different dream-systems at once," he wrote, "no one of which would connect itself either with the others or with my waking life."[4] But the dream speaks more eloquently about the dreamer's identity conflict than it does about a transcendent world, pointing back to the time of his youth when he was divided in anguish by his conflicting ambitions to be a painter, a scientist-doctor, and a philosopher.[5] Erikson cites the dream as being revelatory of "an acute identity confusion," resolved in the reinstatement of the dreamer's mature professional identity by an exercise of the psychologist's "'objective' empathy and systematic compassion" in recording it; but he does so against the necessary, implied background of the "prolonged identity crisis" of James's youth and in the light also of the necessary hint about its source, noting that the son's later philosophy was "a continuation and an abrogation of his father's creed."[6] The covert message of the disturbing dream makes sense only in the light of a much larger context that includes many overt and covert messages of his youth and his old age.

My methodological moral, therefore, is that before unconscious conflict can be reliably inferred and interpreted as a covert message in a text with a different overt message, we should first locate the conflict firmly in a documentable crisis of the author's life. Otherwise the richness and convenience of theory substitute illicitly for the poverty and untidiness of the data. Erikson himself in *Young Man Luther* relies heavily on Luther's supposed fit in the choir, an event that is dubiously derived from testimony by an enemy of Luther's, given some four decades after it was supposed to have taken place, and never mentioned (as Erikson notes) by Luther himself.[7] "We are thus obliged to accept half-legend as half-history," Erikson concludes, "provided only that a reported episode does not contradict other well-established facts; persists in having a ring of truth; and yields a meaning consistent with psychological theory."[8] It is a standard well suited to a historical novelist, who must often supply motives for which the record speaks too softly or not at all; but a historian cannot take the same license without producing a suppositious history of surmises.

Fawn Brodie has written a book on the supposition that the legend about Jefferson's liaison with a young slave girl actually happened, as his enemies claimed. She can show that, being present nine months before Sally's childbirths, Jefferson might have fathered her children, but even this hypothesis does not warrant the literary gothic of Brodie's romantic supposition that Sally Hemings, like Maria Cosway, actually was one of Jefferson's "tragic secret loves."[9] Whereas Victorian biographers were tempted to veil or suppress scandalous evidence of sexuality, Brodie is typically modern in celebrating her "scandal" as proof of her hero's continuing sexual vitality. If he were not sexually involved with Sally and Maria, she concludes, "Jefferson is made out to be something less than a man, and Alexander Hamilton's ancient canard that Jefferson was 'feminine' is perpetuated even in our own time."[10] One might call this standard "the Norman Mailer test" for historical truth. Even if this argument were convincing, however, since she justly shows that "from the beginning of Jefferson's life as a political man and as a lawyer he was caught up not only in the slavery problem but also in the psychological complexities and ambivalences provoked by the issue of miscegenation,"[11] there is no evidence at all that the alleged liaison made any difference to Jefferson's social ideas and political actions. The point of paying attention to the presence of deep-seated emotional conflicts, after all, is to connect them with the agents' historically influential thoughts and actions so that we can understand them better.

Michael Paul Rogin in *Fathers and Children* spins out a psychoanalytical tale about Andrew Jackson, as an explanation of American Indian policy, an account bristling with references to "oral introjection" fantasies of regaining the "primal infant-mother connection," the "death instinct," an insane "oral rage," and the "anal stage" of development, all supposedly showing "a logic of the psyche" that "led from children to mothers, from debt to the bank, from Indian removal to removal of the federal deposits."[12] But if we do not abandon our skepticism in the face of all this facile generalizing, mixing Freud, Erikson, and Melanie Klein in a strange brew, we must ask: What sort of biographical evidence are we dealing with? Rogin's answer is: "We have, of course, no clinical evidence to root Jackson's rages in early childhood experience." Instead we have what are called "suggestive facts," which turn out mainly to be theories: "Problems in infancy, involving feeding, weaning, or holding the child, often intensify infantile rage and accentuate later difficulties in the struggle of the child to break securely free of the mother. . . . Speech difficulties often indicate a problematic oral relationship. . . . Disturbances in the parasympathetic nervous system, like slobbering, commonly derive from tension in the early maternal tie."[13] In this litany of generalities a few facts are visible: Jackson was a posthumous child who suffered recurrently from a long list of medically unspecific symptoms, while often expressing anger and occasionally feeling deep depression. Rogin himself admits that the illnesses may not have been psychosomatic at all, but even if they were, he never puts this material into a datable context by which we could decode the sufferings in relation to specific conflicts in a pattern of development, as Erikson seeks to do with Luther. Rogin's type of argument, too common in "psychohistory," perhaps should be called "poor but honest," like the parents of a nineteenth-century rags-to-riches hero.

My second methodological moral is summed up in this quotation: "To learn to say 'I don't know' is the beginning of intellectual integrity."[14] "Psychohistorians" should paste this remark of Freud's on their mirrors, remembering, alas, that he and William C. Bullitt said it in their tendentious, dogmatic, and denigrating biography of Woodrow Wilson, which actually admitted ignorance only on the question of the strength of Wilson's libido, an issue they then rejected as being unimportant. Very much more in the true spirit of the remark is Erikson's measured observation that the data about Jefferson's alleged liaison with the slave girl "oscillate between conveying something that seems possible to something even probable."[15] The first thing to go in much "psychohistory," however, like truth in wartime, is the willingness to take seriously the Scottish verdict of "not proven." Robert Frost once compared free verse to playing tennis without a net. Too much "psychohistory" is like jumping over the net before the match is over.

Too many interpretations are also monistic, like a player who always runs around his backhand. Oedipus rules with a heavy hand. Erikson's schedule for growth departed from Freud, however, and anticipated current interest in the problems of the aged by alluding to adult crises of personality with their own emotional issues. Freud pointed out that creative writers had dramatized the oedipal crisis before he ever analyzed it, and in Willa Cather's *The Professor's House* or Lionel Trilling's *The Middle of the Journey*, for example, Erikson could have found novelistic evidence for his own concept of a mid-life crisis of "generativity," threatened by stagnation and self-indulgence. Yet the hold of earlier psychoanalytic concepts is tenacious, and some biographers use them even when they have better evidence for Erikson's point. Thus a recent biographer of the historian Frederick Jackson Turner thoroughly documents his extravagance in smoking, eating, buying, and contracting for books which he never wrote; his interest in popularizing his ideas on the lecture circuit, rather than refining them professionally; and his hoarding and underlining of all favorable references to his work, while covering every available surface with his large flowing signature. The author either sees these traits as the charm of "a hedonist in a Victorian world" or as the sign of "a life-size inferiority complex." But the biographer himself records the crucial fact: "the most tragic year" of Turner's life was when two of his three children died when he was thirty-eight.[16] Yet rather than explore this crisis as an explanatory source for Turner's treating himself in such a self-indulgent way, Billington interprets it instead as a way station on the path to maturity, despite the fact that the Turners went into debt permanently on their recuperative European vacation after the death of their children.

If the rule of licensing one's explanations by starting out from a specific disturbed moment in the career of the subject might help to keep us from fixating on the familiar Freudian categories, it also would tend to free us from their causal reference to infancy, where the historian and biographer seldom have any evidence. It is all very well in the name of realism to bring the bedroom, the bathroom, and the nursery back into our historical awareness, but the problem of evidence cannot be solved simply by relying on the abstractions of theory, which is itself continuously under critical revision. Causal knowingness always tends to promote the imperialism of theory and to disguise moral judgments in "scientific" lingo.   Rogin tips his hand to show the moral in his linkage of American expansionism to Jacksonian "oral rage" when the books ends by tying Jacksonianism to the coming "Leviathan" of "corporate power, worldly acquisitiveness, and bureaucratic order." [17]

The psychologically sensitive biographer can have sufficient evidence, if the surviving record includes it, for the career and point of a theme, understood as a conflict of relatively obscured intentions, entangled with conscious aims. A clinician has recently argued that psychoanalysis itself is only the redescription of an action in narrative terms that point to hidden reasons, rather than being a causal explanation of it in terms of conditions. [18] The novelistic form of Freud's case studies is certainly the novel part of psychoanalysis in terms of his innovative break with the organic-disease models for hysteria; but psychoanalytic theory is also traditionally engaged with asserting genetic and causal propositions about psychosexual development, not merely with decoding language and symptoms in terms of unrecognized and conflicting wishes. It is precisely this "scientific" part of the legacy that has led an English literary scholar to believe that "the notion of causality in the emotional life of the individual" must give psychoanalysis the useful function not "to deepen or subtilize the complexities of life or literature, but rather to devise simplifying formulae that make all things clear." [19]

Every narrative is a balance between particulars and generalizations. If it is easy to lose the individual in the role of illustration, which happens in case histories, it is also necessary to look for recurring themes in a biographical subject in order to see it as a life and not "a happening." But these generalizations define patterns, rather than causal mechanisms. Peter Shaw's study, *The Character of John Adams*, for example, is refreshingly free of all clinical jargon, yet he presents Adams in terms which reflect familiarity with psychoanalytic ideas. He shows Adams to be more prostrated by success than by failure, suggests in a footnote that "the common element among Adams's collapses may have been defiance of figures in authority," and points to a recurring pattern by which "in common with his other revolts, once Adams had defeated an individual in authority, he acted to legitimate the principles underlying his opponent's position." [20]

Shaw's note cites Freud's essay on "Those Wrecked by Success," which highlights the way in which the forces of conscience may forbid a person to gain the hoped-for enjoyment brought about by a change in reality, but he does not draw Freud's conclusion. Freud disarms us at first by confessing, after several stabs at explaining why Lady Macbeth should collapse after her success, that he cannot penetrate "the triple obscurity of the bad preservation of the text, the unknown intention of the dramatist, and the hidden purport of the legend." But he abandons this agnosticism when he turns to Ibsen's Rebecca West and finds that "everything that befell her at Rosmersholm, the passion for Rosmer and the enmity towards his wife, was from the first a consequence of the Oedipus-complex, a compulsive replica of her relations with her mother and Dr. West." [21] Freud's literary detour finally brings him back to the certainty of his clinical diagnosis that illness-inducing conscience is always connected with the Oedipus complex. Shaw, on the other hand, as a historian, wants to situate Adams in the village life of eighteenth-century Massachusetts with its Puritan tradition, and he convincingly presents Adams's "anxious uncertainty arising from self-examination" as a translation of "the Puritan concern over salvation into the question of his worthiness for success." [22] Freudian confidence in the universality of the oedipal theory of guilt would blot out this historical context.

Shaw does not tell us why Adams legitimated his opponents, but there is a clue in Erikson's remark about Luther's conservatism: "psychological dialectics" must assume it to be "even probable" that "a great revolutionary's psyche may also harbor a great reactionary."[23] The remark exploits the psychoanalytic idea of ambivalence, one of the most useful concepts, which has entered into our way of interpreting thoughts and actions quite without respect to the psychosexual etiology that Freud developed for it. The clinical encounter has distinct advantages for turning up evidence about fantasies  derived from our feelings as children, and the quest for them is conducted not for theoretical reasons, but in order to find a therapeutic remedy for the patient's problem. The biographer has no such advantage or purpose. It is appropriate therefore to look elsewhere in tracking down Adams's ambivalence. We might find it, for example, in his querulous puritanism, a political religion which provided him with a double legacy, justifying both revolt against authority and submission to it.

Psychoanalytic therapy is notable as a modern mode of understanding that takes the individual seriously. Inevitably, its impact on historiography has been to sponsor studies of what used to be called "great men" in politics, science, philosophy, and art. But Freud's theory also highlighted the matrix of the family and the weight of cultural norms as they are mediated by parental voices. From this point of view "psychohistory" has looked to common child-rearing practices or shared childhood experiences in the hope of finding explanatory keys. "The history of childhood and of the family, collective biography and prosopography," Peter Loewenberg observes, "are now moving to the forefront of historical interest."[24] Erikson's *Childhood and Society*, first published in 1950, had pointed the way. Biography of children or a movement's followers is often empirically hard to come by and the temptation is great to rely on theory to fill the gaps, or to turn every property of an individual life cycle into a property of the community. Rogin cites Erikson's authority, for example, in taking Jackson, whose mother died when he was an adolescent, "to represent antebellum America," because by definition the leader "experiences widely shared social tensions as personal trauma."[25] It is true that Erikson did see Luther as one of those rare individuals who "lift his individual patienthood to the level of a universal one" by trying "to solve for all what he could not solve for himself alone."²⁶ But it is one thing to show the hero using his struggle with his conflicts to develop universal statements of religion or philosophy; it is quite another to identify his psychological conflicts with those of his followers. The issues that the hero defines may, indeed, be shared with his followers; the specific psychological biography that led to focusing on those issues may be very different, precisely because similar conflicts do not necessarily produce similar responses to them.

The language of "identity" has become the common coin of current ethnic, national, and ideological movements without their having any indebtedness to psychoanalytic ideas, which they usually scorn. But a psychology that emphasizes how a person becomes individuated through conflict in the family ought to be able to appreciate how other groups also achieve definition in extrafamilial conflicts; however, to do so it has to transcend the Freudian emphasis on family-centered issues. Erikson has expanded the tradition by taking vocational ambitions as seriously as Freud took sexual wishes, and the departure itself comports with Freud's famous remark about the sign of health being the capacity to love *and* work. But Erikson has also usefully emphasized the developmental need for ideological orientation as part of the identity-making process, thus taking more seriously what Freudians have always been inclined to unmask as mere rationalization of deeper instinctual issues. As a historian and a sociologist have justly emphasized, the sense of identity and self-esteem are always vulnerable to historical events and keyed to social mandates that are not necessarily located in the family context.²⁷ The point ought to constitute a third methodological moral—there are more things in heaven and earth than are dreamed of in our family life.

Like biography and history, novels are narratives that tell stories of change, often imitating their ancestors by a show of presumed documentary validity. For psychological interpreters the text is a disguised autobiographical document. Freudianism assumes that the function of the interpreter of a text is "to reveal significances of which the poet himself was unaware and which (at least in the first instance) he might even strenuously deny."²⁸ D. H. Lawrence has greatly influenced the interpretation of American literature, for example, by his formula, enunciated in *Studies in Classic American Literature*, that we should always "trust the tale and not the teller." This path, however, is booby-trapped. By interpreting Cooper's Leatherstocking saga as "a wish-fulfillment vision" of "the nucleus of a new society" as "a stark, stripped human relationship of two men, deeper than the deeps of sex," Lawrence also projected on Cooper his own romantic wishes for America, and he ignored Cooper's deep fascination with the realistic problem of law and justice in a frontier society.[29] The moral is that a theme does not have to turn on love or death (*pace* Leslie Fiedler) to have an obsessive appeal in a writer's work.

Moreover, messages in a text may be covert to us for historical, rather than psychological, reasons precisely because of our distance from the time-laden concerns of the author and his audience. Today, for example, in reading Hawthorne we are not likely to miss his psychological acuteness about guilt, but we are much less likely to tune in to the extraordinary density of his historical imagination, nurtured by a close reading of colonial sources, which only professional historians now read. We readily see that "My Kinsman, Major Molineux," for example, with its disturbing dream sequence about a boy's witnessing of the tarring and feathering of his wished-for patron, says something about the ambivalent growing pains of the youth, as well as of his country, caught up in the crisis of the Revolution. But we are not likely to appreciate fully the multitude of highly condensed and disguised historical allusions to English May Day riots, Masonry, the Boston Tea Party mob, the raid on the lieutenant governor's house, the political idiom of the conflict between the "country party" and the "court party," and the familial imagery about the mother country's imperial policy. Instead, psychoanalytic critics are inclined to see in young Robin Molineux, whose names conflate two colonial political references, merely a stand-in for "what every young man does and must do" in "destroying an image of paternal authority so that, freed from its restraining influence, he can begin life as an adult."[30] But Hawthorne's best short stories are powerful precisely because they overlap the psychological and historical levels, as if he were himself an unusually subtle "psychohistorian." Roy Harvey Pearce, who has done much to unravel this tale, appropriately decodes Hawthorne's historically oriented symbolism as declaring that "man has no nature, except in his history."[31] One must add, however, that Hawthorne himself used the term "psychological romance" in reference to his stories, and the psychological interest always points to recurrent features of our mental life, to transhistorical issues, however much they are grounded in our historical existence.

One virture of the psychologically oriented critic is to remind us that texts are not anonymous. Nor are they merely verbal patterns. The "most essential event, the dominant category of experience" for reader and writer alike of a Hemingway novel, declares Frederic Jameson, is "the process of writing."[32] This formalism, surprising in a Marxist critic, offers little guidance to the reading of *For Whom the Bell Tolls*. The trouble is not only that it incorporates Hemingway's political experiences, but that it also incorporates his obsession with death. It is not merely hindsight but insight that ought to make us notice the deeply felt quality of Robert Jordan's final dialogue with himself about his father's suicide and his own fear of reenacting it, a theme which led Hemingway to think first of calling his novel *The Undiscovered Country*, that fatal territory from which, as Hamlet said, "no traveller returns." The first title usefully reminds us of how isolated the hero really is in spite of the second title's affirmation about human solidarity. The shadow cast on the novel by the earlier title affects our reading of the hero's final claim that he is "completely integrated now," just as the claim itself distinguishes the hero from his author, who died in a sick despair.

A closer look at another writer may clarify this problem of distinguishing author and character. I shall choose a much-admired and much-discussed story by Henry James because he has misled some critics by sponsoring the modern idea of the artist as a godlike impersonal creator, who does not intervene in his story except to tell it, letting his protagonist be the central intelligence on whom nothing is lost. In fact, James is often profoundly autobiographical in his fiction and never more so than in "The Jolly Corner," published in 1908 when he was sixty-five, thirty-three years after he had left for Europe to make his career abroad. Freud, with his interest in the psychological significance of numbers, would surely not have been surprised to discover that the hero of James's story, also an expatriate returning to America after thirty-three years, had left when he was twenty-three and returned when he was fifty-six, thus exactly reversing the digits in his creator's case. This numerical mirror image is very appropriate to a story about a man confronting his alter ego in the form of a ghost haunting his family mansion. Dismayed by the rampant commercialism of a city that has overwhelmed his fond memories of an earlier New York, the hero's feelings resonate with those James would soon express in *The American Scene*, a travel book recording his mixture of painful nostalgia and shock about his country.

The central situation of the story is a psychoanalyst's gold mine, for it is described in terms similar to those James used in the travel book and in his memoir, *A Small Boy and Others*, where he records his nightmare of confronting a ghost. As a returned expatriate, who was himself the grandson of an immigrant, James had been troubled at Ellis Island by the vast flood of new immigrants, who seemed to invade "the intimacy of his American patriotism," and he spoke of himself as a "questionably privileged person who has had an apparition, seen a ghost in his supposedly safe old house,"[33] just as his story's hero has done. The story is also full of details derived from the author's family situation. The hero's girl friend, Alice, bears the first name of the author's sister and his sister-in-law; the ravaged ghost is afflicted with eye trouble, which the author's psychologist-brother had suffered, and with two amputated fingers, perhaps suggesting the wound suffered by another of the author's brothers in the Civil War, or perhaps his own back injury sustained at the outbreak of the war. In revisiting his birthplace in 1905 to find it supplanted by a high building, James complains of "having been amputated of half my history" and indulges himself in the "free fantasy of the hypothetic rescued identity" of his family mansion.[34] Finally, to cap the connections, the fictional hero experiences a sort of second birth as a result of his troubled fantasies, just as the author's father and brother had done in the disturbing "vastations" and "visitations" which had marked their vocational crises. Seen in this light, the formalist's notion of the text as something detachable from its author seems absurd.

Yet what at first looks like a gold mine for the analyst is also a quagmire. The "dream adventure" and the story differ in one important respect: in the actual nightmare the dreamer turned the tables on the ghost, frightening him away, while in the story the ghost overwhelms the hero, who blacks out in horror at this vision of his possible other self.[35] Furthermore, the haunted man is presented to us as an egocentric hypocrite who as a frivolous expatriate has been living off the money from his leasing of an American skyscraper, while sentimentally keeping up the old house of his boyhood with the profits from his rent. In the story he awakes from his nightmare in the embrace of the girl, who represents his congenial American past; but in reality James returned to Rye to resume his bachelor-expatriate life.

The biographer is entitled to make what he legitimately can out of the relation of this intriguing story to the working out of James's complex feelings, which are as much involved with the different appeals of America and Europe as they are with family feelings. But the story is also detachable from them, insofar as we can appreciate the irony of Spencer Brydon's experience without knowing about the many possible correspondences between the story and the author's life. These correspondences are richer than the conventional Freudian categories take account of. In the forties Saul Rosenzweig's psychoanalytic account reduced the ghost, in accordance with the formula of "the return of the repressed," to a symbol of James's "unlived life," itself the product of "castration anxiety" arising from the identification of his own back injury with that of his one-legged father in the context of an unconscious sense of guilt for not having participated in the Civil War.[36] In this view James finally laid the ghost only by his feverish war-work in England, in an overcompensating identification with the Allied cause. This interpretation, however, would be more plausible if William James had suffered the back injury, for the evidence is overwhelming that he (not Henry) did have a long, troubled overidentification with his father, an eccentric and original theologian. Furthermore, as Peter Buitenhuis has remarked, by emphasizing the theme of the unlived life, this Freudian interpretation distorts the nature of the story's hero, who confesses that far from missing out on experience, he has been living a "scandalous" life. There *are* Jamesian heroes who have an unlived life, yet "Brydon has lived; the point is that he has not lived 'edifyingly,'" but has "followed strange paths and worshipped strange gods." [37]

In the next decade Leon Edel brought to bear another Freudian category in interpreting Henry James's "dream adventure." Edel noticed that James had been provoked in 1911 to discuss the nightmare, whose setting was the Louvre, by recalling his youthful visits to the museum with William James. In those early days the elder brother, unlike Henry, spoke French with assurance and moved confidently in the world of painting. Read in this light, the younger brother's nightmare expressed a persistent sibling rivalry by imagining the elder as a routed ghost, more fearful than frightening. The dream incorporated this wish fulfillment, as well as Henry's mingled fear and love of the past. He has simply been bolder in his dream than in his short story, where the hero succumbed to his horror of the ravaged ghost. Not surprisingly, Edel reads the tale as a vehicle for Henry "laying the ghost of his old rivalry with William." [38]

Edel's theory of the dream is plausible enough, but on Edel's own showing the novelist *may* have dreamed his dream in 1910, a year before he wrote about it, as a part of his recovery from a disabling breakdown of self-confidence, occasioned by the meager response to his collected edition of his works. If true, then the story, written in 1906, antedated the dream rather than reflecting it, and life then imitated art. Furthermore, sibling rivalry with William James as a theme needs to be more plausibly translated from oedipal terms into a larger identity issue, involving the different choice of country each of the brothers made, a decision connected with their work as well as with their much-debated cultural attitudes. Henry James was, in fact, his mother's "darling," and he chose to live in the mother country. "The Jolly Corner" most obviously has to do, as Edel himself puts it, with the author's ambivalent feelings about his "American-European legend," arising from his act of expatriation. In the decade that remained to him, Edel asserts, "all that he did from this time on was intimately related to his American past." [39] Yet if this fact seems to imitate his hero's posture in recognizing his love for the girl, James (as Edel himself shows) would still suffer a few years later in 1910 from a deep depression in which he burned forty years of accumulated papers. Spencer Brydon and Henry James cannot be merged.

Moving back and forth between the life and the text is essential footwork for the critic and the biographer, but one moral of this example is that the journey is as hazardous as Eliza's crossing the ice when she was escaping slavery. Edel's foot slips, tumbling him into the water, at a critical point when he blurs the hero of "The Jolly Corner" with the subject of the biography. "He sees at last his own dual nature," Edel asserts, "the self of intellect and power and the self of imagination and art; the self that for so long had tried to live in his brother's skin but could now shed it, and the self that reflected his creativity." [40]

But these assertions merge the hero and his creator at the price of obscuring the irony of the story. Spencer Brydon never does see himself in the frightening specter of a maimed capitalist. On the contrary, he rejects the creature absolutely: "'He's none of *me*, even as I *might* have been,' Brydon sturdily declared," assuming he was supposed to have known himself. "You couldn't!" his girl friend rightly remarks, recognizing his blindness, which is symbolically reflected in the specter's "poor ruined sight." [41] Edel assumes that the character, like a patient having his inner conflicts explained by his psychoanalyst, comes to a liberating self-recognition, but James portrays him instead as a man who never does learn to see himself quite straight and must be rescued instead by the more discerning love of a woman. She too has dreamed of his American alter ego, but she has always been ready to accept it out of pity, for she knows the specter is also his past self, as well as his alternative self.

Wayne Booth has sensitized modern critics to the difference between the author as a historical person and the author as an implied narrator of his story. Yet the question of their relationship can still be raised. I suggest paradoxically that when the links between author and character are obvious, the differences may usually be more significant. Similarly, when the links are not evident, the similarities may be more important. In the case of "The Jolly Corner" the linkage exists where at first one might least expect to find it—in the ghost's presence as a ravaged man of power, seemingly the foil for James's intellectual career as an expatriate artist. To look for the latent meaning of conflict in James's alleged castration anxiety, sibling rivalry, or even incestuous homosexuality, as modern critics have done, is to ignore the vocational locus of his troubles and to assume that psychological truth must be sexual. The indisputable evidence is the timing of his major depressions; they coincide with the failure of his ambition to have a triumphant commercial success in the theater. The scene of his defeat was the London theater, where, in 1895, he was savagely heckled off the stage for being the author of *Guy Domville*. His friend Robert Louis Stevenson had died in Samoa during the rehearsal of this play in London, and Stevenson's *Dr. Jekyll and Mr. Hyde* had been a smashing commercial success. These circumstances help explain why James, responding in 1906 to William Dean Howells's earlier suggestion that he combine his talents for the gothic and the "international theme," wrote about an "international ghost." In 1910 his theatrical ambition revived, plunging him again into disabling depression.

One detail of the story links up with James's dream of the Louvre and his discussion of it in his autobiography. The parquet floor of Brydon's family house, on which he wakes from his faint, has (he observes) first given him his idea of style and James makes the same remark in his autobiography about the parquet floor of the Louvre's *Galerie d'Apollon*. The gallery itself houses the crown jewels, and its Napoleonic ambience colors James's association of the Louvre with "history and fame and power." Crucially, it is there that he remembers having had a fearful "prevision" of the kind of "queer so-called inward sort" of life that he would have as an artist. In his final days, a stroke would induce him even to believe that he actually was Napoleon, dictating a memorandum about redecorating the Louvre.[42] His doomed search for a commercial success in the theater, which led him to lower his own literary standards, expressed a persistent wish for power. Seen in this light, "The

Jolly Corner" is a remarkably self-critical story, testifying to James's own ability to recognize (without conquering) his own Napoleonic fantasy. The dream turns victory into romantic melodrama; but the story confronts the wider truth with an ironic awareness of the delusion involved in a wish for popular success, alien to James's talents, that has ravaged his own inner poise. While the hero's horror at the commercialism of New York City reflects the same mood expressed in the author's travel book, Alice's acceptance of the other self perpetuates the author's ambivalence towards America, a tension with the literary advantage of preventing him from endorsing tendentiously drawn international contrasts.

James was bolder in his dream than he was in his story about confronting the ghost of his other self. But the bolder vision, however healthy psychologically it may have been for James, even perhaps relieving his depression in 1910, as Edel suggests, would have made for a melodramatic story and left out an ironic truth about Brydon and James. The triumphs of art, unlike dreams of victory, are achieved within the limitations of reality. In this respect Freud was reductive in claiming too simply that the dreams invented by writers stand in the same relation to analysis as do genuine dreams. Only when we pay close attention to the difference between the hero and the author, between a story and a dream, are we prepared to make intelligent discovery of the subtle connections between them. Understanding the literary point of a story as a dramatic statement about a character's experience is not the same act as explaining its latent significance for the biographer of the artist's mind.[43] Yet each mode of analysis helps to bring the other into focus. Edel's footwork in negotiating the hazardous ice floes of psychological criticism is more convincing, for example, in his treatment of Willa Cather's *The Professor's House*, where he shows in detail how a correlated study of a life and a work can deepen our understanding of both.

Cather's official biographer leaves us with something of a mystery. He notes that the artist's study in the elegant Pittsburgh home of her patron, Isabelle McClung, was a former sewing room, like the professor's study in the novel. He notes as well that the fifty-two-year-old hero is the age the author was when the novel was published in 1925, revealing in her a new, surprising attitude "more desolate by far than any fear of the price that worldly success tries to impose, or a disapproval of new forces in American life." He also suggests helpfully that "it is by a scrutiny of the approach to houses that the deepest meaning in the novel will disclose itself," and he even inadvertently provides a further clue by recording that when Willa Cather visited the French house of her recently married patron in 1923, she sadly found herself unable to work there.[44] He does not, however, bring any of these details into relation to each other or to his reading of the story. They remain inert items of fact.

Edel's psychoanalytic curiosity enables him instead to illuminate the professor's mysterious despair, as well as his regressive nostalgia for an idyllic past, by connecting this character's outlook to the author's feelings after her displacement from the security of her patron's home.[45] Edel's analysis, by accounting for the pressure on the novel of Cather's sense of personal loss, not only explains a neurotic strain in her hero, but also the novelist's own mysterious remark that "the world broke in two in 1922 or thereabout." That was the year in which she wrote a story called *A Lost Lady*.[46] Surely the psycho-biographer is helpful in connecting the implied author of this story with the actual writer. The methodological point of Edel's demonstration of how correlating life and text can illuminate both is his use of it to show that *The Professor's House* is "an unsymmetrical and unrealized novel because Willa Cather could not bring the two parts of her broken world together again."[47] The biographer has thus joined together the critic and the psychoanalyst.

This same merger is the high merit, for example, of Justin Kaplan's biography, *Mr. Clemens and Mark Twain*. The novelist lived in Vienna at the same time that Freud was developing psychoanalysis, and the American writer was also fascinated with what he called his "dream self" and with the presence in man of a Dr. Jekyll and Mr. Hyde who, he felt, were "wholly unknown to each other."[48] The biographer was prepared for his work by having spent "a number of rewarding years in psychoanalysis," while being at the same time sharply critical of "doctrinaire Freudianism" with its insensitivity to social history and its "numbing sense of predestination, an inexorable chain of neurotic cause and effect reaching all the way back to earliest childhood." For Twain's biographer, Erikson was "an even greater liberator for the writing of biography," but because of his recognition of the "the possiblities for change at every stage of life," rather than for his "complex schematics." [49] Kaplan's biography is distinguished by its artful rendering of the novelist's multiple conflicts in his sense of himself, as he set out at thirty-one to explore "the literary and psychological options of a new, created identity called Mark Twain," who found "fulfillment and crushing disillusionments" in his engagement with the post–Civil War period that he labelled The Gilded Age. [50]

Kaplan's perspective enables him to see that no sharp distinction can be drawn between autobiography and fiction in Mark Twain's work, and he brings to the surface the rich tangle of emotional ties between "The Private History of a Campaign that Failed," the author's satirical account of his brief service in Missouri as a Confederate ranger, and the satirical novel, *A Connecticut Yankee in King Arthur's Court*, written shortly afterward. The memoir records the author's remorseful participation in the killing of an innocent stranger in civilian clothes, who was mistaken for a Yankee scout. At the time he wrote it, Twain idealized General Grant and was reading proof of the general's memoirs in which he wrote of being accidently wounded while wearing civilian clothes as a stranger in Missouri. Later, in 1887, the novelist read aloud "A Campaign that Failed" to a Union veterans group and added a satirical remark about the incident being the only battle in the history of the world where the opposing force was "utterly exterminated." Kaplan points out that this phrase precisely describes the conclusion of the novel, when the Yankee destroys his Arthurian enemies with gatling guns and electric fences. The novel thus translates "the unresolved tensions of his uncomfortable role as Confederate irregular and deserter" into "the major conflicts of the book itself." [51]

Making this connection between the two texts, Kaplan can more easily call our attention to the implicit parrallels in the novel between Arthur's England and the American South,

between the Yankee's republican, industrial "new deal" program and the ideology of the victorious North, between the two
civil wars which, both in history and in the fiction, destroy an
old order, thus linking the Rebel's encounter with the Yankee
scout and the Yankee's battle with the enemies of his republic.
Kaplan's correlations not only tell us about Mark Twain's feelings about his postwar friendship with Grant, but also about
the raging ambivalence in the novelist's Southern and Northern
loyalties, a conflict that turned his novel into a "curse on both
parts of the 'contrast' and ended his battle of ancients and
moderns with a double defeat." [52]

Critics have fallen out over interpreting the strange switch
in tone from comedy to tragic apocalypse in the novel, and any
close reader must be puzzled by the Yankee's final expression of
a yearning nostalgia for the very order he has been ridiculing
and subverting throughout the story. To clarify these issues in
the light of the comparisons Kaplan has made, we can go even
further by noting a neglected analogy between the memoir and
the novel: both documents end exactly the same way with a
Yankee in the arms of Mark Twain and each dying man is
mumbling about his wife and children. Having seen the
biographer read between the lines, we can now, as it were,
notice this similarity in the "lines" themselves, a parallel we
can then take as further confirmation of the biographer's
analysis and a clue to the incoherences of the novel.

Is there a summary moral we can legitimately draw from
these examples? Let me suggest one: in reading any single work
from a critical perspective on its artistic meaning for us, we use
biographical insight by subordinating it to the service of textual
interpretation and evaluation. In reading any life, however, we
see all its texts, fictional and documentary, as historical actions
within a context of artistic craft, social milieu, and private life.
Every text is then part of a continuing story not only of a canon,
but of a person's self-definition. Neither perspective can ignore
or rule out the other. Speaking of Henry Adams's two novels, R.
P. Blackmur says that "unlike those of a professional novelist,"
they do not "show their full significance except in connection
with his life." [53] Certainly they are illuminated by his life and are
inferior to the works of major novelists, but how do we know

that biography can add nothing to the significance of even the best novels? Aesthetic evaluation and genetic analysis are logically different, but understanding of genesis may not only influence our understanding of the nature of successful art; it may illuminate failures of art as well and so locate points of development and decline in the artist's canon.

John Cheever in a recent interview protests that "any confusion between autobiography and fiction debases fiction." He suggests, however, that "the role autobiography plays in fiction is precisely the role that reality plays in a dream." There is a "not capricious but quite mysterious union of fact and imagination" in both. This, however, is an odd analogy for Cheever to use because from the analyst's point of view the mysterious union of fact and imagination in the dream always speaks covertly about the autobiography, linking the deeper emotional themes of both. Cheever does not clarify the distinction he wishes to preserve by going on to speak of his "morbidly close" relationship to his brother, after his parents' separation, and the persistent recurrence in his work of "the brother theme." [54]

Similarly, René Wellek and Austin Warren in *The Theory of Literature* rightly warn that a work of art has "a quite different relation to reality than a book of memoirs, a diary, or a letter." They also observe that "a work of art may rather embody the 'dream' of an author than his actual life." But the "dream" of an author, as a wish or an ideal, is itself a deeply personal matter of autobiography, and this fact must qualify the validity of their assertion that "even when a work of art contains elements which can be surely identified as biographical, these elements will be so rearranged and transformed in a work that they lose all their specifically personal meaning and become simply concrete human material, integral elements of a work." [55] The word *all* corrects the distortions of merging life and work at the price of producing the distortions of an absolute separation, as if the true work were anonymous, signed merely "artist." No doubt, E. M. Forster was right to suggest that in some sense a work of art wants not to be signed; but it usually is signed because its creator also wants to declare his responsibility. On this issue I share the view of a German Marxist critic who suggests that criticism ought to find "its most rewarding task in discovering and interpreting the very crossing-points and links between the two aspects,"[56] the real author and the fictional narrator.

In this task a heuristic, noncanonical, self-critical use of elements in the psychoanalytic tradition may help us preserve the human concreteness of history, biography, and fiction, while freeing us as well from the prison house of mere language, whether it be "structuralist" or "metapsychological." But it will also require that virtue which Santayana once defined as a skepticism that is "the chastity of the intellect." Erikson can be an ally in this humanism because, as Roy Schafer has observed, although he "retains Freudian drives, defenses, identifications, superego dictates, and stages of development as components of the concept of identity, he tends to view them in the context of life themes and to explain them by reference to these themes. Thus, like the existentialists, he reverses the Freudian priorities which require explanations to move from content to formalistic concepts."[57] It remains to be seen whether psychoanalysis can succeed in reformulating its conflicted tradition in a style more congenial to historical and literary understanding. We need to see Erikson's achievement not as a definitive resting-place, but rather as a crucial step forward in that direction.

Contemporary influential literary movements, however, are virulently antihistorical, preferring the "synchronic" to the "diachronic," formal structure to temporal sequence, "codes" to biographies, archetypes to history. "Indeed," an English critic has remarked, "one of Lévi-Strauss's aphorisms might be nailed to the mast of the entire structuralist enterprise as a message and a warning to the rest of us: 'to reach reality we must first repudiate experience.'"[58]

A sign of the times among intellectual historians is that an editor of papers given at a 1977 conference called attention to the new direction in which younger historians were moving by noting that they felt a "relative indifference" to "the whole realm of literature," Freudian psychology, and the study of distinctive individuals. Whereas a decade ago scholars might have quoted Lionel Trilling, the editor observed, now "virtually the patron saint of the conference" was an anthropologist, Clifford

Geertz.[59] There is, however, an unnoticed irony in this deference to Geertz out of the contributors' "fascination with community." Geertz himself sees anthropology as parallel to the inquiry of "penetrating a literary text" because the culture of a people is "an ensemble of texts," saying something about something. He cites an example from his own field journal as an attempt to construct "actor-oriented descriptions of the involvements of a Berber chieftain, a Jewish merchant, and a French soldier with one another in 1912 Morocco," an "imaginative act," not all that different from Flaubert's constructing "similar descriptions of, say, the involvements with one another of a provincial French doctor, his silly, adulterous wife, and her feckless lover in nineteenth-century France." Moreover, in the very year of the historians' conference, Geertz addressed the Lionel Trilling Memorial Seminar at Columbia University, declared his common concern with Trilling for the relation of culture to the moral imagination, and illustrated his own method by analogical references to three literary critics, two of them oriented to psychoanalytic ideas.[60] In the historians' volume it is hard to catch a glimpse of the anthropologist who not only admired Trilling, but who cited the critic, Kenneth Burke, and the novelist, Walker Percy, even more often than the historians cited Geertz.

Whatever differences divide them, historians, critics, and psychoanalysts are all engaged in imaginative participation in other people's experience. None of these enterprises is a spectator sport. Psychobiography, as an ally of history and criticism, has the merit, in its respect for the personal and concrete, of helping to keep alive our sense of historiography and literary analysis as forms of reflection on experience, actual or vicarious, forms that incorporate and revise our own experience. Incorporate, because the historian must draw on his own experience to interpret the experience of others, whether in documents or texts, and revise, because every written history, biography, or literary interpretation organizes experience in shapes that did not previously exist. Responding to them, we also add to our experience and examine our lives.

Narration, says Ortega, "implies that the narrated events are essentially clear and not problematic."[61] To counter this view is to recognize that psychoanalysis and history share a disciplined attention to disruptive conflicts, which make their stories necessarily complex and remind us that each person and society has to some extent his own language. Communication therefore implies a limited, vulnerable, and problematic world. Freud recognized that his case histories read like short stories. Like modern fiction, as Steven Marcus has pointed out, they are "creative narratives that include their own analysis and interpretation."[62] Reading "Dora" with its plots, double plots, and counterplots, "we know we are in a novel, probably by Proust."[63] But to emphasize "multiplicity, duplicity, and ambiguity of significance"[64] in this case need not imply a skeptical contrast between fictionalizing and truth finding. "There is no communication through objects viewed as wholly impersonal," John W. Miller has argued, "or yet through subjects viewed as wholly personal."[65] History, literature, and biography illustrate this epistemology of a metaphysical "midworld," a region of artifacts, in which articulate order embodies our own responsible acts of interpretation. Recognizing that plural languages, historical time, and inner conflict are the hallmarks of the human, these disciplines can express their truths only in complex narratives.

# Notes

1. Erik H. Erikson, *Dimensions of a New Identity* (New York, 1974), p. 13.

2. Hayden White, "The Historical Text as Literary Artifact," *Clio* 3, no. 3 (1974):277–303; Roy Schafer, *A New Language for Psychoanalysis* (New Haven, Conn., 1976), p. 192.

3. Sigmund Freud, *Psychopathology of Everyday Life* in *The Basic Writings of Sigmund Freud* ed. and trans. A. A. Brill (New York 1938), p. 86.

4. William James, "A Suggestion about Mysticism," in *A William James Reader*, ed. Gay Wilson Allen (Boston, 1971), p. 208.

5. Cushing Strout, "The Pluralistic Identity of William James," *American Quarterly* 23 (May 1971):135–52; see also chapter 11.

6. Erik H. Erikson, *Identity: Youth and Crisis* (New York, 1968), p. 151.

7. Lewis W. Spitz, "Psychohistory and History: The Case of Young Man Luther," *Soundings* 56 (Spring 1973):182–209.

8. Erik H. Erikson, *Young Man Luther: A Study in Psychoanalysis and History* (New York, 1958), p. 37.

9. Fawn M. Brodie, *Thomas Jefferson: An Intimate History* (New York, 1974), p. 470.

10. Ibid., p. 30.

11. Ibid., pp. 92–93.

12. Michael Paul Rogin, *Fathers and Children: Andrew Jackson and the Subjugation of the American Indian* (New York, 1975), p. 280.

13. Ibid., p. 45.

14. Sigmund Freud and William C. Bullitt, *Thomas Woodrow Wilson: A Psychological Study* (Boston, 1967), p. 67.

15. Erikson, *Dimensions of a New Identity*, p. 58.

16. Ray Allen Billington, *Frederick Jackson Turner: Historian, Scholar, Teacher* (New York, 1973), pp. 430, 423, 159. See my review essay in *History and Theory* 13, no. 3 (1974):315–25.

17. Rogin, *Fathers and Children*, p. 313.

18. Schafer, *A New Language for Psychoanalysis*, pp. 210–11. His analysis is consistent with my own in chapter 12, which stresses the descriptive rather than causal nature of the identity-crisis concept. See also my bibliographical essay, "The Uses and Abuses of Psychology in American History," *American Quarterly* 28, no. 3 (1976):324–42, for the mixture of intentional and causal modes in Freud and his historian-followers.

19. George Watson, *The Study of Literature: A New Rationale of Literary History* (New York, 1969), pp. 163–64.

20. Peter Shaw, *The Character of John Adams* (Chapel Hill, N.C., 1976), pp. 66, 129–30.

21. Sigmund Freud, "Those Wrecked by Success," *Character and Culture*, ed. Philip Rieff (New York, 1963), pp. 170, 178.

22. Shaw, *Character of John Adams*, p. 65.

23. Erikson, *Young Man Luther*, p. 231.

24. Peter Loewenberg, "History and Psychoanalysis," *International Encyclopaedia of Psychiatry, Psychology, Psychoanalysis, and Neurology*, vol. 5 (1977), p. 373.

25. Rogin, *Fathers and Children*, p. 14.

26. Erikson, *Young Man Luther*, p. 67.

27. Fred Weinstein and Gerald M. Platt, *Psychoanalytic Sociology: An Essay on the Interpretation of Historical Data and the Phenomena of Collective Behavior* (Baltimore, 1973), pp. 82–84.

28. Watson, *Study of Literature*, p. 160.

29. D. H. Lawrence, "Studies in Classic American Literature," in *The Shock of Recognition*, ed. Edmund Wilson (Garden City, 1943), pp. 953, 956–57.

30. Simon O. Lesser, "Hawthorne and Anderson: Conscious and Unconscious Perception," in *Psychoanalysis and American Fiction* ed. Irving Malin (New York, 1965), p. 98. For the historical allusions see Peter Shaw, "Fathers,

Sons, and the Ambiguities of Revolution, in 'My Kinsman, Major Molineux,'" *New England Quarterly* 49, no. 4 (December 1976):559-76.

31. Roy Harvey Pearce, "Hawthorne and the Sense of the Past; or, the Immortality of Major Molineux," in R. H. Pearce, *Historicism Once More: Problems and Occasions for the American Scholar* (Princeton, N.J., 1969), p. 162.

32. Frederic Jameson, *Marxism and Form: Twentieth Century Dialectical Theories of Literature* (Princeton, N.J. 1971), p. 411.

33. Henry James, *The American Scene* (New York, 1946), p. 85.

34. Ibid., p. 91.

35. Leon Edel, ed., *The Ghostly Tales of Henry James* (New Brunswick, N.J., 1948), p. 724.

36. Saul Rosenzweig, "The Ghost of Henry James," *Partisan Review* 11 (Fall 1944):436-55.

37. Peter Buitenhuis, *The Grasping Imagination: The American Writings of Henry James* (Toronto, 1970), p. 217.

38. Leon Edel, *Henry James: The Untried Years 1843-1870* (Philadelphia, 1953), pp. 79, 313.

39. Ibid., pp. 315-17.

40. Ibid., p. 315.

41. James, "The Jolly Corner," in *Americans and Europe: Selected Tales of Henry James*, ed. Napier Wilt and John Lucas (Boston, 1965), pp. 439-41.

42. For analysis of the dream see Henry James, *Autobiography*, ed. Frederick Dupee (New York, 1956), pp. 196-97; Leon Edel, *Henry James: The Untried Years*, pp. 67-97; Stephen Donadio, *Nietzche, Henry James, and the Artistic Will* (New York, 1978), pp. 228-36. For a fuller exposition of my argument see Cushing Strout, "Henry James's Dream of the Louvre, 'The Jolly Corner,' and Psychological Interpretation," *Psychohistory Review* 8, nos. 1 and 2 (Summer-Fall 1979):47-52. The entire issue is about the James family.

43. E. D. Hirsch, Jr., in distinguishing *meaning* from *significance*, finds a similar distinction in Lucien Goldmann's contrast between *comprehending* a meaningful strength and *explaining* it by inserting it into a larger structure. See Hirsch, *The Aims of Interpretation* (Chicago, 1976), p. 2. In historical analysis something similar occurs, I believe, when we understand past agents in terms that they would have themselves used and explain them in terms that we find intellectually acceptable.

44. E. K. Brown, *Willa Cather: A Critical Biography* (New York, 1953), pp. 97, 239, 240, 236.

45. Leon Edel, "Willa Cather and *The Professor's House*," in Malin, *Psychoanalysis and American Fiction*, pp. 217-21.

46. Brown, *Willa Cather*, p. 44.

47. Edel, "Willa Cather and *The Professor's House*," p. 221.

48. Justin Kaplan, *Mr. Clemens and Mark Twain* (New York, 1966), p. 341.

49. Justin Kaplan to Albert Stone, 7 March 1977.

50. Kaplan, *Mr. Clemens and Mark Twain*, p. 9.

51. Ibid., pp. 274-77, 296.

52. Ibid., p. 297.

53. R. P. Blackmur, "The Novels of Henry Adams," in R. P. Blackmur, *A Primer of Ignorance*, (New York, 1967), p. 201. For a psychological-biographical interpretation of Adams's *Esther* see chapter 13.

54. John Hersey, "John Cheever, Boy and Man," *New York Times Book Review*, 26 March 1978, pp. 31–32.

55. René Wellek and Austin Warren, *The Theory of Literature* (New York, 1949), pp. 71–72.

56. Robert Weimann, *Structure and Society in Literary History: Studies in the History and Theory of Historical Criticism* (Charlottesville, Va. 1976), p. 241.

57. Schafer, *A New Language for Psychoanalysis*, p. 114.

58. David Lodge, *The Modes of Modern Writing: Metaphor, Metonymy, and the Typology of Modern Literature* (Ithaca, N.Y. 1977), p. 64.

59. John Higham, Introduction to *New Directions in American Intellectual History*, ed. John Higham and Paul K. Conkin (Baltimore, 1979), p. xvii.

60. Clifford Geertz *The Interpretation of Cultures* (New York, 1973), pp. 448, 452; Geertz, "Found in Translation: On the Social History of the Moral Imagination," *Georgia Review* 31 (Winter 1977):794, 803. The three critics cited are Paul Fussell, Steven Marcus, and Quentin Anderson.

61. Ortega y Gasset, *Concord and Liberty*, trans. Helene Weyl (New York, 1946), p. 144.

62. Steven Marcus, "Freud and Dora: Story, History, Case History," *Partisan Review*, 41, no. 1 (1974):108.

63. Ibid., p. 100.

64. Ibid., p. 99.

65. John W. Miller, "The Midworld," in J. W. Miller, *The Paradox of Cause and Other Essays* (New York , 1978), p. 122.

# Index